DECENT EXPOSURE

DECENT EXPOSURE

How To Teach Your Children About Sex

CONNIE MARSHNER

LEGACY COMMUNICATIONS
Franklin, Tennessee

Legacy Communications
P.O. Box 680365
Franklin, Tennessee 37068-0365

ISBN: 1-880692-090

For Pearse and Michael and Caroline and Cecilia
and their future children

CONTENTS

INTRODUCTION

WHERE I'M COMING FROM

'm not a saint, I wasn't in my youth, and I know my kids aren't going to be. Chances are, neither are yours. And we both need practical, down to earth advice for the down to earth situations that arise as children grow in awareness.

You need to know whether you can trust me. Where am I coming from? What are my basic premises about Christianity and sexual morality?

Titus 2:12: "God's grace has been revealed and taught so that what we have to do is to give up everything that does not lead us to God."

That verse summarizes this entire book. It's a challenging verse. I believe that any use of the sexual faculty outside of Christian marriage leads us away from God. Compared to greed, wrath, and cold-bloodedness, it may be that sins of the flesh are among the less ferocious sins with which mankind is afflicted, but they are still destructive of our fellowship with God and with our neighbor. We must regard them with great seriousness.

It is not a victory merely if your son or daughter avoids begetting a child out of wedlock, though that certainly is a goal. It is not an adequate definition of success merely that your children postpone coitus until after they are married, though that certainly is a goal.

As an author, I would feel that I had achieved something worthwhile if, through the help of *Decent Exposure,* you were able to raise children who not only have control over their flesh, but who also understand that sexuality is not only an occasion of considerable righteous delight within marriage, but who also understand that, in marriage, it is a means of self-giving, self-sacrificial love for another person; who see their sexual capability as one way to donate themselves in service and love to others.

1

In other words, who know that sexuality in practice must be accompanied by permanent commitment and fidelity. Who understand that sexuality is part of their God-given nature, and part of their path to the Lord.

If the goal isn't that expansive, it will be hard not to end up with a bottom-line that comes across something like this: Don't have sex because you might get diseases, and then you'll suffer. Now, I grant, a self-centered, rebellious teenager might actually hear that, and decide that he has more to lose than to gain by doing the immoral thing. So I'm not disparaging that message—if a rebellious kid listens to it, and does the right thing because of it, it's an effective message.

But there has to be a world view deeper than that. If you are reading this book, you probably already have the Christian view of service and self-giving, though you may not have used those words, and you may not have thought of your sexuality as part of your following of Christ. But it is. And as you read this book, you will see that it is. That knowledge and that practice are what you want to pass on to your children.

The Goal. Put simply, your goal is to teach virtue, to lead your children to understanding virtue, to make them actively desire to practice virtue. But they can't want what they don't know! It is appalling to read the results of surveys which reveal that enormous percentages of Christian young people don't even have the factual knowledge that sexual activity outside of marriage is wrong. They don't even know that 1 Thessalonians 4:3 applies to this day and age: "For this is the will of God, even your sanctification, that ye should abstain from fornication" (KJV). They don't know 1 Corinthians 6:9: "Know ye not that the unrighteous shall not inherit the kingdom of God? Be not deceived: neither fornicators, nor idolaters, nor adulterers, nor effeminate, nor abusers of themselves with mankind . . . nor thieves . . . nor drunkards . . . shall inherit the kingdom of God." I use the King James in these two passages, because that translation uses that good old word *fornication*. The more modern translations have softened it into "sexual immorality"—probably thinking that the bite of the old word might put contemporary people off. Well, the bite of that word is salutary. In an age that thinks of morality more in the context of social or political correctness than in the context of sin and repentance, we need the sharpness of an occasional old word to drive home a point.

The point is: sexual sins separate us from God, and they are to be feared and avoided. We strive to teach our children how to avoid sins of anger, or gluttony, or hatred—and many seem to learn those lessons well.

But we don't have the same success at teaching our children to avoid fornication.

As parents, we want our children's happiness. Nothing is so guaranteed to blight a person's chance at future happiness as a loss of innocence in youth. Parents can understand what children, even (or especially) teenagers, can't. Parents seek their children's protection; motivating them to chastity, and equipping them to practice it, is one of the greatest protections we can give them.

Here are some of my premises about how to get from here to there.

Communication. Kids need to talk with parents about sexuality, sexual behavior, and sexual morality. But they are not going to talk with parents about those dynamite topics if they are not also talking about fashions, friends, music, cars, sports, chores, relatives, neighbors, hopes, fears, and dreams. In other words, a healthy family life greases the skids for everything else.

I wish I didn't have to say this, but I do: many of us don't have healthy patterns of communication with our children, and many of us have never observed healthy patterns of communication with children. Our parents never got us to share our hearts with them, and we don't know how to get our kids to share theirs with us. If that describes your predicament, there is no way around the stark truth: get help. If reading books can get your and your spouse's behavior to change, read books. If it takes sitting down and talking with your pastor or small group, do it. If you know you need to change, and you want to change, you are half way there. All you really need is some technical guidance.

There are parents with good communication skills who think it's not necessary to talk about sex with their kids. But listen: if kids can't talk to their parents, they will talk to someone else, and they'll get pseudo-morality and pseudo-knowledge from peers, pop culture, or the streets. It is a sacred obligation of parents to teach their children about sexual morality. It should be as comfortable as possible, of course; hence this book.

Capability. In order to practice Christian morality, our young adult children must be *capable of controlling their passions*. This means they must have been taught and trained in all the virtues of Christian living that make self-control possible: obedience, patience, unselfishness, kindness, gentleness, fortitude, and so on. This means they must have seen those virtues in their parents. Or at least, they must see their parents struggling in pursuit of those virtues. Don't struggle in silence! Make your struggle a teaching opportunity: share with your children what is going on inside of you, so that they can know how to fight the battles for peace, for patience, for kindness, and so on when those battles are raging inside of them. Remember, the Holy Spirit is as available to children as He is to adults—but parents must allow that grace to flower, and be wary not to smother it with reticence, coolness, or cynicism.

The Spirit can move, and when a person gives his life to God, wonderful changes can happen: lifetimes of bad habits can be broken. After a conversion, the Spirit brings about those wonderful changes by building up certain virtues in the heart of the converted one. Proper upbringing, which instills those virtues from childhood, "prepares the soil", and predisposes the young person to be virtuous. It is the parent's duty to ready the child for conversion.

Some may argue: why not just convert kids and figure all the pieces will fall into place? The data suggest otherwise. Even among seemingly "converted" young people, behavior is not markedly different from national norms.

Motivation. Ultimately, love of God is the only perfect motivation for Christian sexual morality (or any other kind of morality, for that matter). Instilling that motive is the goal of all parenting. But don't let the perfect be the enemy of the good. If the motivation isn't perfect, an imperfect one can still protect a child from much harm. Fear of pregnancy has kept many a woman pure until marriage, which, in turn, made a happy marriage possible where otherwise it might not have been. Today, the fear of AIDS may keep many men and women from lives of promiscuity.

Formula. I wish this book could give a formula. Say thus and so to your children, and they will act accordingly. But of course, as you already know, there are no formulae for rearing children, or for instilling godliness in them. It is part of the wonders of this universe created by our loving God, that no two individuals are alike, and no two of us respond the same way to the same stimuli. Indeed, two children, even close in age, in the same family, with the same parents, will experience the identical teaching very differently. How and what we learn is to a great extent influenced by what's on our minds at the time, what emotional landscape we happen to be traveling in. Nobody can know what a child is capable of internalizing at any given moment.

In this book, I just aim to show that the subject of teaching your children about sex need not intimidate you. For indeed the whole of

Christian family life you are practicing is the education of the affections—and the proper education of the affections is what Christian living is all about. "Sex Ed" is only a small part of affection education.

The traditional family is being attacked in our day as never before. One of the most damaging attacks on it comes through the erosion of sexual morality. In privately raising your children to virtue you are not only teaching them the way of salvation, you are, in the great sweep of history, saving the institution of the family itself. And in doing that, you are making evangelization and conversion of future generations possible.

Chapter 1

NOBODY SAYS NO ANYMORE

J anet is a lovely Christian woman. She and her family always seemed like typical, fine, Christian people. She had a couple of kids and a steady husband, and as the kids got older Janet got a job. They had always been regular church-goers, not overly active in church programs, but the kids did go to Sunday school, at least until they got into high school.

Then something seemed to go wrong, and when you greeted them they weren't so friendly, as if something were distracting them. The family didn't seem to joke or smile much. You didn't notice that at the time, though. It wasn't until June, the high school daughter, stopped coming that anybody began to notice something was different. Then Bob, the husband, stopped coming, too. You were talking about it one day at the Women's Help Society, and one of the other women mentioned that she'd heard Bob was filing for divorce. So you asked the pastor to visit, and then the whole story came out.

June had been at a party one night, and, feeling daring, had had a couple of beers. She lost her normal inhibitions, and the next thing she knew, she was pregnant. But she didn't tell anybody for a long time, so they just thought she was moody and sick. When Janet found out, she and Bob were so ashamed that they felt they didn't dare tell anybody. It wasn't until the sixth month that June got to a doctor, and then in the seventh month she had developed toxemia of pregnancy and had to be in the hospital. The baby came prematurely, after a terribly difficult labor, and had to spend five weeks in the nursery, two of them in intensive care. It turned out that Bob's insurance didn't cover any of this, and Janet's part-time job wasn't enough to pay for everything. As the bills started mounting, Bob got crabbier and crabbier and more and more withdrawn.

He had wanted to throw June out of the house to begin with, but Janet had insisted that this was her home, right or wrong. Now he seemed to hold it against Janet for bringing this disgrace and financial ruin on the family, so he had moved out in anger.

In the meantime, June had gone on welfare so the baby's future medical expenses would be covered by Medicaid. But there was no way she could consider going back to school in the fall, since the baby needed so much care. The doctors weren't sure yet, either, whether the baby was going to be completely normal.

Janet kept saying to the pastor over and over, "How did it happen? Where did we go wrong? What did we fail to do?"

You listen to this story, and you breathe a prayer, "There but for the grace of God go I." Then you remember your children are already in elementary school, and you feel a flicker of fear. *Do I know how to raise mine any differently?*

If you feel that flicker of fear, you need this book.

Question: When was the first time you had sex? *Answer*: The first instant you were conceived, when the forty-six chromosomes that make up your entire physical identity—twenty-three from your mother's ovum and twenty-three from your father's sperm—met and joined to form a single nucleus that grew into you. At that moment you had sex, and you have never stopped having either female or male gender. That is what sex is: part of your identity.

When you read the question above and began to try to remember the first time you had sexual relations with a member of the other sex, you made the common mistake of equating the word sex with the act of sexual intercourse or conjugal relations. But sex is much more than an act; it's a condition of existence.

If you have been wondering how to talk to your children about conjugal relations but haven't thought about teaching them about their sexual nature, you need this book.

Perhaps you're thinking about thoughts like this: *I'm a new Christian. I thank the Lord that He rescued me from the path of immorality and sin and helped me and my husband straighten out our lives and our marriage. When I remember the bitterness we felt toward each other, just three years ago, over the affair I was having and the one he had started to get back at me—I just praise God for His love and care for us. We're new creatures now, and the more we love Him, the more we love each other. Family is a joy now, the way I always wished it could be.*

And I'm so grateful to Him that He did all this before our children were old enough to be hurt by the bad example we were setting without realizing it. But I'm still embarrassed about that past and ashamed of it, and I don't want to think about it at all. My child asked me just yesterday where babies came from, and I was so embarrassed that I stammered and stuttered and finally said something really foolish about going to the popcorn store and finding him hiding in the popcorn bin. That's dumb, and I could tell he was confused, because normally we have good communication.

But I can't have a conversation with my children about sex! I'd want to tell them what God's plan is, and I'd feel like such a hypocrite, considering my own past. I just couldn't bear to "preach" something I hadn't followed myself. I don't feel as if I deserve any credibility at all. Still, I know that parents are the primary sex educators of their children, and there isn't anybody else to teach them. What am I to do?

If you identify with this dilemma, keep reading.

DEFINING THE PROBLEMS

Janet is not alone. If you follow the news at all, you cannot but be aware that teenage pregnancy is a major personal problem for a lot of Americans. So many individuals are affected by it that it is sometimes considered a national problem. Three thousand parents of girls a day begin the same drama Janet is living. That's at least how many new teenage pregnancies occur every day.[1] The mothers of teenage boys have a different kind of drama: when there are suddenly hushed conversations, or when one regular girlfriend disappears from the scene, and there's no explanation readily available, they wonder. They wonder whether they can believe their son's cheerful assurances that he'd never have sex. They know how big is the chasm between a clear head in conversation with adults and a quiet evening with a "hot babe" and lots of privacy. They realize they will probably never be told if a grandchild of theirs is quietly aborted.

There are about 1.2 million teenage pregnancies per year. Throughout the 1980's, eleven percent of U.S. females aged 15–19 became pregnant each year.[2] Even if 31 percent of those pregnancies end in birth to a married girl, as they do for sixteen-year-olds, it doesn't make it all right. Nothing really changes much except the child's last name. Teenage marriages are the most likely to fail, especially if they were forced marriages to begin with.

The facts are clear: for a woman, early childbearing is practically an invitation to lifelong poverty. For the baby, being born to a teenager spells high risk of premature death, low birth weight, and greater likelihood of various other problems. Much of our nation's 14 percent infant mortality rate (seventh highest in the world) comes from babies born to too-young mothers. For the country, half a million births to unmarried girls aged fifteen–nineteen means $16.7 billion in annual welfare costs—more than half the total expenditures on Aid to Families with Dependent Children, food stamps, and Medicaid.[3] Not that you can measure a human life in dollars and cents. Each and every human life is of incalculable value. But it's important to understand that the country is paying heavily for the mistakes of individuals. It isn't just the problem of their families. Nor is it only teenagers who are experiencing an increase in unmarried births. In 1984, 64.9 percent of all births to unmarried women were to women over the age of twenty.[4]

CONSEQUENCES WORSE THAN PREGNANCY

But pregnancy is not the only consequence of promiscuity. More than half of America's seventeen-year-olds have had sexual intercourse, and somewhere around 20 percent of them will get pregnant. But tragically, far more than 20 percent will be afflicted with problems, many of them serious, and many of them lifelong.

On the emotional level, self-devaluation is a regular consequence of early sexual activity. That's psychological talk that means the kids involved think worse of themselves afterwards, have lower self-esteem. Despite all the cultural hype for "doing it", human nature remains human nature: sexual intercourse is a very intimate experience, designed by nature to promote bonding with the partner. The environment which nurtures intimacy and bonding is one of love, stability, and maturity. For a girl to enter into the most intimate of human experiences, only to learn a week later that her partner has done the same thing with somebody else, and made coarse jokes about her intimacy, is a devastating experience. The same devastation can occur to a boy, though a boy is more likely to not even realize what's happening to his emotions. The reaction is the same: it's inevitable to feel disgusted at oneself. Then the anger starts growing. "I'll show her I don't care about her either" leads to more sexual encounters. The pattern continues, and then distrust takes hold.

It is statistically well-documented that the earlier a person starts having sexual intercourse, the more partners he or she is likely to have. In other words, it's the rare person who has the single overwhelming love affair, and then lives chastely in honor of the memory of that great love. Maybe in Victorian novels—maybe in Victorian life. But not today. Promiscuity is the usual next step for American youths who become sexually active.

Next on the ladder is disease. Fifty-six million people—more than one in five Americans—are infected with a viral, sexually transmitted disease. That's not even counting the bacterial diseases, the old standbys like syphilis. Twelve million new sexually transmitted infections occur each year, one-fourth of them to teenagers.[5] That figure comes from a report from by the Alan Guttmacher Institute. The Guttmacher Institute is the research arm of Planned Parenthood—the organization that has gotten rich by aiding and abetting teenage sexual activity. If even they admit this consequence, one can be sure of the figures.

Even if a contemporary American teen were trying to be like the Victorian heroine, he or she still wouldn't be safe from disease. One study in Atlanta found that 24 percent of adolescent women who claimed to have had only one sexual partner nonetheless were infected with chlamydia. As someone recently said: when you go to bed with somebody, you are going to bed with everybody that person has gone to bed with for ten years, and with everybody that all those people have gone to bed with. The girls in Atlanta didn't understand what that meant, if indeed they had ever heard it.

More than 2.5 million teenagers a year in the United States contract some kind of sexually transmitted disease, or STD. That's the current name, by the way, for what used to be called venereal diseases. Even cervical cancer is considered an STD nowadays, because it is so clearly linked with early onset of sexual intercourse, and multiple partners. I'll talk in more detail about the physiological diseases of promiscuity in the next chapter.

And I haven't even mentioned AIDS yet. In the first edition of this book, a mere five years ago, I wrote several paragraphs about AIDS. Today you can find a chapter devoted entirely to that gruesome topic.

HOW DOES OUR NATION RESPOND?

Now, all these trends are well-publicized. None of this data is secret: disease, teen motherhood, poverty that follows teen motherhood, and so on. The body politic is well aware of the problems. How has this august body responded?

With a few notable exceptions, our political and public health leaders have responded to all these dire trends by urging more education in the practice of some imaginary notion called "safe sex." This is supposed to mean you can have sex with anybody at any time it "feels good" without worrying about babies or disease.

"Personal Safe Sex Sampler Kits" are advertised for sale through the mail, offering a selection of condoms, massage lotion, and rubber gloves, along with a pamphlet on reducing the risk of AIDS while enjoying sex in a safer way (never mind that *Good Housekeeping* magazine, known for its seal of approval, at the time would not accept any condom advertising because it won't advertise a product whose reliability it cannot guarantee). Television stations are convinced that it is their civic duty to advertise condoms. Placards on buses advertise hotlines for confidential counseling and testing for disease. Billions of dollars are spent on "education" in "safe sex," creating a burgeoning new industry of providers. Enterprising teachers devise lesson plans to teach fourth-graders how to exercise their sexual faculties with no adverse consequences. Since 1970, Planned Parenthood has been teaching essentially the same message with federal funds—and the results discussed above.

The bottom-line rationale of those who advocate "safe-sex" education to children at younger ages than ever is summarized in the statement: "Boys will be boys, and girls will be girls. They're going to have sex anyway, so all we can do is teach them how to do it safely." This resignation to lust is astonishing. The same opinion makers and political leaders did not lean back and say, "People are going to smoke anyway, so let's just convince them to use low-tar cigarettes." They did not say, "Boys will be boys, and they will drink when they drive, so let's just encourage them to wear seatbelts." Not at all. We didn't see campaigns about "safe smoking" or "how to drink and drive safely." Instead, massive propaganda campaigns against smoking *per se,* and tough laws against any drinking and driving, were the response of the public's leaders. Why are the consequences of sexual behavior dismissed and ignored? Why were students in eleven elementary schools in Chicago *paid* to attend special classes in sex education?

Almost the inverse of the teenage pregnancy problem is another one, as deep and grave for the future of the entire free West as the teenage pregnancy problem is for the individuals who must come to grips with it.

At the end of World War II, the free Western nations of the world accounted for 22 percent of the world's population. With this strength, freedom was bought for most of the world for almost forty years. Now these nations make up 15 percent of the world, and by 2025, we will be a mere 9 percent of the world.

Is it racist to talk like that? No. I imply no superiority of race. It is a fact, though, that most of the undeveloped world depends on the developed world for economic, medical, and technical help—all of which depend on people. And when the underdeveloped parts of the world have their wars and famines, where do they turn for help?

But where does the developed world get the resources to be the world's policeman, commissary, and medical clinic? From the taxes its population pays. We have had no famine, no plague, and less poverty than anywhere else in the world. But we have had fewer babies. We are not replacing ourselves.[6] When the tax burden reaches a certain ratio with the population (and some argue we're there already), something disastrous happens to the productivity of the people. By not replacing our population, are we hastening the decline of our own civilization?

Millions of public dollars are set aside ostensibly to prevent teenagers from giving birth, but in fact the money is used to fund programs that increase the likelihood of premarital sexual activity. Yet the federal government does nothing in its tax laws to make it easier for married couples to support their children. Indeed, the opposite seems to be the case. Do we live in a fundamentally antichild society?

Do we live in a fundamentally "feel good now" society? Do we believe in instant gratification so much that we avoid having any more children than we can help because they detract from our "self-fulfillment?" Do we believe, instead, that gratifying our impulses will make us happy but fear permanent commitments because they are "boring"?

The economic costs associated with alcohol and alcohol abuse were estimated at $116.9 billion in 1982,[7] and there's no reason to believe that figure has done anything but increase since. Another $28 billion was squandered in paying for motor vehicle crashes attributable to alcohol abuse.[8] The number of mental health facilities in the country increased from 3,005 in 1970 to 4,622 in 1984.[9] Does this suggest a happier, saner population? Or is it the cost of pursuing a "feel good now" mentality? Admissions for cocaine abuse increased more than 350 percent just between 1977 and 1981. Was the interruption of careers evidence of the

successful pursuit of "the good life"?[10]
Does anybody still believe that this way lies happiness?

WHAT ARE WE DOING?

Then why do we in the Western world still act as if it did? Why do we, as citizens, tolerate the incessant hype of sexual suggestiveness as the way to sell everything from cigarettes to perfume? Why do we tolerate 10,000 non-marital sexual situations a year in television programming? One can hardly watch a prime-time television show without having to endure lewd jokes. Why do we still watch?

What are we as a nation doing to ourselves by condoning and encouraging this flood of uncontrolled sexual outpouring? By exploiting our deepest feelings, we are making it harder for our real emotional needs to be met. We are desensitizing ourselves to guilt, and that means we are desensitizing ourselves to the exuberant relief of knowing repentance and forgiveness as well. We are desensitizing ourselves to the horror of abortion. Dr. Edward Sheridan, a prominent Washington, D.C., psychiatrist, puts it this way: "We in mental health are kept busy not by conscious guilt and pain, as real as those are, but by unconscious guilt. In the matter of abortion, there is powerful unconscious guilt collectively in the family and in the nation, and in us as individuals."

By undertaking casual relationships and wasting the deepest intimacy of nature on one-night stands, people are making it increasingly difficult to bond into satisfying lifelong marriage; that means they are continually setting the real goal of happiness further and further away from themselves. By engaging in acts they feel are expected of them but which they really don't want, women are hurting themselves, destroying their self-respect, which in turn makes them more vulnerable to exploitation.

Frenetically pursuing momentary pleasure only covers over deep human loneliness. And by attempting to satisfy those longings with sexual relationships, we as a nation are making it impossible for ourselves to achieve true intimacy, profound relationships, and true love.

AN OFFENSE AGAINST GOD

For a Christian, there is something even more disturbing than all the heartache, family agony, shortchanged futures, disease, and economic costs that these facts spell. The approximately 500,000 teenage births each year are all that remain of more than 1 million teenage pregnancies. Fully half of the teenage pregnancies in this nation become abortion statistics.

Think what that means: 500,000 young women submitting to abortions, perhaps voluntarily but more likely semivoluntarily, driven by panic, fear, or persuasion bordering on force from boyfriends, girlfriends, or family. Think of the scars in their hearts and on their consciences. Think of the sleepless nights as they grow older and the impact of the deed sinks in on them. Think of the psychological timebombs planted in their minds and hearts, waiting to go off in later years.

Think of the offense to the Creator: the offense of abortion piled on top of the offense of promiscuity. God's prohibition of both is equally certain: virtue is as dear to His heart as life is. The only difference in the severity of the evil is that a living person has many chances to repent and to live virtuously later on, but an unborn child has only one chance to live. (See, e.g., Rom.6:12–14; Phil.2:15; 1 John 3:1–3; Ps. 139:13–16.)

Speaking of virtue, when was the last time you heard that word in a secular context? How about from a pulpit? Whatever became of virtue? Does anybody say no anymore?

"EVERYBODY" IS NOT "DOING IT"

Fortunately, some people still say no to promiscuous sex. In the midst of all the discussion, it should be noted that 46 percent of teens are *not* sexually active.[11] That means that 65 percent of high school females under age 18 are virgins.[12] It should also be noted that many sexually experienced teens opt later for "secondary virginity"; that is, they return to the practice of chastity. In one national survey, 12 percent of teens had had only one sexual experience. Yet in statistical categories, they are considered "sexually active." Year after year, the *Who's Who Among American High School Students* finds that the majority of high school students with A and B averages avoid illegal drug use and premarital sex. The 1987 survey found that 73 percent of those students said they had never had sexual intercourse.[13]

Of one thing we can be certain: more teenagers are having sex than really want to. Survey after survey, when asking high school students what they really want to know about sex, turns up findings like the one at the teen services program at Grady Memorial Hospital in Atlanta. What did those kids most want to know? Nine out of ten wanted to learn how to say no. Even Christian lecturers report that Christian young people come to them after talks and say, their voices tense with disbelief, "You mean I don't have to have sex?"

Especially distressing is the fact that the behavior of Christian youth is only slightly more moral than the behavior of other youth. Josh McDowell reports that 43 percent of evangelical Christian students are no longer virgin by the time they graduate from high school.[14]

What do we know about the young people who are not sexually active? Quite a bit. We know they tend to live with both their parents; their parents tend to be visibly interested in them; they tend to have at least a C average in schoolwork; they have plans for the future; they didn't date until later than other kids; their parents have moderately strict discipline and a moderately large number of rules about dating; they tend to be churchgoers and they tend to take their religion seriously.

Planned Parenthood is militant about providing its services to teens without notifying their parents; it has gone to court to defend the "right to privacy" of teenagers. Proponents of this tactic of undermining parental authority insist that if teens had to talk to their parents about sexuality, it might prevent the young people from getting contraceptives, but not from engaging in sexual activity. The facts seem to fly in the face of this rhetoric, however: Minnesota law requiring parents to be notified of minors' abortions resulted in a dramatic reduction in teen pregnancy, abortion, and births.[15] It seems that when teenagers know their parents will have to be involved sooner or later, they adjust themselves to their parents' expectations.

We know three absolutely indispensable things about chaste teens: (1) Their parents have talked to them about sexuality and sexual morality.[16] (2) They believe that premarital sexual intercourse is wrong. (3) They are capable of practicing their beliefs.

This, then, is the challenge for us as Christian parents in our decadent and sex-saturated age: communicate with our children, teach them Christian values, and equip them to live those values. Like some of the other truly tall orders of life, it is disarmingly simple. In the rest of this book, we'll look more closely at the influences and values we're up against, as well as how specifically we can teach our children to say yes to God's best for them and no to the tragic mistake of premarital sex.

Chapter 2

THE WORLD
OF ADOLESCENCE

I t's easy to communicate with a six-month-old: an infant is thrilled to her toes when you communicate with her by merely making eye contact and repeating her gurgles. But when we're talking about sixteen-year-olds, it's another matter. Things change as kids grow up.

One day, it seems, your boy would do anything for you—with an angelic smile to boot—if you promised to buy hot cocoa on your next trip to the supermarket. The next day, when you propose that as a treat, he looks at you with his head cocked at an unnatural angle, his hair carefully flopping casually over his right eye, his lips curled just right, and says, "Mom, uh, that's okay" in an accent that he thinks is California-skater-cool. Or you presently notice he's coming to the table with three buttons on his shirt undone. You suggest he button up a couple. "Mom!" comes the indignant response, "only nerds button the top button!" You find yourself humbly explaining that you weren't requesting the top one be buttoned—only the next two.

And then you ask yourself, why am I humbly explaining? Am I not the mom? And what is a nerd anyway?

Or the day your little angel is in the grocery story with you, and as you ponder the different cuts of meat, you glance at him, and he is standing there with hands cutting rhythmic patterns in the air, pelvis rocking back and forth, one foot going up and down as its corresponding hip juts in and out. His mouth is hanging open, his head jerking back and forth, his eyes staring vacantly into space. For a split second you fear he is having a seizure. Then you realize all the jerks and rocks are in rhythm with each other . . . and all are in rhythm with what seems to be some shrieking females on the Muzak. Something you've never heard, but obviously a tune with which his existence vibrates.

What has happened, and so suddenly? The youth culture has stretched out its tentacles to grab your child, that's what.

Or what about the day that your usually-willing helper seems so reluctant to unload the groceries from the car, and you get stern. Only later do you realize that the cause of the unwillingness was that a playmate was hanging around. "Mom, I wish you wouldn't embarass me in front of my friends," is the translation of "Don't expect me to obey you cheerfully when anybody my age is around."

One of the biggest influences as children grow into adolescence is the youth culture, that all-pervasive atmosphere that most American teenagers inhabit during most of their waking hours: listening to the radio, on the bus, at school, at after-school jobs, watching television, in the movies, and reflected in their friends. This culture gives no respect to parents. (To give you some idea of what you're up against: rock videos show parents being thrown out of windows and the like.) Indeed, one of the main messages of the culture is that the teen is isolated and unloved, and certainly misunderstood, except by fellow inhabitants of the teen culture, and that parents are the worst offenders.

If your youngster is already headed into this culture, you will have to act fast. If your youngster is already in it, you will have to be decisive in building bridges of communication that are possibly already burned. After considering briefly our responsibility as parents, the rest of this chapter will explore the nature of today's youth culture.

A PARENT'S RESPONSIBILITY

You should operate on the assumption that nobody is going to help your child except you. Certainly no one cares about your child as much as you do. While it would be helpful if the institutions of the modern world were more supportive of parents, don't forget that Christian tradition, from the beginning, gives parents prime responsibility for their children.

God said through Moses in Deuteronomy 6, "These commandments that I give you today are to be upon your hearts. Impress them on your children. Talk about them when you sit at home and when you walk along the road, when you lie down and when you get up" (vv.6–7).

"What greater work is there than training the mind and forming the habits of the young?" wondered John Chrysostom in the fourth century.

"What would it avail if we possessed and performed all else, and became perfect saints, if we neglect that for which we chiefly live, namely, to care for the young? In my judgment, there is no other outward offense that in the sight of God so heavily burdens the world, and deserves such heavy reproach, as the neglect to educate children." Thus stated Martin Luther in the sixteenth century.[1] A visit to some of the teen spots of our suburbs would convince Luther that the moral education of today's children had been sadly neglected—never mind what he would think of what goes on, or fails to go on, in today's classrooms.

"It is the duty of parents . . . to make absolutely sure that the education of their children remains under their own control, in keeping with their Christian duty, and above all to refuse to send them to those schools in which there is danger of imbibing the deadly poison of impiety." This warning in 1890 by Pope Leo XIII is explicit on the point that Christian parents cannot trust anybody else to rear their children in a Christian manner.[2] But of course, it's not just Christian tradition. In the Tractate Sanhedrin of the Talmud, Rabbi Chisda gives his married daughters advice on how to please their husbands, both intimately and in public matters. Orthodox Jews consider this passage one of authoritative example that parents are to be the teachers of their children in all matters, at appropriate times.

It should not surprise us that diverse religious traditions say the same thing, for indeed, it is written in our hearts as human beings that parents nurture and teach their children. Why else, anthropologically speaking, have we created a society in which our young take so many years to mature and need more help than the young of any other species in attaining maturity? The only real question is, Who will be the major influence during those long, formative years: parents or nonloving others?

Contemporary American society (and while I write of America, I know that all over the Western world things are the same) has forgotten the wisdom of relying on parents as the major influence. Professionals tell us when to feed our babies and what to feed them. Exasperated by our own ignorance of how to civilize them, we prop our young children in front of television to buy ourselves some peace and quiet. There they are taught, by imitation, how to behave—by robots or walking stuffed toys that are caricatures of human beings.

We send them to school at a tender age, though they frequently tell us by their difficulties that they aren't ready to be there. While there they are influenced and trained by people whom we have never met, know nothing of, and who may or may not believe as we do. The teachers have, at best, an impersonal, professional "caring responsibility" for our tender young buds. But the other children have only the example of their parents, who may or may not be Christian, to guide their relationships. But we tell ourselves, in contravention of our own instincts for tenderness, "That's the real world, the kid has to get used to it."

From sunup to sundown, once out of the diaper and bottle stage, our children spend fewer and fewer hours a day in interactive company with people of other ages. The nursery school teacher may be an adult, but it's the other kids who are important to our kids. The school-age youngster who likes to linger after school to talk to the teacher is immediately ostracized and labelled "weird" by the other children. By high school, many a sixteen-year-old would rather die than be seen by his peers talking pleasantly to an adult. If we were talking about different races or religions, instead of about different age groups, our society would not tolerate the segregation we inflict on our children.

Thus, it should be no surprise that, as they get older, they isolate themselves in their electronically generated world of personal stereos and videos and televisions and seek companionship only with isolated fellow teens. Fellow victims of the teen culture are the only people they know how to associate with, because we haven't given them any opportunity to learn how to associate with people of other ages. But this isolation goes against the way we're built. Our human nature seeks companionship and intimacy. And when one has not learned how to be a companion of the mind and heart, one will respond to the surge of hormones and follow where it leads, hoping that pursuit will satisfy the yearnings the heart is feeling.

This is why educating a child to resist casual sex is more than teaching anatomy and right values. Instruction in these matters is essential (it teaches the what and the why), but young people must be equipped to resist the lures that will come at them. They must also be taught the how of saying no. Our children must learn how to relate to people at many different levels, how to overcome their loneliness on levels other than the physical. Only through such practice and such discipline can the real intimacy we seek be achieved. But that is precisely what our society does *not* teach and what the youth culture is militant in resisting. Without development of the full range of social capability, the temptation to instant gratification, which disguises itself as instant intimacy, will prove irresistible.

WHAT IS THIS YOUTH CULTURE?

I have said the secular youth culture is a grave enemy of the Christian parent's desire to prepare his or her child to receive the Lord and to have full, satisfying human relationships. Do I sound extreme? Are you saying to yourself, "Come on, Connie, the older generation has always complained about the entertainments of the young. I remember my parents' complaining about the music I listened to, but it didn't ruin me." Well, in one sense you're right. Beethoven's parents probably wouldn't have liked the kind of music he wrote, either. "Too modern," they would have said. But I'm not talking about musical quality here. Entertainment is only a small part of this vicious youth culture.

One day not too long ago I was sitting in a comfy chair in our local public library, waiting to be picked up. My eye roamed at random down the magazines on display in the "young adult" section there in the entryway. On just one teen magazine cover, these were the teasers: "Body-aware swimwear"; "First Date: What's Really on His Mind"; "Countdown to Prom—a politically correct approach to prom night"; "Help! I Don't Fit In!"; "Fly! The Hottest Workout." Articles inside included "In Search of Her" about two adopted sisters searching for their birthmother, and "I got an AIDS test." Not very savory stuff. Nothing uplifting.[3] The paperback fiction on display in the racks was no better. Of twelve covers visible, two were clearly about drugs, four about the occult, three about boy/girl romance, and one that seemed to stress multiculturalism. Another rack of six featured five fantasy/occult covers, and one romance.

This is just a random sample of what the minds of our literate young people are being filled with: somebody's idea of fun that doesn't match your or my idea. These magazine covers and book covers hint at a world view. And there is a world view out there, underlying the youth culture. The youth culture I am trying to alert you to uses entertainment as a tool for selling a world view that is by its nature hostile to Christianity.

The lifelong struggle of a Christian is to control one's fleshly self, to become the "new creature" that Christ's sacrificial death on the cross enabled us to become. Christ died that we might have new life, and become new creatures in Him. We count ourselves dead to sin, but alive to God in Christ Jesus (See Romans 6:11 ff). Through the blood of Christ we have received a spirit of love and of self-control, that we might forgive others their trespasses against us, that we might put our mind in the heavenlies, even though our bodies are on earth for a time. The fall of Adam has guaranteed that this is a lifelong struggle, because the self does not want to be crucified with Christ. It rises up, demanding authority.

Ever since the time of Christ, the western world understood that though we were created in the image of Christ, we had to struggle our whole life to take on His likeness. In other words, human nature was fallen. But at the end of the 18th century, the ideologues who also invented the French Revolution rejected this idea. Man is basically good, opined Jean-Jacques Rousseau; it is society which corrupts him. Mind you, this is the same Rousseau who abandoned all his illegitimate children at an orphanage. And then wrote theoretical treatises on education which have been the basis of public school ideology ever since, treatises in which he put an intellectual gloss on his guilty conscience and maintained that collective education was really best for children.

Man is born basically good? Do we really believe that? Then why do two-year-olds tear each other's hair out if they're not controlled, fighting over a toy? Then why does three-year-old Johnny have a temper tantrum when Mom takes away the sharp knife that he was playing with? Never mind what twelve and thirteen-year-olds are capable of if they're not given correct formation!

To a Christian, in short, it is patent nonsense to maintain that "kids are basically good." Kids are basically selfish, mean, lazy, wanting what gives them physical pleasure right now, and prepared to do anything to get it. Sounds like a lot of teenagers and adults I know. And not surprisingly. Without training in self-control, and self-sacrifice, without a conscience carefully developed, without a deliberate struggle to conquer the selfishness that flesh is heir to—that's what we all would be.

The contemporary youth culture says: Hey, be selfish. Man, life is short, you gotta go for it. Break on through to the other side. Climb the stairway to the heaven of drugs. There's no right and wrong. If it feels good, do it. Other people don't matter. Use 'em like toys, forget 'em later. Hey, if brutality turns you on, go for it. You gotta fulfill yourself. Nobody else cares about you. It's the survival of the fittest. Tomorrow may never come. You gotta hate your parents, they just want to deprive you of fun. Churches, religion—they're just lies invented to oppress you. Nothing lasts, nothing matters.

The so-called musicians idolized by the young live according to what they sing. Scarcely a week goes by without headlines about one or another rock writer, singer, or musician who is charged with some deviant sexual assault, or some drug offense, or inciting a riot, or corrupting the morals of a minor (of either gender), or assaulting somebody, or brandishing a gun, or showing pornography to a minor. Yet time and again, surveys of American teenagers seeking to find who the heroes are of the next generation—find that these degenerates are the heroes of our youth. It's enough to make Charles Lindbergh and Nathan Hale—real heroes, who were appreciated as such by previous generations—roll over in their graves.

It's not just the music, though that subculture is the most publicized. Hollywood is no friend of traditional values either. A recent survey found that 77 percent of the public knows that the movie industry does not portray their values, while only 16 percent said it does portray their values.[4] That sounds about right to me. I'm willing to believe that 16 percent of the public think there's nothing wrong with profanity, obscenity, fornication, murder, larceny, adultery, cheating, lying, stealing, at least in some combination. What I'd like to ask that 77 percent is: why do you still go to the movies?

A *Time*/CNN survey in 1989 found that 67 percent of the public believe that violent images in movies are "mainly to blame" for the national epidemic of teenage violence. Seventy percent of the public endorsed the concept of greater restraint on showing sex and violence in movies.[5] What I'd like to know is, why hasn't that idea ever been the subject of a national debate? A *Los Angeles Times* survey the same year reported that 63 percent of the public believe that television encourages crime.[6] I'd like to ask those 67 percent, and those 77 percent, why they still watch television. It's not just kids who are influenced by it, though clearly they are more impressionable than adults.

Actually, many Americans are skipping the movies; Hollywood's revenues are down. And the television network executives are pulling their hair out because the public "grazes" more than they watch; that is, viewers don't sit through a program til it ends; they flip channels constantly. But they're still watching. In 1992, according to Nielsen Media Research, each household in America watched an average of 7 hours and 4 minutes of television *every day*. This is two hours more than it was in 1960.[7] Is the television on in your house for seven hours a day? Somehow, if you're reading this book, I doubt it. But I'll bet it's on for two or three.

But these are adults' opinions—kids, who are the most easily impressed, don't know what values they're absorbing. If they're told, often they don't care. By definition, almost, tomorrow is not real to youth. They have to watch TV because it's what "everybody else" does. It would be downright un-cool to admit your parents wouldn't let you watch a certain movie.

The contemporary youth culture is, basically, another manifestation of Yankee ingenuity, an American invention. It came out of post-World War II affluence. That affluence allowed us to require compulsory school attendance until age eighteen, which meant that a lot of kids who otherwise would have been busy learning trades and pursuing useful activity found themselves forced, against their inclination, to sit in classrooms. Being herded around a school building all day did not create intellectual ambitions, but it did create a heady atmosphere. Entrepreneurs were quick to discover that these numerous youngsters had money at their disposal and very few real needs their parents couldn't meet, so they set about making fashion a real need, and that included fashion in music.

Then came the Sixties, and the idolization of youth and rebellion. The let-it-all-hang-out hippies of the 60's are now not only the lawyers and politicians of our nation, they are also its cultural leaders. And if you have the feeling that some ex-hippies are reliving their glory days by writing scripts for *90210* that read like action plans for organizing campus demonstrations, you're right. And if the message in news, movies, and other programming aimed supposedly at adults seems to you more and more to resemble the old agenda of acid, amnesty, and abortion, you're right again.

Today, the *Wall Street Journal* estimates the annual spending in the United States of girls under twenty at $30 billion.[8] There are entire nations that don't have budgets that size! *Rolling Stone* magazine put Bruce Springsteen's gross income from concerts alone (not counting his record income) at close to $40 million for just one year. It takes a lot of kids to spend that much money on concerts in one year.

Another aspect of the youth culture is the obsession with sex, and this also feeds a huge industry. The pornography business regards boys aged twelve to fourteen as its major target market, according to the Attorney General's Commission on Pornography. At the time of that Commission, the porn industry took in around $7 billion a year, most of it free from tax liability because it was underground. By way of comparison, the budget of the entire U.S. Department of Justice the same year was about $7 billion a year.

The atmosphere is right for the growth of this culture because young people in their teens are without purposeful function in today's society. Labor regulations effectively keep them out of real participation in the job market. Education laws require their bodies in a school building for the average daily attendance count. Thanks to high protein diets, they reach physical maturity earlier than their ancestors, but thanks to other factors, they reach social maturity far later, if ever. Their functions inside the family are almost nil unless they happen to be a member of a large family or a farm family, where their help is genuinely needed.

Yet every standard by which our modern, technological society measures self-worth tells them that they must accomplish something, they must have a function, in order to be worth something. We as a society are forgetting to value relationships ("You are valuable because you are my son") in our romance with accomplishments ("You are valuable because you earned $600 last month"). In the course of all this, education for the sake of ideas has been lost, and that is a sad irony, because while liberal education may seem to be useless in functional terms, it is the ideas acquired through a liberal education that would enable young people to find their value in a very real sense.

WHERE HAVE ALL THE HEROES GONE?

The youth culture is very successful at simultaneously focusing on and maintaining the idea of a "generation gap." In all media, parents are ridiculed and the group is elevated to the role of king and judge.

Peers are all that matters, the culture says. What "the other kids" think of a person is the highest value. And the esteem of peers is based on looks and clothes and affluence (not necessarily family affluence—one's own spending money is status enough, no questions asked how it was obtained). In the inner city, where youth culture takes on some forms of its own, the harassment and outright persecution of academically achieving youngsters by their looks-and-muscles-oriented peers is one of the pervasive tragedies of the day.

In the larger culture's pursuit of eternal youth, adult fashions imitate youth fashions. The "punk" style of dressing began with some of the most far-out rock groups, then trickled into respectability. In the 1960s, when sexual promiscuity and drugs first became fashionable, it was among young people, but the fashions and lifestyle quickly moved up the age ladder. When parents are trying to look like teenagers, when Mom and Dad are experimenting with cocaine or getting drunk every weekend or "playing around," where is Junior going to find a voice of moderation to encourage him to resist?

The relativistic philosophy that has pervaded public education for thirty years is a great source of aid and comfort for the youth culture.[9] Adolescence is a time of psychological individuation: the young person is seeking to view himself as an individual independent of his parents and family. This is a legitimate psychological task. But a relativistic philosophy in the classroom, which teaches that old values no longer apply (even if not in so many words) can be a great reassurance to an experimenting adolescent who may wonder if he's going too far in his individuation process.

The prejudice of teachers who see themselves, not as perpetuators of Western civilization and its achievements, but as "agents of social change," can reinforce the tendency to rebellion in subtle but effective ways: the teacher who encourages students to come to her with their problems and then arranges covert abortions for them is an extreme and, mercifully, unusual example. But the general disposition of the education establishment, when confronted with evidence of its own failures (illiteracy, for instance), to blame parents first is an example not lost on young people looking for things to blame on their own parents.

The youth culture feeds mainly, of course, on the media. Young people watch an average of eighteen hours of television a week. They are the nation's most frequent moviegoers. They are the buyers of Walkmen, tapes, and records. They play them while getting dressed in the morning, driving or riding to school, walking the corridors at school, studying, playing, socializing, running or working out, eating—and even set the clock-radio to go off after they're asleep.

Total immersion was what made the Berlitz course famous because it taught a foreign language so quickly. Total immersion in music teaches the message of the music equally fast. And the main message of the music is a false view of reality, a world view of profound self-centeredness and self-absorption.

Are any of the songs about helping people in need? Are any of them about responding appropriately to the emotional needs of unattractive kids in the class? Do any of them express fondness for little brothers or sisters and a protectiveness toward them? Are there songs about the challenges of chastity, joyfully met, and temptation overcome? Are there stories of obedience to elders? How about hopes for the future? Patriotism? Self-sacrifice? You know I'm asking rhetorical questions.

What are the songs about? Today's songs will have different words from the ones high on the charts six months ago. But the themes are not likely to be much different. "I am the anti-Christ . . . I want to be anarchy," sang the Sex Pistols not long ago. "Straight to Hell" was the title of a song by a British group called The Clash. "Come on, have a good time and get blinded out of your mind" encouraged "Have a Drink on Me" by AC/DC. (In case you don't know, AC/DC is a code word for bisexuality). "I don't really wanna dance, girl / I want to get in your pants" was the theme line from a song incongruously called "I Need Lunch" by a group with the delightful name of Dead Boys.

"We shall survive / let us take ourselves along / where we fight our parents out in the streets / to find out who's right and who's wrong" urged Elton John a few years ago in a forthright appeal to anarchy. "People call me rude / I wish we were all nude / I wish there was no black and white / I wish there were no rules" sang Prince not too long ago, after reciting the Lord's Prayer in concert. The challenge to logic in his train of thought is almost as profound as his challenge to social order. "Romeo and Juliet, together in eternity / Forty thousand men and women every day / More than forty thousand every day / Come on, baby, don't fear the reaper" are the words the Blue Oyster Cult used to lure listeners to suicide. And there are cases where young people, after listening for hours and hours to such messages, finally psyched themselves up enough to do just that.

Obscenity. Sexual preoccupation. Hatred of oneself, of parents, of the world, and even of the object of one's lust. These are typical moods reflected in the music of the youth culture. Suicide, Satan, bestiality— these are the themes of heavy metal rock.

You may be saying to yourself, well, there's the Parents Music Resource Center, to monitor all this sex, violence, and substance abuse in rock music. Two Christian mothers started that in 1985, and their efforts got lots of coverage in Christian and secular media when they asked record companies to put warning labels on explicit recordings. Ostensibly, some companies agreed to do that, but after a few years, the PMRC found that less than half of the recordings needing lables had them. The kids were seeing the labels, not the parents. And then, in 1990, PMRC even stopped monitoring what the industry produces. No doubt, one of its co-founders, Tipper Gore, had by then gotten the message that if she kept on trying to protect children her husband's political career would come to a grinding halt. So in 1990, PMRC basically quit, and we all know where Al Gore's political career went. Nowadays, PMRC seems more interested in defending the industry against the threat of legislation that might mandate labeling than it is in protecting children against the evils in the recordings.[10]

Robert Pattison is an intellectual who has analyzed rock music from a scholarly perspective and concludes: "Rock asserts that everything the senses apprehend is properly part of self, and the object of selfhood is to reach full growth, when self becomes synonymous with the universe. . . . Solipsism is the invariable mental disposition of the vulgar pantheist, because in solipsism there is no transcendent anything, only infinite me."[11]

Nor is there relief from this "infinite me" mentality. And don't believe that Madonna sings pro-life songs. When rock comes close to being pro-life, it's in conjunction with glamorizing teen pregnancy or single motherhood, extolling motherhood as an extension of the ego. "Daddy Don't Preach," which made Madonna a temporary sensation in right-to-life circles, made no pitch to avoid abortion; in fact, it made a pitch for teenage rebellion. In this case, the rebellion took the form of marrying the fellow and having the baby, but the self-sacrifice of motherhood and the well-being of the child weren't even hinted at. I'm still waiting for the first rock song that encourages teen mothers to place their babies for adoption, the truly loving alternative.

If Madonna is the best example rock culture puts forth for young women, consider the typical role models available for youth. Apart from an occasional athlete who urges kids to avoid drugs or drunk driving or teen pregnancy (all pitched to the theme that such actions will hurt the "infinite me") consider the models held up for imitation. Sarcastic, disrespectful, manipulative, flippant, out for themselves—from the earliest exposure to mass media, these are the characteristics that will imprint themselves on the minds of children and youth.

When my son was six years old, he became enamored of *Star Wars*, like most boys his age. That movie series was basically unobjectionable for adults. But it took years for Pearse's self-conscious and deliberate imitation of Han Solo's sarcastic quips to disappear, and Pearse will always have some of that in him because of that exposure. To this day, he and his brother can, at the drop of a hat, launch into the dialogue from any part of any one of those three movies. So can some of their friends at school, too. Just last night at dinner Pearse was telling us how much he wanted to be Han Solo when he was younger, and how that is still a deep down part of him. I took some heart by reminding myself that, at least, Han did do the noble and heroic thing when it mattered—he was only selfish up to the next-to-the-last minute. Things could have been worse: he could have wanted to be Darth Vader, who was positively evil up to the last minute.

But I grieve when I hear this, and realize that Pearse has never even read about the semi-historic El Cid, who saved Christianity from the Moors, and never wanted to be the real historic Sam Houston or the other leaders at the Alamo, who really lived difficult and heroic deeds. He knows who Robert E. Lee was, but he never suffered with Lee as he did with Han Solo. The closest any real person came to being a hero was Jeremiah Denton, the longest-held Vietnam P.O.W. and later U.S. Senator (and, incidentally, strongest advocate Congress ever had for chastity and virtue!).

My point is this: youth naturally models itself on heroes, learns the details of their lives, identifies with their struggles, wants to be like them, thinks about them, imagines how they felt and thought, is inspired by them. Han Solo is the closest this generation of boys has come to a hero—and our sons are the poorer because they were deprived of real-life heroes. When adversity comes, it will surprise them, because they have not already vicariously experienced it through their heroes or heroines.

THE CULT OF "COOL"

In keeping with its nature of glorifying the "infinite me," the youth culture values those things that feed youthful egos and harshly devalues anything that bespeaks loyalty to objective reality. Virtue, for instance, is despised and laughed at. This is true of all virtue, but particularly sexual virtue. A girl who is still a virgin and foolish enough to confide that fact will experience anguish because of the scorn heaped upon her. A boy observed being respectful to his parents will be ridiculed. If his parents are lucky, once he gets in the car and drives off, he'll phase into civility. But while he's on the sidewalk with his friends in full view, he'll be obliged to say something demeaning about his folks.

Self-centeredness reigns supreme. Teens view their time as theirs by sacred right, along with their money. You have seen middle-aged fathers mowing the lawn or shoveling snow while teenage sons lounge in front of television sets (or, perhaps, over their schoolbooks). Though Junior was clearly able, Dad found it wasn't worth the hassle that would have been required to get his son off the couch. The notion that a child owes some obligation of time or effort to his family is one that Junior would not have received from the youth culture.

Incompetence in personal relationships is standard, though not necessarily by choice at all. The time-tested advice "To have a friend you must be one" means little, because kids don't know how to be a friend. They are lonely, isolated, and wallowing in self-absorption and self-pity. They don't know how to recognize such weaknesses in anybody else, let alone alleviate the symptoms. Having not learned respect as children, and for other children, there isn't even that foundation for knowing how to treat another person. The familiarity induced in sex education classes has long since destroyed the innate awe young people are meant to feel for the opposite sex, so there particularly is no respect between the sexes.

Further complicating the establishment of friendship relationships is the "cool" syndrome. Everyone, particularly boys, wants to be "cool," to put on a mask of confidence, without commitment, to appear safely scornful and aloof, perpetuating a distance between himself and the rest of the world. The "cool" mask prevents intimacy and the healing of underlying problems: when you are unreachable, nobody can help you. And yet if you're not "cool" you'd rather be dead, because those are the standards set by the youth culture. Of course, you can have sexual encounters and still be cool as long as the encounters are physical conquests and occasions of self-congratulation instead of sharings of the soul. Girls yearn for more in a relationship, but all too frequently they lack the discernment to know what they're really getting and the self-confidence to resist the deceptive overtures that come at them.

FRUITS OF THE YOUTH CULTURE

The fruits of the youth culture are all too well known. You read the figures on teen pregnancy in the last chapter. Youth suicide, too, has reached critical proportions: nineteen out of every hundred thousand young people between the ages of fifteen and twenty-four will kill themselves every year. Charlotte Ross of the Youth Suicide National Center says that a main reason for youth suicide is that young people do not know how to cope with the bad times and the disappointments of life. And not surprisingly, lessons like that are not available to be learned in the youth culture.

But how does our function-oriented society attempt to stem the tide of youth suicide? By making movies about it and inventing curriculum programs around the topic. And research experts find that youth suicide rates increase every time one of those "sensitive, made-for-TV" movies is aired.[12] The curriculum plans, designed and executed by "professionals," focus on discovering what students' attitudes toward suicide and improving their knowledge about it. Nobody, however, looks at the real reasons behind the despair and hopelessness of youth. Stephen Stack, a sociologist at Auburn University, has found that divorce rates and nonattendance at church are far more reliable predictors of youth suicide than unemployment or other factors. Yet do the opinion makers of society exhort parents to patch up their marriages in an effort to prevent teen suicide? No, because that is not a message our society wants to hear.

Parental divorce and non-attendance at church are also among the better predictors of teen pregnancy. The kids who have the least buffer zone between themselves and the youth culture are the most likely to be its victims. The kids who follow the examples of their rock-star heroes are the ones who do drugs and booze, and they, in turn, become the ones who cannot adjust to adult responsibilities, can't hold a job, and can't maintain a marriage.

WHY DOES IT CONTINUE?

Why does this destructive youth culture continue to flourish? Because parents allow it! Loving, Christian parents fail to realize the gravity of the danger. What little they know of the rock scene seems repulsive, and they assume their children are equally repulsed. Or perhaps they feel they don't need to worry because their children go to church and Sunday school, and doesn't that counterbalance the evil in the world?

Parents are taught by women's magazines to fear "overprotecting" their children, to "let them experiment with independence." We are conditioned to expect rebellion and lifestyle changes as our children get older, so we're afraid to inquire too deeply into their habits and tastes. We're afraid of causing a "backlash." Transactional analysis rather than authority is the fundamental principle behind such advice.

As parents, increasingly, we have our own interests to pursue as well. They may even be fine and commendable interests. But does our distraction with our own interests cause us to be too readily assured that our kids are doing fine when a more attentive examination might show us otherwise? Mothers who have to take employment outside the home have no easy row to hoe, and the additional responsibility and independence their children experience can be big boosts toward maturity. But the same independence can be the cause of emotional isolation and an occasion of temptation. It can force kids into looking to sources other than their parents for guidance and instruction.

What parent has time to attend to every word the kids are reading? It's tough enough to maintain veto power over what books they check out of the library, and the effort becomes more of a contest of wills as every month passes. To say nothing of laws and policies which may deny a cardholder the right to know what books are checked out on another person's card. As they get older, they have access to magazine racks. And what mother has time to read the magazines? What parent has time, or tolerance, to listen to the songs the kids are hearing? And doesn't every parent just wish he or she had the time to plop in front of the boob tube the way the kids do?

It's hard to fight against the youth culture. It's natural to want our children to "like" us, to interact pleasantly with us. If this means giving them their own way, it's an attractive prospect, particularly if the alternative is stern words and angry shouts and adrenalin pumping through everybody's veins. Fathers want peace in the home more than anything else in life. The course of least resistance is appealing, so parents avoid confronting the issue head-on until Mom gets overwhelmed by the rebelliousness of the kids and complains to Dad, who did not want to hear these problems for the fifteenth time—and then reacts in anger. This plays into the hands of the Enemy and proves how lacking in sympathy parents are, just as the songs say. And the reaction of anger makes rebellious children feel that much more justified in their rationalization of rebellion.

If we never learned to discipline them effectively when they were one and two and three, they respect us less and less as they become eleven, twelve, and thirteen. If they never knew obedience before, they are hard put to learn it now—and we are harder put to teach them anything.

We know, however, that we can't compete with schools and other kids for popularity with our children. We know that we must account to God, not for whether our kids liked us, but for whether we reared them in a godly fashion. We know these things, but we still grow weary.

Thus, the fault isn't only in the external environment, the youth culture. The fault is also within us and our weaknesses. Do we send conflicting signals to our children? We say, "Be sober," but do they see us take a few drops too many? Or we say that "Daddy is the boss in this household," and Mom expects the kids to obey her as they would him. But when she wants her own way contrary to Dad's order, do the kids observe her proceeding to get it? Or maybe Mom whines at Dad until he gives in to what she wants, but then she wonders why the kids drive her crazy with whining. Mostly, though, it continues because Satan is pursuing our children, yet we don't believe it enough to take the threat seriously.

Chapter 3

THE WRONG KIND OF EDUCATION

There was one aspect of the youth culture that I didn't talk about in the last chapter. It's not much talked about, but it's a very real part of what young people in the world today live with. And not just young people.

STD. Sexually-transmitted disease. The politically correct name for what used to be called "venereal disease." But VD developed a stigma, so the more neutral phrase was popularized, lest people feel condemned for having VD and not seek medical treatment.

The irony is that today, more and more of the STD's that afflict millions of people are untreatable. But nobody tells kids that before they become sexually active. They're just told enough to peak their curiosity.

A boy named Toby used to live around the corner from us. He was a nice boy, a year ahead of my elder son in school, but interested in similar things. Toby played the violin and chess, two things we had been encouraging Pearse to do. He also treated his little sister well, was always respectful and helpful, an example that we thought was positive. Toby was in the Gifted and Talented program in the Fairfax County Public Schools, however. And in seventh grade he got a whole semester of sex education. Once in that class, he began to talk a lot about sex with my boys.

Consequently, my boys began asking me questions that I could tell were inspired by Toby's conversation. Ten-year-old Michael, for instance, strolled into the kitchen one afternoon as I was peeling carrots and casually asked, "Hey, Mom, what's bisexuality?" I decided they needed some facts to counter the impressions Toby was probably giving, so Pearse and I spent a couple of hours during our home schooling one week to go over the facts of life. After those two hours, Pearse said to me,

"Well, Mom, I think we've just about covered it. How come Toby has to spend a whole semester on it?"

Wisdom out of the mouths of babes. How come indeed?

The reason is that some educators somewhere, responding to pressure from bureaucrats above them, decided that the children of Fairfax County needed to spend a semester being force-fed sexual preoccupation. They call it sex education, and no less than the Surgeon General of the United States has urged it for the nation. Progressive educators have been promoting it for thirty years. But in this chapter, we're going to see that as it's practiced, it's the wrong kind of education for your child and mine.

ARGUMENTS FOR SEX EDUCATION

There are four basic arguments used to sell sex education.

Argument one: "Kids will have sex no matter what we tell them. All we can do is minimize the risks of venereal disease and unwanted pregnancy."

Argument two: Our society is full of Victorian, religious hangups. If kids can learn early to accept and enjoy sex, we'll be a less-violent society. As Carol Cassell, one-time education director of Planned Parenthood, put it, "My vision for the future involves happier, more sexually adjusted individuals, with a more positive feeling about themselves and others, and a reduction of sexual dysfunction in marriage."[1]

Argument three: The first argument was losing credibility in the face of ever-escalating teen pregnancy and disease rates. The second had lost its validity in the wake of the explosion of sexual self-help and free-expression fashions from the 1960s and 1970s. But just when the sex education movement needed a boost, along came AIDS and a Surgeon General to call for AIDS education in the schools. It restored the sagging credibility of the movement and even honored it with the heavy responsibility of leading the nation in the most crucial public health battle of the late twentieth century: the safe sex campaign. In response to the AIDS threat, states began passing laws requiring sex education from the early elementary years on up.

Argument four: This one is never spoken, and it makes me sound like a Marxist to even mention it, but there is a lot of money being made on sex education, and, in recent years, on certain responses to AIDS. The provision of sex services and the funding of sex education has created some wealthy interest groups.

Refutation of argument one: Argument one begins with the assumption that human adolescents are essentially, and will act like, animals. But human beings are not animals and should not be expected to act like them. Liberal black columnist William Raspberry asks, "Are we prepared to concede that [teenagers] will do things we know are not in their best interest? Well, some of us aren't. Some of us will insist . . . that when it comes to sex, the only acceptable instruction adults can offer to adolescents is: Don't."[2] But it is the rare classroom that mentions abstinence as an option, let alone teaches how to carry out the option effectively.

Refutation of argument two: School sex education courses presume that relationships between the genders will pretty much be genital in nature. But if a relationship begins with sex, it most likely ends there. Human relationship skills suffer if sex is the resolution of interpersonal relationship problems. The data of increasing divorce and mental health problems bear this out. As psychologist Melvin Anchell put it, "The truth is that typical sex-education courses are almost perfect recipes for producing personality problems and even perversions later in life."[3] So not only do the courses demean an adolescent's human dignity, but they also help guarantee future problems and dependency on the sex-therapy professions.

Refutation of argument three: If the courses were teaching what the Surgeon General has said in his extended remarks, that "the only way to be really safe from AIDS is to be faithful in a monogamous relationship," this argument might have some value. But instead what is taught is how to put a condom on a partner. The former might be preventing disease and distress; the latter only creates a false sense of security dependent on technology.

Refutation of argument four: In one year's response to the AIDS crisis, the federal government spent at least a billion dollars, and not all of it in ways you and I would have endorsed. For instance, close to $700,000 was awarded over two years to the Gay Men's Health Clinic to conduct surveys and hold rap sessions on homosexuality. The grant application that GMHC submitted to the Center for Disease Control indicated that the rap sessions would include debunking such "myths" as the one that heterosexuality is superior to homosexuality. This is just one example of who has been making money off the latest hype of AIDS education, and I'll grant it is an extreme one.

State bureaucracies find their budgets and staffs growing as well. California is a good example. In 1973, the first year of California's Office of Family Planning, it had a budget of less than $5 million. But as the teen pregnancy rate escalated so did the size of the agency's budget. By 1982, its budget was $40 million. Even allowing for inflation, that's a growth industry!

At the federal level, the trend is magnified: the first year of federal expenditures on family planning was 1971, when there were 68 pregnancies per 1,000 women aged 15 to 19. Federal expenditures that year were $93 million. By 1985, there were 95 pregnancies per 1,000 teenage women, and the federal expenditures had risen to $480.4 million. [4]

One doesn't have to be a terrible cynic to speculate that many bureaucrats realize they would have to find different jobs if the youth of America were virtuous. But then, tens of thousands of public workers wouldn't have their jobs if the citizenry as a whole were virtuous.

EFFECTS OF SEX EDUCATION

By 1985, 70 percent of all high-school seniors had taken sex-education courses.[5] Over half of America's youth have had sexual intercourse by the time they are seventeen years old; 40 percent of today's fourteen-year-old girls will become pregnant by the time they are nineteen.[6] More than a million teenage girls in the United States become pregnant each year: 13.4 percent are already married when they get pregnant; 10.9 percent get married before the birth occurs; 39.6 percent have abortions; and 22.8 percent become single parents.

Meanwhile, more than one in five Americans are infected with a viral sexually transmitted disease. That's just viral infections: bacterial infections like syphilis or gonorrhea are a whole different category. There are scores of sexually-transmitted diseases. Viral infections generally cannot be cured. Twelve million new sexually-transmitted infections occur each year, two-thirds of them to people under 25, and one-fourth to teenagers. Women usually show fewer symptoms, and so go untreated longer, until the infection flares up into a generalized pelvic inflammatory disease, which often requires three days in the hospital, and often has a consequence of infertility. As many as 150,000 women a year become infertile because of sexually transmitted diseases.[7] This is not Christian-right-wing-terrorist data, either—it's from no less impeccable source than the Alan Guttmacher Institute, Planned Parenthood's research affiliate.

Breast cancer is a politically correct disease right now. It's quite the thing to lament the inadequate dollars spent on research into this disease that affects only women. But, did you know that women who have abortions are far more likely to have breast cancer than are those women who carry their pregnancies to birth? You're not likely to hear about it from the Women's Studies Department of your local university, either, though it is a well-established conclusion of carefully ignored medical research. As far back as 1981, published research was finding that the incidence of breast cancer was 2.4 times greater in women who had had abortions than in others.[8] Yet the "sex education" courses which are supposed to be preparing young people for the risks of sexual activity breathe not a word of this risk. Abortion, remember, is the preferred solution to an unwanted consequence of sexual activity, and as such nothing must be heard that would portray abortion in a negative light.

Nor are the sexually-transmitted diseases just the obvious suspects. Cervical cancer is now considered a sexually-transmitted disease. Mortality rates for this disease were tapering off; women under age 30 with cancer of the cervix were very few. Then came the sexual revolution, and the rates surged upward, among younger and younger women. Cervical cancer, like penile cancer, usually follows a nasty little virus called HPV, or human papillomavirus. Teenage girls have HPV at rates from 15 percent to 38 percent, depending on the population studied.[9] One study at a university health service, of 467 undergraduate women coming in for a routine annual gynecological exam, found fully 46 percent of the women already infected with HPV.[10]

As I tell my nearly-grown sons, if you go to bed with somebody, know that you are not only going to bed, emotionally, with every other person your lover has ever been to bed with, but bacteriologically, with every person every one of those persons has ever been to bed with. Diseases have consequences. There is no way to have multiple sexual partners without having multiple diseases. In other words, stay chaste, marry a virgin, and be faithful. That spells security in this age. If you don't want to follow that advice, prepare to have lots of discomfort and disease, and to spend lots of dollars, your own and other people's, in avoidable health care. There is only one way to be free of risk. "A woman who has sex with only one individual will not contact an STD . . . provided her partner is also monogamous." Thus states Willard Cates, Jr., of the Centers for Disease Control in Atlanta, in a letter to the editor, responding to a critique from another doctor, in the *Journal of the American Medical Association*.[11] Why a hidden letter to the editor? Why not a front-page headline in *Rolling Stone* or *Sassy?* Surgeon General Everett Koop, who launched the biggest sex education program in the history of the world in the name of combatting AIDS, said the same thing about abstinence being safest sex . . . in the small print.

But if people practice chastity, the middle men don't make money by selling them drugs and devices to give the illusion of safety and to try to minimize the itching and burning of their lesions. The hype continues. . . .

Does sex education promote promiscuity? Wait—I use a judgmental term. Few youth today practice promiscuity. That is un-cool—if it is defined as having sex with more than one person at a time. What is quite cool is serial monogamy. You only have sex with the person you're currently in a relationship with. Now, the "relationship" may last only a couple weeks, and then, of course, both parties are free to pick other partners with whom to be sexually active. That is the current rule of teen sexuality, at any rate. The psychological wisdom of our age tells us teenagers do better if they are given more say in making their own rules than they usually are, so these rules must be right. Got it?

So let me re-phrase my question. Does sex education encourage the early onset of sexual activity? How's that for neutral wording? From the beginning of sex ed, of course, common sense said, of course it will. For a long time it was only common sense that said so. But lately scholarship is coming to the same conclusion. One study, done by William Marsiglio and Frank Mott and published in the journal *Family Planning Perspectives,* found that teenagers who have had sex education are *more likely to have sex at age fifteen or sixteen* than are teenagers who have not.[12] That was a dramatic admission, particularly since it was published in the journal of the Guttmacher Institute, Planned Parenthood's own research arm.

But that wasn't all. The author of another study, Deborah Anne Dawson, found that "prior contraceptive education increases the odds of starting intercourse at fourteen by a factor of 1.5."[13] In other words, if a girl under fourteen has had a class that taught contraception, she is 50 percent more likely to have premarital intercourse than a girl who has not. Since just about all sex education classes teach contraception, this finding makes it pretty clear that having a class on how to prevent pregnancy helps a lot of fourteen-year-olds decide there's no reason to be virtuous anymore. No doubt there are other powerful influences at work as well, such as the youth culture and peer pressure, but the data conclusively show that sex education as taught in the public schools *is* a contributing factor to teen sexual promiscuity.

The logic is supported by fiscal evidence as well. Jacqueline Kasun, an economist at Humboldt State University in California, has found that the states that spend most heavily to provide contraceptives and abortions for free have the *highest* rates of premarital teenage pregnancy. California's premarital teen pregnancy rate is twice as high as Idaho's or South Dakota's, and California spends more than four times as much per capita as the other two states.[14] The message seems clear: if kids think their actions will be free of consequences, they are more likely to engage in the risky activity and, since the promised protections don't really work, suffer the consequences.

SCHOOL-BASED CLINICS

But common sense is not to prevail. Confronted with the evidence that more sex ed equals more sexual activity, the sex-education establishment responded by calling for more services to be delivered to youth. Years of classroom sex education had not reduced the teen pregnancy rates. Years of government-funded family planning clinics in every county in the nation with services free to teenagers had not reduced the teen pregnancy rates. The public was asking tough questions of the sex-education establishment. It needed a new response, and it found one in school-based clinics. This is the latest achievement of the sex-education lobby. The next achievement will be the use of Norplant in teenagers, even if only semi-voluntarily.

The reasoning goes like this: Kids are going to have sex, and they know about contraception, but they don't use it enough because it's hard for them to get to the clinics. If we have the clinics right on the school grounds, however, they'll be able to pick up their equipment before they leave school, and everything will be fine. They'll be "protected" for their date. Besides, if we have medical personnel on campus, they'll be able to reach out to kids when the kids need help.

The rhetoric used at school board meetings may not be so blunt with that reasoning, of course. You'll probably have to read between the lines.

Frequently, the public relations campaign will talk about "sports medicine" or "adolescent medicine," and press releases will be written about the underweight students who are discovered in routine checkups in school-based health clinics. This is for camouflage. Also for reasons of camouflage, Planned Parenthood does not set the clinics up directly. The Center for Population Options, a fellow-traveller organization with Planned Parenthood, has taken the lead in the school-based clinic campaigns.

Michael Schwartz is one of the main critics of school-based clinics. He wrote in *Family Protection Report*[15] that school-based clinics "serve as marketing stations for the abortion industry. . . . Nothing speaks more eloquently to this point than the fact that in at least two communities where school officials refused to put clinics in school, local abortionists have set up free birth control dispensaries near the high schools. . . . Both are private, for-profit corporations whose primary source of income is abortion. Business executives, even in the abortion industry, do not incur the expense of giving away free products if they think this giveaway is going to reduce sales." Likewise, Ortho Pharmaceutical Company and other drug manufactures wouldn't incur the expense of sending sex education kits to high schools unless they expected to gain customers from the investment.

But the general public doesn't get these glimpses behind the scenes. What we typically will see is a good government-sounding campaign. In Illinois, for instance, the March of Dimes and the American Red Cross created community pressure for clinics in schools. They joined with two community-action groups, Parents Too Soon and Ounce of Prevention (both of which are recipients of Title XX federal tax money), which in turn were connected with charitable foundations that were ready to provide start-up money for the clinics.

Joy Dryfoos of the Center for Population Options has urged people planning local clinics to "avoid local controversy by starting with primary health care and then adding family planning services"[16] Paul Shaheen, executive director of the Michigan Council for Maternal and Child Health, has been more explicit about his strategy:

> We follow a strategy that says, "Go to the conservatives." Prevention is a conservative concept so when we wanted to get family planning, I went to the middle of the Republican party and said, "Gee, guys and ladies, you say your welfare rolls are growing too fast and you say you don't like abortion. Well, neither do I. But you've got a four to eight week waiting list at your family

planning clinics. People don't stand around and wait. They find things to do with those four to eight weeks."

We used the most conservative physicians we could find. They go to their conservative friends and say, "This isn't a question of politics. This is a question of human pain and suffering."

In addition to gullible doctors and "middle of the road" Republicans, sex clinic organizers frequently involve clergymen to give a patina of respectability to their programs. Teachers are involved as well, along with a carefully chosen parent or two with progressive views, you may be sure. Media support is easy to come by. The famous Lichter-Rothman study a few years ago surveyed the attitudes of journalists in the major media outlets and found that 54 percent of them thought adultery is not wrong; 76 percent believe homosexuality is not wrong, and 90 percent think abortion should be legal. School sex clinics were not an issue at the time of the survey, but the other indicators suggest where opinions on that topic might lie.

The strategists and organizers who promote school-based clinics are masterful manipulators. Jacqueline Manley, of the Center for Population Options, told the Third Annual Conference on School Based Clinics of her experience in Indianapolis. The assistant superintendent had liked the *Life Planning* curriculum she was trying to sell, but he knew he would face controversy because of the values section and asked her to delete it. She agreed with his request, but then she said, "I went back to the motel room and I started to look at the Values chapter and I thought, 'You know what we can do. We can take the activity called Family Messages and put that in the Communications section. And we can take Rank Your Values and we can switch that around.' I found someplace to stick all the exercises without calling them values." The assistant superintendent was pleased with Manley's changes, and according to her the entire program was put in place in Indianapolis.[17]

School-based clinics are not cheap to operate, either. But its advocates manage to minimize its up-front expenses to the school district. Frequently, private foundations will promise to pay the expenses for the first year or two; "seed money," this is called. The Robert Wood Johnson Foundation is a major donor to such enterprises, frequently committing up to $300,000 in the first year, $200,000 the second, and $100,000 the third. By the third year, the school district is scrambling to find the funds, but by then a self-perpetuating interest group has been created. Douglas

Kirby of the Center for Population Options estimates a cost between $100 and $125 per student per year.[18] The *Chicago Tribune* estimated that the annual cost a few years ago of operating two Chicago-area school-based clinics was $500,000 a year.[19] One can't help wondering whether Chicago could have done quite a bit more good with half a million more dollars in its teacher salary budget.

Any way you look at it, school-based clinics are terribly expensive, especially when nobody officially has any idea whether they can do the job of reducing teenage pregnancy. (Never mind for the moment that reducing teenage *sexual activity* ought to be the goal; the people who make decisions about things like this rarely think in such terms.)

There is no reason to suppose, however, that the clinics will make a bit of difference. More teenagers are already using contraceptives than ever before, yet the number and rate of premarital pregnancies continue to rise.[20] Within two years after first obtaining a prescription for a contraceptive method, one out of four unmarried teenagers becomes pregnant.[21]

When the results begin to be publicized about school-based clinics, the public will probably hear headlines about how teenage births declined in such and such an area after the school clinic was opened. Rounds of congratulations will be exchanged among school board members, and the statistics may be accurate. But watch for what is not reported. Has teenage pregnancy declined, or just teenage births? Stan Weed, at the Institute for Research and Evaluation in Salt Lake City, studied some of the claims of family planning clinics that specialize in the teen market. What he found was that as the number of teenage clients increased, the pregnancy rate increased. The birthrate did go down, however. What accounts for the difference? Abortion rates increased.[22] Is that not, then, a worsening of the problem?

It's not lack of access to contraceptives that causes teenagers to become pregnant. Urging contraception on teenagers, all the while telling them how much fun it is to have sexual intercourse, is like telling a drinker he shouldn't get drunk as you continue to refill his glass with whiskey. It's a double message.

And the biggest double message is just beginning to be sent now. It's called Norplant. Norplant is a lot more than an item in the teenage promiscuity debate. It could be a point of no return for Christian ethics in our society. In California, a judge made use of it a condition of probation for a mother convicted of child abuse. Within a year, thirteen states were considering legislation mandating use of it as part of the punishment for certain crimes, or as part of financial incentive packages for poor women. The trend is growing. Close this book for a moment and think about the implication of what you just read: the government will soon be requiring contraceptive use of some women. Government controlling fertility. Isn't that God's department—the gift of fertility? What right does government have to mandate contraceptive use by anybody?

None, in principle. But our society has lost sight of principle. We wouldn't have the sexuality innundation that is producing so many secondary problems. Americans have a love affair with technology, but antipathy to philosophy. If you can stick a device in a woman's body, and avoid dealing with the deeper level of the problem, go for it—at least, in the pragmatic view of overburdened policymakers. Just one more proof of how the lack of self-control invites government control. Or how too much "freedom," as the word is commonly used, leads inevitably to a deprivation of liberty, in the true sense.

Norplant's first encounter with youth came in Baltimore. The city of Baltimore has a teen birth rate three times the nation's average, and it also has Johns Hopkins University within its limits. The medical establishment organized a consortium of hospitals, doctors, clinics, and a foundation, got the Mayor to support it, and bingo, all of a sudden Norplant was available in all eight of Baltimore's school-based clinics.

Predictably, the media cheered and hurrahed this initiative. It was a dream come true to population planners and reproductive service providers and their public relations teams. Imagine! Five years of fail-proof contraception for just $500. Just what teenagers need. Never mind the adverse reactions—prolonged bleeding, increased risk of sexually transmitted disease, toxic shock syndrome, and HIV transmission. Never mind the niggling questions of coercion or freedom. What a great way to end the problem.

The New York Times reported on the varying opinions of teenage women in Baltimore schools about the prospect. The principal of the school said she favors Norplant because it's a way to "buy time for young women to discover themselves and another way of life" beyond welfare. One of the students, age 19, had a year-old baby, her second. Her first baby was five years old. This mother told the reporter that her second child was not an accident, but a decision she made because her older daughter "had gotten so big and I felt like she didn't need me."

How could any mother feel a three-year-old didn't need her? And yet time and again, that is the voice coming out of the beleaguered inner city. Teenagers have babies because they want somebody to love, they want somebody to love them. Not because they don't have knowledge of and access to drugs and devices and abortions. Because, for reasons that are at root quite normal, they want babies. Since society has, through welfare and other social policies, structured their universe so that no man is obligated to remain attached to them, and since a lack of training and formation has fractured their other family relationships, who else is there to love them?

There are deep reasons for teenage sexual activity. Sometimes, it's just animal lust. But often, it is a lust born of profound human need. Contraceptives are merely technological bandages for serious emotional needs and human problems. And as with other bandages, if the wound is serious enough, it will only fester if you try to hide it with a bandage. Sooner or later, the bandage is going to fall off, and a putrid infection will be staring you in the face. A better policy would be to treat the wounds from the beginning.

THE ABSTINENCE EDUCATION MOVEMENT

In a sense, treating the wounds from the beginning is what the Abstinence Education Movement is all about. This growing movement takes a look at the reasons kids have sex, recognizes that it is because there is some emotional hole that kids are unconsciously trying to fill, and tries to fill the emotional gap. Building up self-esteem, giving a sense of future, and instilling good old-fashioned self-respect are part of the abstinence movement.

If there is an item of good news in this chapter, this is it. There are alternatives to the standard Planned Parenthood-type of sex education. There are numerous curricula that can be, and are being, used as substitutes for the usual "try it, you'll like it, anything goes" sex-ed material— and in public schools, too! Just a few years ago, you would not have had that. Now, there is a proliferation. See "Resources" appendix for the address of the National Association of Abstinence Education, which can provide information about many different curricula.

How that came about is an interesting story. Do you remember I earlier mentioned Senator Jeremiah Denton of Alabama? Not only was he a hero in Vietnam, to me he was even more of a hero in the U.S. Senate. He came up with a bill called the Adolescent Family Life Act, which he forced his reluctant Senate colleagues to debate and vote on. Lo and behold, it was passed. As a result of it, a small office was created within the Department of Health and Human Services, to develop pro-moral sex education curriculum programs.

Numerous curricula were launched with help from the Office of Adolescent Family Life before Bill Clinton killed it. You may have heard some of the names: TeenAid, Sex Respect, Teen Choice, and more. Nor did all abstinence programs have the seed money from Washington; as the trend grew, there was a proliferation from all sources, such as Josh McDowell's Why Wait? From time to time one of them makes headlines, when a court somewhere declares it unconstitutional (on the grounds that teaching abstinence is forcing religious views on students), or when a court declares it constitutional. The Illinois legislature, for instance, gives Sex Respect a yearly grant of several hundred thousand dollars—and Illinois is hardly a right-wing-conservative state.

How does this come about? Kathleen Sullivan, of Sex Respect, freely admits that 15 to 20 percent of students are not going to listen to anything anybody says.[23] But the vast middle, the sixty to eighty percent, need to hear from school that abstinence from sex, as from drugs and alcohol, is reasonable, attainable, and expected behavior. And if in the course of the education, young people get the glimmer of an idea that, perhaps, other people aren't just objects to be used, but persons to be loved, well, then, so much the better.

The point is: it's not just right-wing-conservatives who believe that abstinence makes better sense for kids.

No less an agent of the other side than an editor of *Rolling Stone* magazine has boldly stated as much. In an op-ed in that journalistic dreadnought of the enemy, *The New York Times,* the day after Christmas of 1992, Ellen Hopkins made a liberal, feminist argument for pushing abstinence in the schools. Her argument went as follows: Sex education doesn't work. Even if sex education worked, birth control doesn't. Let's follow one sexually active teen-ager who does just what she's statistically likely to do. Her options are bleak. Even a ruined life may be better than a life cut short by AIDS. Current recommendations for "safer" sex are unrealistic. Promoting abstinence can be done intelligently and effectively. Sex is for adults. An amazing conclusion, no?

A lot of liberals develop common sense as their children, particularly their daughters, enter adolescence. And a lot of teachers have common sense and are eager to have something worthwhile to teach the students whose needs they know so well. Some interesting coalitions can be made at school board and county levels of educators, politicians, and parents trying to find something worthwhile to fill the requirement for safe sex education.

There are a few purists to whom any kind of abstinence education looks like compromise. They feel there's something undesirable about teaching or encouraging the right behavior for less than the noblest reason. As if it isn't good enough for kids to say no out of self-interest, because they should be saying it for correct spiritual reasons. I have encountered people like this, and as we discuss it further, it usually emerges that they don't think the schools ought to teach any sex education. In other words, they're standing in a station from which the train left about fifty years ago. To be sure, if I had my druthers and could re-fashion society from the ground up, I wouldn't want sex education in the public schools either, because in my ideal society kids would be getting virtues education from their parents their whole life long. But enough of my pipedream: this is the real world, and sex-ed is a problem on the agenda. As to whether it's going to be Planned Parenthood's version or something less evil, any Christian involved in making decisions for the public schools should have an easy choice.

COPING WITH SEX EDUCATION COURSES

Suppose you live in a state that instituted elementary through senior high sex education courses as it rode the AIDS bandwagon of the late 1980's. Your children are currently in public schools. What are your options?

Can you afford a private or Christian school? Is there one convenient to you? Are you comfortable with it? Don't assume that all private schools or all religiously-affiliated schools are free from the plague of sex education. Some are as much trend-followers as the public schools.

If another school is not an option, have you considered home schooling? It's not as hard as it seems. Lots of curriculum programs are available, and because personalized attention escalates the pace of learning, you may be surprised to discover that home schooling requires less time than you might expect. The movement is becoming well-organized, and it is also now widely accepted, not only legally but also socially, and there are abundant parent-support groups to help you get started, and to fellow-ship with after you're into it. By having your own children at home, you as parent have lots more control over how much of the youth culture they are exposed to, since they no longer have the peer group at school to teach them the songs and fill their minds with the television shows you may not want them to hear or see. So don't dismiss the home-schooling option without due consideration.

If taking your child out of public school is not an option, you might try to exempt your child from the sex education course. This is not usually very successful. Only about 3 percent of parents nationwide succeed in this course of action.[24] District policies and state laws differ. If the course is required for graduation from high school, a different battleplan is required than if it is merely an offering in fourth grade. And increasingly, the "family life" instruction is taught in discrete modules that are infiltrated throughout the curriculum.

A word of warning: The very effort to try for exemption could stigmatize your child, both in the eyes of other students and in the eyes of the teachers and administrators. If his academic future lies in that school, that could be a serious setback. Depending on the child's age and disposition, the fear of peer ridicule could be counterproductive as well. Since you're not likely to succeed, you might want to think very seriously before trying.

Sometimes there is strength in unity. If you can find twenty other parents who want their children exempted, you have a much better chance than if you are a lone ranger. Be aware, however, that organizing a parent group to operate en masse could turn into a full-time volunteer job for you. But there is a lot of potential in parental grassroots movements. For example, groups of parent activists have defeated plans to establish school-based clinics at various locales in the nation. Years ago I wrote an entire book on the topic of how to organize grassroots parental action groups. If you can find it anywhere, it might give you some guidance if you decide to go this route.[25]

HOW TO EVALUATE A SEX EDUCATION PROGRAM

If the options of switching schools or changing curricula are not available to you, the next step in protecting your child is to at least know the enemy. Know the curriculum he's being taught, and know it inside out. Know exactly what is being fed to him every week—this is essential if you are to counteract successfully the harmful messages that may be contained in the material.

It may not be all bad, however. Don't assume that it is either good or bad before you have evaluated it, slowly and carefully, paragraph by paragraph.

What is the character, tone, and general orientation of the program? Is chastity presented as something positive and purposeful? Is the innocence of the young protected? Is proper and respectful terminology used at all times? Is the instruction given on a sex-separate basis (i.e., non-coed classrooms)?

How does the program handle the problems associated with promiscuity, contraception, and abortion? Is the possibility of contracting venereal disease without realizing it stressed? Are the dangers of VD stressed, as well as the fact that some of them are not curable? Is it explicitly taught that the best way to avoid VD or AIDS is to be chaste?

What is taught about human development? Are facts about fetal development before birth taught thoroughly, preferably with illustrations? Are differences between human beings and animals stressed, or are just the similarities mentioned? Are human freedom and personal responsibility emphasized? Is the fact that the sexual appetite can be controlled acknowledged and given due importance? Is practical information given on how to say no, how to avoid dangerous situations, and so forth?

What about the bigger picture, the global perspective? Is the old "population explosion" nonsense taught, or does the program give the real truth about the birth dearth facing the Western world today?

What kind of values are implicit or explicit in the program? Is the idea that "all values are just choices" the dominant theme? Do consequentialist ideas underlie the philosophy behind the book—namely, that if something produces a good result, it must be the right thing to do? Are certain dangerous techniques employed in the program, such as hypothetical lifeboat exercises (in which students decide which persons to throw overboard in order to save which other persons)? Is personal or family privacy probed, either in assignments or in class discussions? Are negative feelings focused on and students forced to think about them? Are there a lot of "unfinished statement" exercises, such as "I would like to have sex with somebody who . . . "?

With these questions in mind, read through the material that your child will be taught. It may not be easy to get it. You may have to go to the school, the teacher, and even the principal to be allowed to see the text-book or teacher's guide. Your child may not be allowed to bring his book or workbook home. Against that possibility, while you have the material, make a copy of what is in each chapter. That way you'll have an idea of what is being taught over the semester, and you'll be able to address the same topics with your child at home from the proper moral perspective.

INOCULATING YOUR CHILDREN

If your child is in a public school, it really comes down to inoculating your child against the undesirable material being shoved at him in the classroom. Of course, alert parents do this all the time anyway. It's one of the main reasons to help your child with homework in any subject, so you know what ideas are being taught. If you know your second-grader is learning to add double digits in his head, as you're driving along in the car you can give him double-digit problems to add. If you know your fourth-grader is studying knights and castles, you might choose a Christmas present of a book about King Arthur.

Such general involvement can be occasional. But when it comes to counterbalancing sex education instruction, your involvement has to be early and often. Be explicit. Tell your child you're displeased he has to take that course. Let him know what you did to protect him from having to take it and that you feel it's something to be protected against. To the extent he can understand, tell him why, in a manner something like this: "We're your parents, and God has given us the responsibility to teach you right and wrong. From what I've heard, Mrs. Jones may be trying to teach you something different in the classroom from what we believe. Now when she teaches math, you can believe her, but when she gets into some things about how people should treat each other, she may not have the right ideas. She's still your teacher, so you have to respect her, but you don't have to believe her when she contradicts what we've taught. This might be confusing to you, so I want to make sure we talk about it at the dinner table each night so we can help you. We want to make sure you aren't taught something that's a mistake and might confuse you later on."

Try to have the review one-on-one with the child who is in the program. But if that doesn't work out, do it at the dinner table. Don't worry too much if younger children hear some clinical or mature conversations during this semester. They may not be listening to it anyhow. But if they are, you're doing some full family teaching, and you're inoculating the younger ones, too. If they know it already when it's their turn to get it in school, they will probably pay even less attention to it then.

The best protection a child can have against the teaching of deviant values is to have a full set of right ones already. Before entering the first classroom, a Christian child should have grasped some concepts of privacy and virtue, without even realizing it (see chapters 7–8). But those grasps of morality and virtue should deepen steadily and should recognize the enemy. Often, in our parental zeal to protect innocence, we allow ignorance to hold sway in our children's minds. This cannot protect them from evil influences.

When the material gets around to explicit things, if your child already knows what they're trying to teach him, he will be able to criticize and reject what is wrong in the teaching. If he has intuitively grasped some basic principles of sexual morality, now is the time to make that intuitive understanding into a conscious, articulate defense of those values. If he has already enjoyed family intimacy, he knows, probably without realizing it, that human relationships take time to develop, and that they're worth waiting for. If he has been well-disciplined, he knows, for example, that things that may seem attractive can nonetheless be bad for himself and others.

Most of all, probably the most helpful thing you can do to help your child cope with organized sexual hyperconsciousness is to be his friend. Keep all your channels of communication open. Be careful to keep his self-esteem up. Catch him doing things right—or even just trying—so you can commend him on his increasing maturity, thoughtfulness, and responsibility. Be sensitive to his emotional states. Realize he will be under a lot of pressure, getting a lot of stimulation from the ideas and conversations he is going to hear. He'll be torn between trying to react to it all in a manner his peers find acceptable and not wanting to betray his deeper loyalty to his parents. This stimulation will cause behavioral effects he will not realize and that will have to be disciplined if they go too far. So be sure that he senses his family's love and involvement and concern for his happiness in other ways. He may be self-conscious, particularly around the other sex, and may worry about things he knew nothing of before.

All I've suggested so far you can do to help minimize damage to your own child. But what about the rest of the classroom? What about the children yours will be playing with, going out with, working alongside? How can they be helped to avoid a promiscuous lifestyle?

What behavioral science data there are on factors correlating with a moral lifestyle suggest that what all American children need is not sex education programs, but church values and a stable home life. As Eunice Kennedy Shriver put it, "Absence of love and lack of family connectedness are the underlying causes of most adolescent pathology, which no pills or devices can cure."[26] A University of North Carolina study found that "adolescent girls reared without fathers are much more likely to be sexually active" than girls raised by two parents.[27] This study also found that boys become more sexually active when parents divorce.

Jacqueline Kasun has found that a young woman who attends church at least once a week is much less likely to engage in premarital intercourse than one who does not, from age fourteen on up. Indeed, regular church attendance has a stronger effect on the behavior of girls over age seventeen than any other factor![28] This is particularly notable in the inner cities.

If our children are going to be in public schools, however, we need to monitor closely what they're being taught so that we can correct or counteract as necessary. This requires time and effort—make no mistake about that. And it may only be successful as long as childhood lasts. Adolescents legitimately need privacy, and mom prying into what they get taught at school can be an area of unnecessary conflict. But, considering what's at stake, for as long as you can, it's worth the effort to try.

And take heart. In 1993, the New York City School superintendent had to resign after he tried to force a pro-homosexual family life curriculum into the elementary schools. That victory may suggest that even this corrupt generation may find limits in what it is willing to tolerate in the brainwashing of young children. But in the meanwhile, be exceedingly watchful, and protect your children yourself.

Chapter 4

THE ORIGINS OF CONSCIENCE

The word *holy* means "set apart for God." The basic goal of Christian parents is to make the home holy, set apart for God as far as possible in the areas that matter.

This does not mean that our goal is to make our kids weird. We want them to look and sound normal. They will know, to a greater or lesser degree, the things that preoccupy their peers. They will not, most likely, be innocent or ignorant of the perversions that afflict the world. But God willing, *they will not be preoccupied with these things.* That will be the biggest difference between them and their peers. Of course, if they associate too much with friends who are thus preoccupied, they will be corrupted. To the extent that they can be trained properly, however, the holy influence of the home can make its impact.

Children reared in a holy atmosphere will be swimming against the tide of values and peer pressure. But they will be willing to do so because they will understand the reasons. And what's more, they will want to pursue the higher good because their wills will have been trained.

Ultimately, children reared thus may find themselves very successful in the world, in their education or career. Despite the glamor of the rock culture, after all, those who take it seriously and emulate its lifestyle are more likely to end up digging ditches than designing the plans.

The prerequisite for any effective child-rearing is that the parents must be struggling to be holy themselves. The parents must swim against the tide, must set apart their own time for prayer, must humble themselves before God, must discipline themselves in a thousand small and large ways. Tranquility will be the watchword of the home: "Be still and know that I am God" (Ps. 46:10) is practical advice for the home. When radios are blaring and voices are escalating, how is one to hear the Lord?

Christian sex education, you see, is not education in sex; it is education in affection and in relating to others. But before it makes sense to talk about teaching children to relate to others, first they have to know how to relate to themselves and to God. And that is the first task of the conscience. In this chapter, we'll look at the basic Christian atmosphere that needs to be created in a home before the right kind of sex education can take place.

CONSCIENCE

In training a child, remember you are training the will, which acts but does not think. The mind is taught; the will is trained. Andrew Murray put it this way: habits precede principles. The conscience, the internalized disposition to judge right or wrong, contains some elements of both habits and principles.

Ambrose Bierce, that cynical wag, said that the conscience was that part of you that felt bad when every other part felt good. More precisely, the conscience is a person's supply, or fund, of moral information. The voice of conscience is the judgment spontaneously formed when one brings that fund of information to bear on an action.

The parents' task is to form the child's conscience so the child knows the difference between right and wrong, and to form the child's will so he can fight against what is wrong. The parent should ask himself, *Is my own conscience formed correctly? Is my own will strong in avoiding sin?* If an honest examination finds me lacking, that's no reason to abandon the effort to form my child's conscience. After all, the Christian journey is a continuous road to be traveled, a continual process of daily trying to be a little more Christlike. As I learn to strengthen my own will, I can be imparting strength to my children. It is only Satan who would deceive me into thinking that I must be perfect before I can begin to teach my children to avoid sin.

How does a child learn right and wrong? His first idea is that right is what pleases Mom, and wrong is what displeases her. It's a natural, beautiful, and perfectly planned first step.

The eventual goal is for the child to understand that something is right because it pleases God and wrong because it displeases Him. This is the only foundation for a healthy conscience. It is completely based on love. In between Mom and God, of course, come Dad, Brother, Sister, Teacher, and other authority figures. The concept of God does not come early to our fallen minds; we form the concept by analogy with our human parents and caretakers.

But is this how most of us understand right and wrong? If it were, I suspect our sad world would not be in the shabby shape it is. Unfortunately, even Christian parents tend to fall into several common alternatives—understandably enough, because we probably were raised according to one or another of them ourselves.

If Mom or Dad is never satisfied by a child's efforts, if nothing is "right enough" or "good enough" and all the child hears about is his failings, it is hard for a child to care about pleasing that person who can never be pleased. Besides producing workaholics as a side effect, such parental dissatisfaction produces a conscience that isn't satisfied with doing right. With the coming of adolescence, the conscience can become totally indifferent, the mind having decided that "nothing I do is good enough anyhow, so why bother." Or it can become hyperscrupulous and prudish, scanning each thought and word with a magnifying glass, looking for faults. Neither is a healthy alternative, and neither is likely to produce morality and happiness.

Perhaps an equally common phenomenon is the conscience built on fear. How many children believe that right is what they can get away with and wrong is what will get them punished? "Do what you're told or you'll be punished" is the lesson perhaps most commonly learned. Behind all that, somewhere, is God, who set down rules, waiting to be discovered, and who frequently allows Himself to be discovered and loved. But for most children, growing up in an atmosphere of a fear-based morality, a sense of divine love is seriously obscured, if not absent. "Well, kids can't understand such things anyhow," those who practice such habits of child-rearing will argue.

Maybe not at first. But if right and wrong are explained correctly over and over, and if children observe others feeling remorse at the thought of displeasing or causing pain to God, the concept can get through. The Holy Spirit fills children far more than we adults might believe—at least until by our cynicism we teach them to ignore or resist His gentle impulses.

Following the path of Christian virtue is a journey without a lot of visible and tangible rewards. To be courageous in following it, a young person needs to be satisfied with having virtue as its own reward. And that can only happen when one knows with emotional as well as intellectual certainty that God is pleased. That knowledge is the reward. But how can virtue be its own reward when a fear-formed conscience has deprived the person of the joy of knowing he has pleased God by doing right? Parents are a child's first image of God, remember.

Do you see what a self-destructive path it is to try to train a child to virtue through instilling fear? It deprives the child of joy.

I do not mean to imply that fear of punishment, human and divine, should not be real to a child. Indeed it should. But it should be a back-up mechanism to the parent who uses it and to the child who thinks about it. When the more noble motivation of altruistic love fails, there is a less noble one to reinforce the correct decision. Yes, one should do what one does for the love of God and love of others. Hope of heavenly reward is the ideal motivator. But fear of punishment is an equally strong human emotion. Who among us has not, in moments of great temptation, asked himself, *But what if I die on the way home?* as a way to strengthen his will to resist a delicious temptation? A hardened conscience can ignore even that question, however, for a hardened conscience has lost even the fear of punishment.

My friend Andre Leyva, a family counselor, has invented a visual aid to explain something very important about parent/child interaction, and how it evolves into certain types of behavior patterns in adolescents.

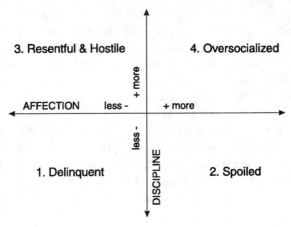

At the center of both axes are moderate amounts of both discipline and affection—obviously, as with so much in life, moderation is the goal. The further you move out on either axis, the more you invite problems. The child who receives a lot of discipline, and very little affection is likely to become resentful and hostile. Naturally enough he doesn't feel loved, and hence is hard put to love others. The child who receives very little discipline and very little affection is the one likely to become a juvenile delinquent. He'll be rebelling against parents who give him neither limits nor love. The child who receives little discipline, but much affection—the Dr. Spock type of upbringing—is liable to become spoiled, with an excessive ego. He feels terribly important, expects things to go his way throughout life, and does not know how to cope with adversity. The child who receives too much discipline and too much affection is not free of problems, either. Such a child is called "oversocialized," which means likely to be too compliant, thus failing to develop sufficient individuality and self-reliance to enable him or her to cope with life on a healthy basis.

Graphic depictions of human dynamics are, of course, seriously imperfect. I generally steer quite clear of them myself. But when I first encountered this chart in a Christian parenting course taught by Dr. Leyva, it rang true to my experience, and showed me with crystal clearness something I had been groping for in my own experience as a parent.[1] It also gives a hint why the children of well-disciplined, high-achieving parents sometimes don't turn out to be so well-disciplined—the children of these usually busy parents have perceived the discipline, but not the affection. I think all parents of teenagers would do well to find out whether their children *feel* loved. Most kids *know* (with their intellect) they are loved—but it's *feeling loved* that gives the emotional energy to make the right choices.

CHILDREN AND SIN

It should be obvious that I believe sin is possible for children. This is not a fashionable notion today, however. Ever since the Enlightenment, at the end of the eighteenth century, liberal and fashionable circles have maintained that children are born perfect, coming into the world "naturally good." Jean-Jacques Rousseau called it the "noble savage": man is born virtuous but everywhere inflicts and endures misery. Why? Because of his upbringing. Much secular child psychology begins with the premise that children are born naturally good.

Can we agree that this is so much baloney? Some people say adults aren't capable of sin, either, that they just act the way they do because they grew up in adverse circumstances or were conditioned to act a certain way. The same people, however, would not have corrected these adults even when they were children, because then, they would have maintained, they were incapable of sin. Well, naturally, if you don't correct a child, he's going to grow up into an adult who acts like a beast. If that means you also can't correct the adult, there's no hope for the future of the human race!

It's easier for parents to see that children can sin than it is for doting grandparents. And a person whose conscience is unhappily fear-formed can understandably argue, "How can God punish a child?" and therefore logically end up uncertain whether a child can really sin. Then, too, a parent who is not clear in his own mind that a child is capable of sin will have poor motivation to discipline the child and will not be in a good position to form the conscience of the child.

One point of confusion might be this: everything wrong is not a sin. In our family, for instance, bad table manners and insufficiently formal church clothes produced as many parent-son confrontations as any real sins. This was a mistake on our part as parents. I don't think we ever said it was a sin (we knew better), but from the reaction sometimes, how would the kids know we don't think it's a matter of grave moral concern? (In case you've had the same scene played out in your home, take heart: when they attained the age at which they won the right to pick their own clothes, their choices were on the whole quite good, and they looked down their noses at the kids whose parents did not insist on shirts and ties at church!)

Kids have unerring perceptions of parents' faults. If Daddy blows his top, Junior will notice that and conveniently overlook what he did to provoke the explosion. Technically, he's correct in observing that Dad lost his temper. But if he makes that observation out loud, chances are he will be punished more severely for his honesty (which Dad will call "freshness") than for the original misbehavior. Yet Junior's observation, while it may sound "fresh," may reflect no sin, but instead, be nothing worse than a lack of diplomacy on his part. Kids' reactions to parents' faults are not sins. Say Mom wants her nap—indeed, legitimately needs her nap in order to do her job. It is wrong for the kids to make noise and interrupt her nap. But it isn't a sin to interrupt Mom's nap, and it would be wrong to tell exuberant Johnny that it is. It would be excessive of Mom to think of it as a sin.

What is real sin in a child? Selfishness. Deliberate, planned, self-seeking self-centeredness—putting what "I" want and "I" desire before everything else, and everybody else, in the world. This is the mentality, the set of habits, that makes happiness in this life impossible and renders salvation difficult. It was selfishness that made Eve want to be better than God. It is selfishness that produces pride, covetousness, lust, anger, gluttony, envy, and sloth—which, in turn, produce lying, stealing, cheating, fighting, exploiting, anger, and all the rest. Those sins deserve to be punished in and of themselves. But their root causes should be noted, and in childhood the roots can be extirpated. Adult sexual indulgence outside of marriage is just another form of uninhibited selfishness, the natural and logical consequence of a lifetime of putting what "I" want before other considerations. The earlier a child can spot selfishness in himself and root it out, the greater favor the parent has done him.

At what age is a child capable of sin? If not at ten, then why would it be at twelve? Why at fourteen? And if at ten, why not at eight? What's the difference between two years? A Catholic priest has written of a child who repents to him, saying, "I spent a whole week wishing a terrible accident would happen to my mother and really hurt her." Is that a sin? For a child to spend a week absorbed in one evil idea, no matter what his chronological age, certainly does not please a loving God. If you want to argue that it's not a sin and say that God would not punish a seven-year-old for this, then consider this practical question: If such a tendency toward selfish hatred goes uncorrected, what will the child be thinking five years hence? What is he likely to be doing ten years hence? Better to nip an evil flower in its bud than to wait for it to get strong and woody.

Consider the misery the child could be causing himself by this sin. Suppose that during that week of wishing ill to his mother, she had indeed met with a fatal accident and died. What would the load of guilt on his young heart have been then? Might it not have overshadowed the rest of his life? And would he not then clearly be the victim of his own sin? Are we not all ultimately the victims of our own sins?

The year before my husband and I went to Australia on a speaking tour, we had cut down a sweet gum tree in our front yard. That spring hundreds of suckers had sprung up on the lawn from the root system of the tree. But there were a myriad of details to arrange before the trip, and every time we mowed the lawn, the extra fifteen minutes to mow down the suckers just didn't seem to be available. When we got back from Australia, the suckers were tall and strong, and the front yard looked like an abandoned shack. One afternoon I went out with some hedge trimmers, expecting to snip them down. But no go; they were too woody. I got snippers and tried to cut them one at a time. Still no go. I ended up having to pry them out, one at a time, tearing them from the root by brute force. They were simply too strong to cut, even by hand. I couldn't get them all that day, either, because I got so many blisters after a short time that I couldn't continue. Then, a few days later, I began having problems with my pregnancy and couldn't do any more physical work.

So it is with sin: if we don't pluck it out when it's young and easily removed, we have a bigger problem later. And we never know when time may run out on our opportunity to tear it out later.

As parents whose job it is to form the consciences of our children, we must continuously form our own consciences. How can we teach our kids if we don't know how to do it ourselves? So we must examine ourselves daily to make sure we are not separating ourselves from God's love. We must repent daily, if not more frequently. We must not excuse ourselves for our own faults, our temper outbursts, our moments of self-pity, our desires for selfishness, our materialistic attachments, our impatience. We must give our little sins their just due, call them sins, and treat them as such so that we can give our big sins their due. The job of a conscience is to tell us when we need to repent, and to help us do so. If we go through life ignoring our little sins, then we'll ignore our big sins, and pretty soon we won't be able to hear our consciences at all.

This is why, from the youngest age, our children should be corrected. It will develop their conscience. And the sooner that happens, the better. There is so little time available to parents to help develop a child's conscience. By age thirteen, most children are reluctant to receive highly personalized help with their repenting, even if they have been accustomed to it since childhood. At that age, the yearning toward privacy, which is a healthy tendency, will be growing strong and should be respected.

A word from Dad, spoken privately and gently, often carries more weight than one from Mom as years advance. And sometimes Dad can make a deeper impression on a daughter than he might think. But as adolescence advances, the neck is arched over the pasture fence. This is why youth groups become important, and why as parents we must be so careful of the values of the leaders of those groups. A church with an active youth group and an involved, reliable pastor is a great blessing. A youth's involvement should be a family priority, and the involvement should be made a pleasant experience—no arguments about what he wears to meetings, for instance, and willingness to arrange transportation without complaint.

SHARE THE STRUGGLE

Make no mistake, the Christian life is a constant struggle. It has its rewards: peace that passes understanding, for instance, is one that will pretty much always be available to one who has repented of sin. But comfort and ease are not to be expected. A state of being continually "up" is not a part of genuine Christianity, either, though no one will deny that there are occasional moments of spiritual bliss.

It is a lie to give children any other impression. They need to know that, in following their conscience, formed in accordance with the Word of God, they are going to be struggling all the time. In their formative years, seeing their parents struggle is good preparation for their own struggle, as well as encouragement along the way.

When your faults are visible, later on, perhaps at evening prayer, ask for your child's forgiveness, and then God's, for that temper. It may be years before the child asks your forgiveness for his temper, but having seen you do it will give him an example to follow. It makes God real to your child if he sees you talking to Him.

Avoid double standards in the home, where tantrums are allowable for the parents but the kids are expected to control their anger. Daddy can't be allowed his dirty magazine but Junior be expected to turn his eyes away from them, to take an extreme example. Hypocrisy can be smelled by kids, and the reaction is a loss of trust. When there's a loss of trust, the child's conscience, which has been fortifying itself for its own struggle by pointing to the parent as an example of strength, finds itself without reinforcements.

Parents aren't perfect. Why should we pretend to be? Our children will only believe it for a few of their earliest years anyhow, and if they later figure out that we tried to create a false impression of perfection, they'll be skeptical of everything we tell them. It's not worth it to deceive them. If our egos are so weak that we can't be honest with our own children, we have a lot of work to do. Besides, repenting to our children is a good exercise in humility for a parent, a good antidote to the pride in our station that we are prone to developing along the way.

Remember, it's discouraging for our children to think they are struggling alone. If they know that we, too, are struggling, it offers them heart for their own trials. I'm talking here about little things—garden-variety faults, if you will. When lavish catalogues temptingly arrayed arrive in the mailbox, I conspicuously throw them in the trash, deliberately telling my children that these things are simply invitations to covet things I don't need and shouldn't want. When I find myself chattering on about acquaintances of neighbors in front of the boys, I have been known to stop myself out loud and tell them I'm talking too much and shouldn't gossip. As they get older, they think they can tell when I'm mad. And when their observations are correct, I may tell them I am being tempted to be mad but am trying hard not to be, and would they please do such and such before I give in to the temptation!

In years gone by, I edited a newsletter called *Family Protection Report.* I'll never forget one father's account of how he told his teenaged sons of his experience in Europe while attending a conference. Each day, walking from his hotel to the conference site, he walked two blocks out of his way to avoid a display of pornography in a shop window. He told his son of his experience, and the son's reaction was a startled, "Gosh, Dad, you mean you have to struggle with that, too?" Sharing that confidence probably did more to encourage the son in his fight for custody of his eyes than the father could have done in a year any other way. However, a parent should not confide his failures to a child. Yes, be honest and admit "I have my sins, too," and share strategies on resisting temptation, but sharing accounts of specific sin is more likely to do harm than good. Parents are role models and leaders, and leaders give encouragement, not discouragement.

By training the consciences of our children along these lines, being honest about our own struggles and offering the encouragement that God's help and forgiveness are always available, we create an environment in which truly Biblical sex education can take place.

Chapter 5

TOO LITTLE TOO LATE

C an parents seize control of the youth culture? That's a question of major proportions. Are there enough motivated and concerned parents in our nation to change the viciousness of the youth culture? No, there probably are not. Although organized groups of parents have had some success in specific areas of concern—groups like Mothers Against Drunk Driving come to mind—no group has or probably could set for itself the goal of liberating our young people from the entire self-destructive youth culture. It may be that such is not the way to proceed given such a vast series of vested financial interests, and given the general obliviousness of the American people to the problem.

All of us as parents, however, are responsible for how the culture is allowed into our homes. While we cannot seize control of the entire culture, we *can* prevent our children from being sucked into it. We can limit its incursions into our homes. This is essentially playing a defensive game; if we are starting when our children are young enough, we can play more of an offensive game and create a genuine Christian culture in our homes. For more on that, see the last chapter. But in this chapter, let's consider specific ways in which we can minimize the influence of the youth, or rock, culture in our homes.

MINIMIZING THE ROCK CULTURE

Monitoring the popular rock culture is, theoretically, relatively easy—about as easy as monitoring the whereabouts and activities of your adolescent. If you have an adolescent, you catch the sarcasm in my last sentence. Even apart from the nature of adolescents to roam ever further from the home pasture, by the time kids get to adolescence, parents tend to be ready for a break and are just plain tired. Or Mom has gone to work in anticipation of college bills, and there's only so much time, attention, and ability left over to keep track of every waking minute of the offspring.

Even worse, most other mothers and fathers are taking a laid-back, permissive approach, telling themselves and you that "the public schools aren't as bad as you think," "teens are pretty sensible, really," or "the kids today know so much of the dangers of the world that they're not going to make the mistakes our generation made." When the rest of the world seems to be going permissive, it's hard to resist the trend. But the first prerequisite for resisting the sway of the popular culture is to resist, vigorously, the temptation of permissiveness.

All limits will be tested during adolescence: clothing, table manners, language, habits, church attendance, doing homework, family relationships. Everything is fair game for a storm-tossed teen. It's easy to think that as parents we are being singled out for special opprobrium by our kids, especially when they look at us with snapping eyes and say, "I got up in a perfectly good mood, and you were just mad like you always are." Coming from a person for whom we have made—and intend to keep on making—countless sacrifices, that hurts, never mind the objective injustice of the charge. In such circumstances, it's so attractive and easy to say to yourself, *Why did I bother to make an issue out of the language he used toward his brother? Why didn't I just let it pass and keep peace at the breakfast table?* And you might even decide to let more pass the next time before you react.

In such a situation, you have to remind yourself that both you and he will suffer under such a course of action. You'll suffer in the short-term, because the immediate problem will only get worse, but he'll suffer in the long term. Whether he knows it or not, that rebellious teenager wants to know what your limits are. And deep down inside, he secretly wants to be held to them. It may be ten or twenty years before he realizes that he wants those limits, but when he's grown up, he'll appreciate it. Psychologists will vouch for the deep-seated desire adolescents have for standards to be upheld, despite their testing of them and rebellion against them.

One woman who heard my request for personal stories on James Dobson's "Weekend" program wrote me the story of her life. At age 13 she began dating, and soon got into the drug scene and led a tragic life until she met the Lord. "I would never want to say that it is my parents' fault I did what I did," she wrote to me, "but I do think maybe I was searching for some more restrictions in my life. As I recall, as soon as I really made my parents angry enough to discipline me harshly, I quit doing that particular thing . . . "

HOLD THE STANDARDS HIGH

We want our children to love us. We fear losing their love. And as typical Americans, we can be gulled into thinking that love is a feeling. When a hot-eyed, teenage offspring is shooting angry words at us, it's obvious that the feelings foremost in him are not warm fuzzies. At such a moment, we need to remind ourselves that love is not a feeling but a way of acting. And love to our children requires first of all that we demand, and receive, their respect. If we relax our standards, the first thing that will evaporate is the respect of our children. We should fear losing their respect more than we fear losing their feelings of love.

So let's say we hold the standards and continue to hold them, and they rebel and continue to rebel. The battle of the wills escalates to unendurable proportions. Do we still hold the standards? Do we meet the rebel halfway, agree to look the other way when his girlfriend spends the night, stop asking what he's smoking? This is probably the most common resolution of the problem. But take it a step further. If this is the course of action followed, what happens to the young person when he becomes satiated and disgusted with his own life? Where, then, can he turn for an alternative? If the parents have abandoned their standards, where is he going to find help when the adolescent becomes mature, and wants standards?

A rebellious child can always, with grace, return to the parents' standards. A child who has been deprived of standards will have nothing to return to.

A rebel who has made his own life miserable and ten or twenty years after adolescence finds himself divorced, lonely, and generally miserable will look back to his stormy teen years and muse. *My parents knew I would end up like this,* he may well conclude. If he can say, *They loved me and tried to prevent his; why was I so stupid to resist them?* the prodigal has a point from which to launch a return, from which to stage a comeback. But if he realizes his parents didn't try to stop him but allowed him to proceed easily down the road to ruin, he may well conclude that they didn't love him. In a depressed person, that is a point from which to begin contemplating suicide.

Columnist John Lofton has written of how his son rebelled for three years and made his own—and his parents'—life hell on earth. "For almost three years Andrew used drugs almost every day and most any kind of drugs he could get his hands on: alcohol, marijuana, PCP, LSD and once cocaine. Andrew also stole. . . . In addition, Andrew fornicated, he stayed out many nights, all night, without telling us where he was, and he failed the tenth grade twice." This is hideous torture for a family to endure. John continued, "As Andrew became more rebellious, he and I clashed more violently. We were constantly at war. His mother and I were at the end of our rope—although we prayed for him continuously for nearly three years." John warned his wife to prepare herself for Andrew's death by accident or suicide.

But then, one night while he was high on drugs, Andrew broke down and cried, saying he wanted to stop using drugs. His parents found a Christian treatment center for him, and within days Andrew accepted the Lord. The standards had always been held high, and when he began to feel the pain of his self-inflicted lifestyle, young Andrew knew where to look for help. He knew there was another way to live. Suppose that years earlier, however, his parents had given up the fight and decided to "go along to get along" with him. Where would Andrew have turned in his search?

PATTERNS FROM THE BEGINNING

The younger your child is, the easier it will be to lay down patterns to control the incursions of the youth culture. So much of the influences on our children as they grow up is decided by their early playmates. And for most of us, that is simply a matter of luck of the draw: who happens to live on the street where you move in will be an influence on your child for years, perhaps for life. Have you ever thought of the significance of that? Yet we make our decisions to move into a neighborhood or away from family and friends without thinking about the implications for our children. Many homeschoolers are acutely aware of the difficulty of finding like-minded children for their kids to play with, and many a homeschool mom has worn out herself and a car with driving her homeschooled children to the social opportunities she has carefully organized.

When our boys were young, they didn't have a consistent set of friends because I never trusted the parents of the neighborhood kids, and the boys they knew at church they never saw any time except Sundays. But God is good, and we learned from that mistake. Now, our pre-school girls have a far different situation: we live in a neighborhood where dozens of other families with a similar commitment to the Lord have deliberately moved. We don't have the big yard my husband loved, or the fireplace we all cherished in our old single-family home. But living on our court, within a thirty-second perfectly safe walk of our townhouse, are six little girls the same ages as our two—girls whose parents go to the same prayer meeting we do, and who are committed to raising their children in a godly manner.

When my boys were little, I worried what might be on television in a friend's house, or what games the friend might want to play. My fears were well-founded: their first glimpse of a stack of *Playboy* was in a friend's big brother's closet. Now, with my girls, I am able to trust the other moms, and so my girls are free to have friendships. I expect that, because of their childhood freedom to form friendships, as they mature they will have an easier time than my boys did coming to understand the expectation of Jesus that his people love one another. After all, they will have experienced a little bit of it.

I, too, am far freer. Just the other day, two other moms and I were chatting on the sidewalk, and before we parted we had taken a minute to pray for each other. Because of the shared commitment to seeking God, we can share important things, without lengthy explanation, and without worry about "what will they think of me?" I have a similar relationship with the mothers of teenagers: at times, I have called another mom on the phone in the middle of dinner preparation, and said only "please pray for me right now, there's a crisis brewing here." And she understood, and I have no doubt her prayers helped.

What a wonderful privilege! What a luxury, in this secular and impersonal world, to have that level of Christian sisterhood. But we had to look for it, and we had to move (again) into this community. In a metropolitan area such as Washington, D.C., people have to make extraordinary efforts to ensure that ordinary human relationships can flourish. In the real world, beyond the Capital Beltway, it is easier—though not as easy as it formerly was. I wonder whether it might not make sense for other people to try to consciously move near to other families, or near to their church—in order to try to consciously create Christian neighborhoods.

Many of us can choose to live nearer or farther from our own relatives, however. If our family members are generally emotionally healthy, and share our values and standards, living nearer can be a great boon in our childrearing. The advantages of being close to family exceed the play-mate-selection factor. As children grow up, it's good for them to have other adults besides their parents to whom they can complain about their parents. No, of course, they shouldn't complain about us. But let's face it, despite our best efforts, they are going to. Our choice is, do we want them complaining to their pals, who will undoubtedly take their side of any case they may present, or to their friends' parents, who could have some off-the-wall reactions, or do we want them complaining to an aunt or uncle, who is more likely to give a reasonable response? At the very least, your sister or brother is likely to hear the story from an adult's perspective. And the ensuing comments, no matter how diplomatic, are likely to be more in-clined to fairness than another teenager's would be. Even a doting grand-mother will sooner or later see the faults in the apple of her eye. At the time, this apple may think Grandma is just in a bad mood—*she couldn't possibly be criticizing me*—but eventually, reality will sink in.

Maybe cousins get to watch things on TV that are forbidden at home. Or maybe Grandma allows just about anything to be watched. But it also may be that Aunt and Uncle and Grandma have standards for conduct that are closer to ours than anybody else's around. Even if our relatives don't analyze the problem the same and don't share our concern to limit exposure to the popular culture, if they let it be known that they desire the same outcomes, our children will have that much more reinforcement for those standards. It will not be, "Only Mom and Dad in the whole world feel that way."

There's another reward in living close to relatives, too—one that I had no inkling of until my son started baby-sitting for his cousins. He came home one afternoon full of criticisms for the way his aunt was disciplin-ing her boys. "Boy, Mom," he said, "we never got away with what they do. You know what Aunt Sue does? If he doesn't want his broccoli, she gives him his dessert anyway! She lets him get away with it!" The right-eous indignation was coupled with a submerged sense of superiority about the way he had been raised. So while externally I chided him about not criticizing his aunt, internally I was delighted that he had found something to like in the way he had been raised. And a short while later, when Aunt Sue began to withhold desserts if the broccoli hadn't been eaten, Pearse learned another lesson: the standards were really the same, even though they didn't seem so for a while. He learned something important about flexibility.

Having frequent contact with adult relatives also presents the possibility that the growing youngster is going to hear about Daddy's and Mommy's faults, too, much to his delight. It may embarrass us, but when you think about it, isn't it better for a child to know his parents aren't perfect than to believe them to be perfect and therefore see himself as worse, since he knows he can't possibly hope to achieve such perfection?

But maybe you don't have any relatives in the area, or maybe the ones you do have are not, for one reason or other, good influences on your family life, so you don't have that option. You're stuck in a typical American suburb, having uprooted yourself from family and friends in pursuit of a better job. Are you defenseless?

Not at all. From the beginning, have a list of acceptable companions for your child, and stick to it. Let him know there are some kids he's allowed to play with and some he's not. Period. And before you allow your child into another child's house, know the parents. My friends Pat and Teresa Fagan have the custom of inviting any new neighbors over for something to eat, thus ensuring that they get a fairly good spell of time alone with them. In a couple of hours, my friends can pretty well size up their new neighbors in terms of how seriously they take their parental responsibilities, what their cultural and religious orientations are, and how concerned they are for their own children's welfare. Those are all very revealing things, and astute parents can quickly know if these parents are likely to be raising their children in a compatible manner.

Don't be surprised if you end up finding that your neighbors don't want other children in their houses. Deep down, many people don't really want their own children messing up their houses. Be glad if your home becomes the gathering place for the neighborhood. At least that way you can keep track of what's going on.

One word of caution: make sure that all the little friends play in the public areas of the house from the very beginning. I had never thought of this rule until one day when a bunch of boys were clustered in our boys' room. I went in on some innocent business and smelled burning. When I asked what was burning, the hangdog looks of every single boy sent my suspicions sky high. Only after they had all been sent home did my younger son show me the cardboard box Toby had set on fire. Experimental pyromania. You better believe I called Toby's mom when I found that out. Then we imposed the "public spaces" rule, with exceptions made only when some toy was already confined to the bedroom. Since it's hard for more than two people to work or play together on a computer, having the computer in a bedroom was no great handicap to social life. "Public spaces," by the way, is defined pretty generously at our house. The basement room that served as a schoolroom qualified as a "public space" to satisfy the rule, even though, being downstairs, it offered ample privacy. That it was a public space and liable to interruptions at any moment was the crucial factor in the definition.

SET TASTES EARLY

There are plenty of things we can do to build resistance to the popular culture even before children get to the playmate stage. For example, musical taste is developed early. Even unborn babies can hear music. So, from the earliest days, have music in the house. If a child grows up with Handel's *Water Music* as background music, it is more likely that rock will sound unpleasant in his ears. Sure, the desire to conform will make him say he likes rock, and he'll even believe it. But if the music at home has always been of high-quality, time at least is on your side. Too much television can be an enemy here, because the background music to children's programs is often rock in nature, as are the jingles of commercials, to say the least.

Another way to foster good taste in music is to encourage music lessons with an instrument like piano or in singing, if a church choir is available. Unfortunately, children's choirs have all but disappeared, and you have to ask a few questions to find a piano teacher who will assign classics to learn.

At the very least, from the time a child is born, ban the pop radio stations. Simply don't play them. It may be a sacrifice to you if you like popular music. But ban them anyway. Doing so is buying time for your child to be insulated from the attack of the rock culture. If he does acquire good taste at his mother's knee, it will be just that much longer until it gets corrupted.

From early on, minimize electronic paraphernalia of all kinds in your home. This will be hard to do, but if you must have a television, have *a* television, not one for each member of the family. And don't have it in the living room, like an altar to be worshipped. Hide it somewhere else so guests in the living room can receive your undivided attention. Similarly, one stereo set in the living room, where the record and tapes are collected, is fine. A child does not need personal duplicates. A personal tape player is something to be cherished as a child grows older, but watch out for the boom boxes which allow anything to be dubbed off the radio. Until you trust your child's own judgment, you might want to hold off on that particular gift idea. Whenever the personal radio or tape player does enter the family, it has an unseen benefit: leverage. "If you come home more than five minutes late, I keep your radio next week" can be a sobering sentence coming from a father.

If your child already has a stereo, set tight rules on when it can be played. Three times to ban its use would be upon first arising, while doing homework, and on Sunday mornings. Better than radios are cassette players: that way you can tell what they're listening to. And since cassettes cost money to buy, for a long time you can keep track of what tapes he's getting. Our children got a lot of enjoyment out of cassette players when they were small. I used to make tapes for them of nursery rhymes, songs, and stories with musical accompaniment taped off of records. They used to listen to them over and over again and would fall asleep with them playing whenever they were away from home. Later on, Michael would make tapes of his spelling words and listen to them repeatedly for studying. Interestingly, that's when he began to draw A's in spelling. (That says something for how powerfully we learn through our ears, doesn't it.)

And no Walkmen, for goodness' sake, unless your child is a serious runner who never uses the machine any other time. Around the house, it is a downright insult to the rest of the family to wear one in another person's presence. (What better way not to hear Mom when she calls?) To wear one while bike riding is a safety hazard. To wear one while driving, as I see teens doing frequently, is a worse safety hazard. Sure, I'd love to have a Walkman myself so I could plug into the tapes of my choice while I fix dinner and not have to listen to the arguments of the squabbling boys down the hall. I'd enjoy it tremendously. But that's not what a mother is supposed to do. She's supposed to listen to those arguments and know what's going on between her children. That's her job. I have to decide each time whether I intervene or not, and that's another question. But for sure God put me in this family to know about the relationships going on around me. And you know what? That's why God put children into families, too, to get them involved in life around them. Strolling through life tuned in to their own beat and dropped out of the real world is not healthy.

Once your child gets to the age that he has his own radio, you will have to declare certain stations—the ones with the heavy metal music and the dirty disc jockeys—off limits. That presupposes that you know which stations they are, which means you have to do your homework. Read the media section of the newspaper, talk to your friends and co-workers, and use your commuting time to and from work to monitor different stations instead of relaxing with your own favorite.

Especially if your child is still young enough that his tastes haven't been corrupted, you should ban the worst stations. That's all there is to it. If your child is disposed to challenge limits and act as if rules were made to be broken, you will have to announce ahead the punishments for violation and be prepared to enforce them. Unless you're willing to do the enforcing, don't bother to make the rule. One punishment we've used is that the child is not allowed to stay home alone. When this has meant he sits in the car in the grocery store parking lot for an hour on a summer's day, we remind him that his disobedience is the cause of his misery. Obviously, you can't play endless cat-and-mouse games over this. Children's ages have to be considered, too. If there are compromise stations that adolescents find satisfactory to their social needs but which don't violate your standards too much, be willing to compromise. A reasonable compromise is more likely to be obeyed than a rigid rule. And remember, a large part of the reason a child may listen is not because he likes the music, but because he wants to be like his peer set. A country and oldies station, for instance, might be something you could both live with when you have banned the hard rock stations.

As your child gets older, you can analyze songs with him. This is assuming, of course, that the song has actual words and portrays relationships. A series of repetitions fifty times doesn't withstand much analysis. This can be an opportunity for instruction in many values, by the way. My son Pearse got to like country music because he discerned that might be more acceptable to his parents than rock. He was allowed to make tapes of the least rock-sounding songs, and then he could play the tapes occasionally. Whenever he makes lunch for the family, for instance, or scrubs the kitchen floor, I allow him to listen to his tapes. When I would listen to the tapes, I'd follow the song and point out to him what was really going on in the song.

Sometimes he'd be surprised. "Do you realize what the message is in 'Good Hearted Woman'?" I asked. He had the impression the singer was admiring a tolerant wife. It gave me the opportunity to point out that by admiring his tolerant wife, the fellow was excusing and justifying his own misbehavior. "He thinks he's doing fine to go partying all night as long as she doesn't complain," I pointed out, noting that the fellow was thereby revealing himself as a selfish cad. With the song "Jolene," I showed Pearse how the singer was pleading with another woman not to take her man. "Where's her self-respect, crying over one fellow?" I asked him, assuming this was a boyfriend-girlfriend situation being sung about (not a safe assumption, perhaps, but at least in this song not contradicted by the words). "If that fellow wants to go chasing after another girl just because she makes eyes at him, let him. He's obviously not worth having." And then I drew the analogy the other way: "When you get older and there's some girl you're crazy about, but she's interested in another fellow, don't go begging her to pay attention to you. If she's not interested in you, don't try to make her be. There are lots more fish in the sea. Don't lose your self-respect over one girl."

And in the case of other songs, such as those that talk about "sleeping single in a double bed" or other obvious sexual references, I would point out, "Do you realize this song is praising adultery?" Usually, it would never have occurred to him, and when he realized it, he would like the song less, even if he had already decided he liked the singer.

I always thought that, to help our children not get caught up in the materialism of the popular culture, it would be good to have a rule about money the children earn or receive as gifts. Ten percent should go to the church; 50 percent to savings; and we, the parents, should have veto power over how the rest is spent. Now, I still think that's a reasonable plan. But my husband Bill didn't, though he agreed for a period of time to let me try it. Well, no teenager is going to agree to parting with money unless he or she has grown up with the policy, and unless both parents are a rock wall of agreement about it. So that high ideal did not work in our family. Which is why you should have the conversation about this with your spouse as soon as your children learn the difference between coins and paper money. It takes that long to get it established, and a part of automatic behavior.

It's a rule for the children's own protection. Teens I know who have gotten into drugs were able to do so because they had money for which they didn't have to give any accounting. When Mom cashes the paychecks, Mom knows where the money goes. At the very least, Mom or Dad should receive the paycheck stubs and receive an accounting of how it was spent. The fact that they end up with only 40 percent of their earnings as disposable income may discourage some youngsters from earning money. But as they get older, they'll accept the limitations and work hard for what they want. And when they have real motivation, such as college, they'll also have the real discipline to enable them to earn, and save, real money.

Don't be afraid that giving 10 percent will make them resent the church, either. For a long time, they may not understand why they have to do it, but by being obedient they will begin a lifelong habit the Lord will bless. And when they become young adults and have their own budgets to make up, putting the tithe at the top of the list will come a lot more easily to them than if they had never done it before.

And if you're trying to develop a heart for the needy, you're probably better off having one yourself. Let your child see you taking food to a homeless shelter, or visiting a nursing home, and they'll get a sense of concern for others a lot quicker than if they merely are forced to contribute to a worthy cause.

TELEVISION: THE SHINY-FACED MONSTER

There is a monster that lies in wait for each of us every day. Usually it's in our living rooms, but more and more we find it in our bedrooms, in our kitchens, and by our sewing machines. Everywhere we look, a deceptively innocent looking monster lurks. It exists to waste our time, stimulate our concupiscence, set us a bad example, make us worry, and worse, all the while making us think that we are wiser, more knowledgeable, and better informed because of it. This monster seeks to rearrange our family relationships, form our opinions, and gradually replace our values and suck us into the popular culture.

This monster is, of course, the television. And if you're really serious about controlling the incursions of the rock culture into your home, you will get rid of the television.

I know that sounds drastic, and it is. I suppose some people are more resistant to television than others. Perhaps my family is peculiarly unable to resist it. Maybe that's because we never got enough of it in our formative years, but somehow I doubt it. I know I can have a radio on and go about my daily business. Some women can do their ironing in front of the television; I never could. If the darn thing is on, I have to watch it. Some people can carry on conversations in front of it as if it weren't there. Not me. I'd hush anybody who was talking, irritated at the distraction, even though I knew what I was watching wasn't worth paying attention to. And my husband is just as bad. No matter what else needs doing, no matter how badly he needs sleep, no matter how worthless the show on the tube might be, he'd watch it in lieu of anything else. Why? I don't know, and I don't presume that we're a typical family. But let me tell you how we came to this drastic conclusion.

At one time or another, we tried all the half-measures. We put the television in our bedroom so the kids couldn't sneak up early on Saturday morning to watch the cartoons at low volume in the living room (and then act like embodied He-men or Smurfs all day long). We got a cabinet with a key and locked it up when not in use (but eventually the key got lost). We got a VCR and allowed the kids to make tapes of their choice. We had an account book and had them earn an hour of TV privileges by doing a certain amount of time of this or that. We had cable so that "good" channels and public television stations were available. We had rules about asking permission before turning on the television.

And no matter what the situation was at the time, our children felt sorry for themselves and deprived because they weren't allowed to watch what other kids were or as much as they wanted. The complaints were endless. And then one day after three days in a row of the "Ask permission" rule's being violated and one of the banned "kids' comic shows" being viewed, Daddy said this was enough, he wasn't going to put up with an entire summer of this. He was putting the thing in the attic. And I said, "Oh, Daddy, don't do anything so drastic as that," and then I took the boys to baseball practice.

When we returned the TV was in the attic. And you know, I wish it had happened years earlier. The change was wonderful. The very first thing I noticed was how nice and leisurely Saturday dinners became. We were no longer rushing to get the dinner finished and the dishes washed before the Disney movie came on. The next thing we noticed was that the boys started playing with each other better: a little less squabbling than before, a little more cooperation. After all, there wasn't the television to retreat to anymore if they antagonized each other.

Then I gradually noticed that taking the boys grocery shopping wasn't the hassle it had been before. I wasn't being besieged with requests to buy this or that so often. A few months later and Michael was reading entire books—something he had never done before, though he had long been capable of it. That fall we had football, and grades at school didn't suffer. There was time for football and good grades, but there wouldn't have been time for football, television, and good grades. Within a year, Michael, the learning-disabled boy, was writing ten-page stories.

By the fall, we were going regularly to prayer meeting, whereas in the spring, our Sunday nights had been planned around *Masterpiece Theatre*. And I think that exemplifies my major complaint with television. True, the pull toward the rock culture is deadly, from McDonald's commercials that try to be as much like music videos as they can be to the actual MTV itself (the cable system didn't allow the option of refusing that channel), all the way through the host of other programs. But my deepest objection is that time spent worshipping at the electronic altar is time not spent doing more-important things, things that matter, things that make life more meaningful and worth living, things that involve other people.

As long as they could retreat to television, the boys didn't bother to develop their interior resources and didn't work on their relationship with each other. Flick a switch and immediate gratification: entertainment, fun, pleasure. This was much more alluring than having to apologize and give up a little of what they wanted in order to get somebody else to play with them. And isn't it the same with our teens when they discover sex? If you can persuade the girl to have sex with you, how much more gratifying than having to spend money entertaining her, inventing a conversation to keep her interested, or having to make yourself an interesting person.

So not only is the predominant message on television one that we want to minimize in our children's ears and eyes, but the medium itself builds bad habits of shortcuts and avoidance of the more-challenging—but ultimately more-rewarding—task of really relating to each other.

I must not fail to mention that after a year and a half of hiding in the attic, the TV came down. It was presidential election year, and Mom and Dad needed (or was it only wanted?) to see the presidential debates, for one thing. Also, Pearse was becoming conscious of his need to know current events, but was disinclined to read the papers. We wanted to encourage the civic-minded interest. For another thing, we didn't want to be so rigid that we inadvertently caused a backlash. I was grateful to note that Pearse had developed some critical faculties in the meantime, but we asked my brother-in-law to install a lockbox just the same, mainly to keep temptation out of the reach of younger ones on those occasions when being home alone might make it irresistible.

It was about four months until the boys figured out how to short-circuit the lockbox without using the key. By this time, watching TV had become a cat-and-mouse game. We tried a few more compromises, including cable for a month to make lots of videos. Finally, we put the television in the unheated basement garage. If you want to watch in winter, you have to plan ahead to light the kerosene heater an hour earlier. There's no antenna hookup, so no television reception, just VCR.

It's great. I'd never go back to the old ways. Neither would Bill. The garage has become the gathering place for teenage boys far and wide. With the presence of the machine there to assure them that if conversation fails, there is rescue, conversations can get fast and furious. About once every two months in his senior year of public high school, Pearse would gather a random assortment of his friends to come and beg Dad to lecture them on the proofs of the existence of God.

I earmarked something in the budget for entertainment, with which to buy about a video a month for the little ones. And I didn't worry if they saw some TV at friends' houses, because they know that they don't see it at their house. Besides, most of the little kids in our community don't watch TV shows; their mothers have bought or made videos for them. Occasionally, I would sit with my girls to watch one of their videos, but more often than not, the videoplayer is something to which she is exiled when Mom needs quiet time. There was an unexpected side-effect. Caroline came home one day from her dearest friend's house, obviously exasperated. "I don't like to go to Anna's house if she's going to just sit glued to that machine!" she explained. Without my having said a thing against TV, she had developed a dislike of the passive state of TV viewing. She wanted to have fun with her friends. May her ideas of entertainment never change!

WHERE NOT TO LOOK FOR HELP

If you are interested in minimizing the rock culture in your home, some of what I'm saying may be intriguing to you. Perhaps you aren't willing to make the drastic move of banning the television, but you're thinking of cutting back. You're thinking of ways to put yourself more in charge of the cultural climate of your home. You're wondering where you can look for support. Let me give you one clue about where not to look. Institutional churches.

It pains me to say it, but it's true. Our entire society probably wouldn't be in the mess it is if the church had been doing its job and sounding a clear moral trumpet. Culture follows morality, but in our lifetime, standards of morality have simply been shifted to accommodate the prevailing culture. It's as if Satan had decided systematically to go after the church.

Consider the decline just within the past 100 years or so. In 1873, Anthony Comstock lobbied Congress to pass laws to prevent contraceptives from being sent through the mails. Today, as if by reflex, the presumption is that the only person who ever opposed contraception was the Pope of Rome. But not so. Comstock was a Protestant reformer, drawing his sexual morality from the well of Luther and Calvin. During the same era, most states were passing anti-abortion laws—lobbied by Protestants all.

The prevailing Protestant view of sexual morality was a Scripturally sound linkage of sexual privileges with the married state, and with the potential consequence of children. Thus had been the linkage for Catholics, Protestants, and Jews from time immemorial. Though theological disputes had soured relations among and between them, none of the major faiths had yet so grievously offended the Lord of creation as to presume that man, not God, was free to set the rules for sexual behavior and consequences.

The erosion didn't actually begin until 1930—just over sixty years ago, but an incalculable distance in morality. In England that year, the Lambeth conference of Anglican bishops approved of contraception, provided it was done "in light of . . . Christian principles."[1] The next year, the U.S. Federal Council of Churches, a predecessor of the National Council of Churches (NCC), like a good colonial offspring, followed the lead of the mother country. Technically, it was a committee report, not binding on member churches, that was issued, but that was a minor detail overlooked in the furor that followed.

It is amusing to note that one of the most outraged responses came from the *Washington Post,* which today is editorially quite liberal in the lifestyle and morals department. Said the *Post* on March 22, 1931:

> Carried to its logical conclusion, the committee's report, if carried into effect, would sound the death-knell of marriage as a holy institution by establishing degrading practices which would encourage indiscriminate immorality. The suggestion that the use of legalized contraceptives would be "careful and restrained" is preposterous.

Nor were all the denominations equally liberal. "The whole disgusting movement rests on the assumption of man's sameness with the brutes," commented Bishop Warren Chandler of the Methodist Episcopal Church South. Dr. Walter A. Maier of Concordia Lutheran Theological Seminary in St. Louis said it represented "a renewal of pagan bankruptcy." *The Presbyterian* magazine was of the opinion that this pronouncement "should be enough reason, if there were no other, to withdraw" from the Federal Council of Churches.

But the pronouncement stuck. This was, after all, just past the Roaring Twenties, in many ways comparable to the 1960s for the rapid decay of public and private virtue. The years of the Depression were upon the nation, offering the excuse of hard times as a pretext for seeking to be excused from hard rules.

In 1958, Lambeth restated its 1930 stand with more enthusiasm, stating in its pronouncement that the number of children was a decision for man to make. In 1961, our own NCC went along with Lambeth II. Was this paving the way for the sexual revolution, which, as if on cue, shortly thereafter burst upon Western society? Or was it putting its finger in the wind, noting the direction of the coming hurricane, and deciding to be "relevant and meaningful" in the face of it?

At least, however, there was some firmness in the next logical area, abortion, although on February 23, 1961, the NCC issued this guarded statement: "Protestant Christians are agreed in condemning abortion or any method which destroys human life except where the health or life of the mother is at stake."

The exception for health of the mother was, of course, wide enough to drive a truck through, which is why today an exception like that would never be approved by a pro-life thinker. Perhaps someone who negotiated the wording of that resolution knew exactly what was being said and wanted that loophole there. But on the other hand, it may have been a loophole left in innocent ignorance. In any case, we can assume that the level of feeling, even among NCC denominations, was strong enough against abortion that the Council was compelled to make a statement condemning abortion for destroying human life.

Meanwhile, the makers of the law were acting, and in 1965, the *Griswold v. Connecticut* decision of the U.S. Supreme Court invented the doctrine of privacy to render any state laws pertaining to contraception unconstitutional. This was the first major overturning by the courts of what had been a major Protestant political campaign of the previous century. In 1965, this right of privacy extended to the marriage bedroom. But it didn't stay there for long.

In 1972, the Court extended the same right of privacy to any unmarried person in *Eisenstadt v. Baird,* making it clear that the family rationale used in *Griswold* was essentially window dressing for the sentiment of the times. By 1972, such window dressing acknowledging a special role for matrimony was no longer deemed necessary by the Court.

And one year later, the Court, with its keen sense of what the people would tolerate, gave *Roe v. Wade* to the nation, declaring that a woman's right to privacy was more important than an unborn child's right to life. This time, the State led the Church in setting the moral standards for the country.

And how did churches respond, the denominations that a mere twelve years earlier had been willing to "agree in condemning abortion?" Were they out in front condemning this usurpation of their prerogative to form the moral conscience of the nation? Were they out there protesting this sweeping judicial fiat?

Hardly. Some of them had been on record already urging liberalized access to abortion. Others were scrambling to get on the bandwagon as fast as they could.[2]

Where was the trumpet? Where was the sword to divide the followers of Christ from the world? And then they wondered why people began leaving the mainline denominations in droves, headed for the more "fundamental" Bible-believing churches, where the preaching would be inspired by the Bible instead of by the Supreme Court. Then the slander campaign against those churches began. They were dubbed "extremist" and "reactionary." And the campaign is getting hotter by the year.

CHRISTIAN SEX EDUCATION IS NOT EDUCATION FOR SEX

Notice also the position of the mainline denominations toward sex education. Which denominations are quick to jump on bandwagons of public school sex education? Liberal theologians are not much different from liberal sex educators in their ideas of how to educate children in sexuality. Some of the curriculum programs in some denominational schools reflect this as well.

But the premise of this book is that Christian sex education is not sex education at all; it is not education about sex. Two hours with a biology book that has anatomical illustrations can tell any intelligent person all he needs to know about sex. My eleven-year-old summed that up aptly after a couple of hours with just such a book. In public schools, however, to embellish the program, the curriculum takes off from there into discussions of physiological details: where the pleasure comes from, different ways to achieve the pleasure, how to provide pleasure to the partner, and, of course, how to avoid the consequences. All of this is, arguably, very good education for sex. And since sex produces babies, it is eminently understandable why this kind of education produces the raft of illegitimate pregnancies that the headlines purport to be so concerned about.

We as a nation have been reaping what we have sown. We have been educating for sex, not for affection, intimacy, marriage, or successful human relations. That's one root of the problem. In the most formative years of life, children are allowed to indulge themselves, care nothing for another person's feelings, be indifferent to another person's needs, and as long as they stay out of trouble, absorb a minimum of internal discipline. Then, when they hit adolescence and the hormones let loose, they are attracted to the other sex, but they still don't know how to treat each other as human beings. So school reacts with a flurry of bandages known as sex education. They don't need that. What they need is virtues education, affection education, education in values, education in human relationships. This is not to be confused with what schools call "values education," which in many cases is yet one more attempt to systematically break down what traditional values may have managed to be imparted. Former Secretary of Education William Bennett called the right kind of education "character education," and that's a good term. Indeed, don't we think of a person who treats his fellow man and woman well as a person "with character"?

But affection education has to start long before the hormones begin circulating in the blood.

AFFECTION EDUCATION BEGINS IN THE PARENTS' MINDS

Affection education probably begins the moment a woman knows she is pregnant. That's when she and her husband start forming feelings about this new child. The parents' minds, therefore, are where it begins.

A parent's attitude toward sexuality and sexual expression must be as comfortable as possible. A mother should not be embarrassed by bodily functions. Changing diapers or nursing her infant, things that women frequently are embarrassed to do in front of other people, should not be a cause of concern. Nobody wants to be an exhibitionist, obviously, but neither is there any need to be reclusive and embarrassed. Bodily functions are just that, bodily functions; they are neither "dirty" nor "clean." They are necessary, God-designed, and God-given.

A parent's attitude will be subtly but strongly affected by his or her level of satisfaction within the marriage relationship. If there's difficulty there, sexual or otherwise, the discomfort may come across as discomfort with sexuality in general when speaking to the children. This will give children the impression that Mom or Dad does not want to talk about this subject, for reasons about which they can only speculate. That, of course, is exactly opposite the impression that should be given.

A busy married life with children may indeed leave little time for introspection on the part of parents. But the whole job of parenting will be done better if parents take the time to analyze their feelings and communicate them with each other on every subject, not just bedroom topics. Even if the conjugal act is not as thrilling as a parent may have expected it to be, its deficiencies are a private matter between the spouses (and a counselor if they wish to involve one). Such private matters will never be a topic of conversation with children. So if there is anxiety for fear that children will ask too personal questions, rest assured on that point.

Ignorance is not always bliss. One 51-year-old woman wrote to me from Montana saying, "I remember when I was a high school age student, I used to absolutely long for my parents to tell me about sex." This woman was, in fact, sexually molested by her teenage brother from the time she was four years old, but, she said, "The atmosphere was not so I could tell [my parents] and what is more, I didn't even know the words."

Ignorance of anatomy and biology often accounts for parental discomfort in being the primary educators of their children in matters of human reproduction. Expectant mother books frequently have diagrams of the female anatomy, so Dad, now you know where to read up. Or go to a library and read a medical book with diagrams. You may not want to bring it home, but you can at least peruse the diagrams at the library. (I have read through all such books in our public library, and because of the relativistic moral message they contain would not bring them under my roof.)

Another barrier to thoughtful, deliberate education of children may be scars in a parent from his or her own upbringing. One man I know had been taken by his mother, without any advance explanation, to a strange doctor. The boy, whose own mother had been hospitalized several times with illnesses that were never explained to the child but which he understood to be grave in nature, knew ahead of time that he was going to be seeing this new doctor. But when he asked his mother why, she would give him no reason. Upon arriving there, he was taken into a small room alone by the doctor and sat down and told the facts of life. That over with, his mother never said another word on the subject, nor did his father. It was a traumatic and unpleasant experience for my friend, and he attributed some of his own discomfort with his children to the scars left by that.

There's encouragement to be found in the rest of his story, however. The sex education part of his children's affection education may have been less than ideal, but the other, more important, ingredients were in order. In all other respects, this man had a wonderful relationship with his five children, all of whom are now in their twenties. "The talk" was an acutely uncomfortable experience for my friend and his children (and not much better for his wife in her attempts). But the children did not stray off the path of sexual virtue. They learned God's laws, and their parents gave them affection education through the myriad of subtle and explicit ways unique to each family.

If you have scars from experiences of your upbringing, by all means work and pray for healing of the wounds in your mind and heart. But take some comfort from knowing that there is a lot more to educating your children for virtue than being comfortable with sexuality. As Robert Walker, President of Christian Life Missions and for years editor of *Christian Life* magazine, said, noting that his parents had no access to books or tapes such as today's parents can obtain: "Moreover, if they had resorted to them, I doubt that the result would have been much different.

For above and beyond anything they might have quoted to me or asked me to read, was the exemplary lives which they lived. . . . I am persuaded that our children respond to our guidance and direction in direct proportion to their perception of our love for them—not the fine-tuned or expert advice we give them."

One area that may cause great discomfort to parents as they begin to broach this subject with their children is the matter of guilt. Lingering or subconscious guilt will put you on edge as you answer questions or impart education to innocent children. Remember: it is not the will of God that one who has repented should suffer guilt. Satan would like to paralyze you by keeping the emotion of guilt alive in you, because it helps him keep his hold on you. But if you have repented, corrected the sin, confessed it, and been forgiven, you are free to put it out of your mind. Nay, more: you are obliged to put it out of your mind and cooperate with the loving God who wants to put your guilt as far from you as the east is from the west.

. . . AND CONTINUES IN THE HOME

Parents, be aware that you are a model to your children from day one. Maybe it's technically day fifteen before a newborn baby actually focuses his eyes on his mother, but you don't know when the exact moment will be. It may be sooner and it may be later. Be sure, however, that what is noticed will be significant that first time and every other time. So act as if every day and every moment matters, for they do.

To prepare yourself to be a worthy model, examine your behavior and your conscience. If you didn't do it before you were married, now is the time to sit down with your husband and learn general parenting skills. There are abundant resources for that in any Christian bookstore and on every Christian radio station.

The hinges on the doors of communication are set very early in life, and they are either set at an "open" or a "closed" position. Yes, they can be changed later on by circumstances or emotions. But like anything in nature, they will always tend in the direction they were first set. Sexual topics are no different from any other. If a parent signals to his children that his interest in the adventures of Peter Rabbit (or whatever has captured the imagination of the toddler) is genuine, and he then continues up the ladder with beginning reading and older games and concerns, the child will be willing to ask questions.

To a child, "Why do the leaves fall from the trees?" is no different a question from "Why do mommies have breasts but not daddies?" It is only the caliber of the parents' response that alerts the child that he is treading on sensitive ground. A tense, embarrassed, or, worse, angry response will dry up the well of conversation. An explanation of "Later, Honey. Right now Mommy has to pay attention to what Grandma is saying" can camouflage discomfort for those occasions when the timing of the question is absolutely inconvenient. But if Mommy is fixing dinner, she shouldn't try to deflect the question unless she needs to consult with Daddy on what the family position is. This may occur more than one might expect. Parents who haven't actually discussed their moral values much with each other may not know what the partner thinks ought to be taught to children. In such a case, it's a good idea to make sure that Mom and Dad are both singing off the same sheet of music before they start teaching the child any songs.

IF YOU HAVE NO SPOUSE

If you have no spouse, at the very least you don't have to worry about singing in harmony with another parent. You probably wish you had, however. The disadvantages to a child of growing up in a one-parent family are particularly acute where the formation of attitudes toward the opposite sex is concerned.

For lots of good reasons, a single parent should try to arrange for the supportive involvement in a child's life of exemplary members of the other sex. Frequent, regular contact with one such person would be a goal to strive for. Perhaps through friendship networks, church, uncles, Big Brother and Sister programs, or other such contacts can the appropriate person be found. The need is more crucial for boys raised by single mothers than for girls raised by their mothers, at least in the young years.

It isn't easy to find such a person, to be sure. You're looking for someone who is not only a man or woman you can trust implicitly, but also somebody who has the time to spend—and is willing to spend it— with your children. The search for this individual should be the subject of fervent prayer.

But look inside at your own attitude toward the opposite sex, too. Your attitude may have been jaundiced by your own unhappy experiences. For the sake of the child's future, try with all your might to keep your biases from showing to your child. At the very least, no matter how much effort it may take from you, do not condemn your ex-mate in front of your child and then add for good measure something like, "And besides, all men are rats."

If your passion against your ex-mate persists, master your emotions. Be objective about your feelings, and control them for the sake of your child. No good is to be gained by raising a child of either gender with an innate bias against the opposite gender. As soon as your child is capable of understanding, explain to him, in the case of divorce, "You know, Daddy hurt Mommy's feelings very, very badly, and Mommy's feelings still hurt when she thinks of Daddy. That's why sometimes if you mention Daddy, I may seem to be mad. I'm not mad at you, I'm just feeling my hurt all over again. But all men aren't like that, and I'm sure when you're a man you'll be a real gentleman. Let me tell you what a real gentleman is." In other words, don't hold the faults of one person against the entire gender. And certainly don't burden your child with attitudes formed by your own experiences. Naturally, if you're single for some other reason such as the death of your spouse, a different kind of explanation is called for, but it should be just as objective and balanced in accounting for your emotions.

THE CHALLENGE

The values and suggestions offered in this chapter certainly represent a minority view in today's popular culture. And just as there will be peer pressure on our children as they seek to lead distinctly Christian lives, so also will we face pressure from other parents and the society as a whole to "go with the flow." Thus, establishing and maintaining a Christian culture within the home is a major challenge. If we didn't have the Lord on our side, the struggle would be hopeless. But we *do* have Him with us, so who can be against us? And what do we care who in this corrupt world tries to be against us?

Chapter 6

AIDS: VIRTUE IS
ITS OWN REWARD

The first edition of this book went to press shortly before my daughter Caroline was born. In that edition, there were the five pages, more or less, about homosexuality that you read in chapter 8. AIDS was a news topic, but not yet a headline topic. Caroline is now five and a half years old. AIDS has gone from being a headline topic to being an industry. It has progressed from a medical curiosity to an epidemic. Neither the epidemic nor the industry shows any signs of slowing their rates of growth.

When Caroline was born, homosexuality was still a little bit taboo. The first federal legislation to protect homosexuals against discrimination had been introduced a couple years earlier, but it showed no likelihood of passing. The first Gay Rights march in Wahsington had been in 1980, but then anybody can organize a march in Washington — and usually does. But just last month, there was a whole weekend of gay extravaganza in Washington. From all over the country, with much marketing and promotion in all the respectable media, gays and lesbians of all varieties descended on Washington and copulated in the streets (quite literally). The networks covered the story with full honors.

This came as no surprise. After all, only a few months earlier, at President Bill Clinton's Inauguration, there had been a Gay Inauguration Ball. The gay lobbies were a pressure group during the Presidential campaign, accorded all the legitimacy that any other pressure group, whether veterans or environmentalists or unions, was accorded by the news media. School districts like New York City mandated teaching kindergartners about homosexuality—so as to inculcate politically correct attitudes, using books specially written to confuse children's ideas of family life.

Every time somebody says "How much further can the degeneration of our society go?" they wish they hadn't asked the question. Incest now has its advocates; perhaps that taboo will be the next to go. Well, why not? If both parties consent to the incest, who has the right to interfere with their freedom to do it? Liberals certainly don't think they have any such right. Already, there have been several highly-acclaimed (by the critics) movies featuring cannibalism. Well, why not? Who says dead bodies have to be treated as if they were sacred anyhow?

In just five years, our culture has sunk to these new lows. O Lord, save your people and bless your inheritance.

What is AIDS?

In case there is a literate person on the face of the earth who does not know, AIDS stands for Acquired Immune Deficiency Syndrome. Originally, scientists wanted to name the disease Gay-Related Immune Deficiency, attributing it to its place of origin. But AIDS it became, and a more politically protected disease there will never be again. As of 1991, the Centers for Disease Control reported a cumulative 179,136 cases in the United States.[1]

It is a grim disease. It can take years for symptoms to emerge, but when they come, death follows within usually three years. Frequently, there are neurological changes before there are any other symptoms. Neurological changes can be subtle, such as slight changes in one's perception of light, or they can be profound personality changes, or dementia. The body's normal immune defenses gradually break down, leaving the person susceptible to any and every other bacteria or virus or mycoplasma that comes along. A cut on the toe can become a gangrenous infection. Hepatitis and pneumonia are more common. The body wastes away, slowly or quickly, as the organs give up their functions one by one. There is little if any treatment. The drug zidovudine, AZT, is of limited effectiveness, and indeed toxic. New drugs are, of course, being researched all the time.

And so the disease destroys its victims. It gets long and tedious and painful. Friends fall away, too, for one reason or another, leaving victims at the mercy of medical staff for their only taste of human affection. A few fortunate ones get into AIDS hospices, usually staffed by Christians who are trying to take literally Christ's injunction to love one another. If, in the course of careering through the gay life, one has been lucky enough to have not fractured relationships with blood relatives, there may be family members near. But for most, it is a lonely and painful end.

How is AIDS transmitted? There's no mystery about that. It is transmitted by the intimate exchange of bodily fluids. That means: Sexual intercourse or sharing of blood. Intravenous drug users have high rates of this disease, because they usually share needles with other IV drug users. AIDS rates in Africa are far higher than they are in America; one reason for that may be that mass immunization programs in Africa, to save expense, would boil or otherwise inadequately sterilize needles, thus, in effect, while immunizing for one disease, transmit another. There are other suggested reasons as well. Homosexual intercourse, by definition, utilizes bodily parts in ways not intended by the natural design of the body, and so tearing of skin and blood vessels, even microscopically, is almost inevitable in most such intercourse.

Who gets AIDS? Actually, there's some debate about that. Officially, as of 1992, 66 percent of AIDS cases in America began with homosexual behavior. Twenty-two percent began with intravenous drug use (sharing needles with other AIDS cases). Six percent were wives, lovers, or babies of people with AIDS.[2] Three percent got the disease from contaminated blood supply. And, for another three percent, or 6,492 people, the exposure to AIDS is undetermined.[3]

But the disease is not staying put with homosexuals and IV drug users. It is spreading beyond those categories. Since it is largely transmitted sexually, many expect that AIDS, like other STD's, will end up inordinately affecting the adolescent population.

What causes AIDS? A microscopic virus, called HIV, which stands for Human Immunodeficiency Virus, is officially believed to cause the disease. When the human body is exposed to a virus, it produces an antibody to that virus. That's how a woman finds out before getting married whether or not she needs a German measles vaccination: a blood test will reveal whether she has antibodies to German measles. If she has the antibodies, she will not get the disease. Someone who has HIV antibodies is defined as "HIV seropositive", and current medical expectations are that that person will sooner or later develop full-blown AIDS. "Later" might be more than a decade later, however.

But these are all official views, promulgated or otherwise endorsed by the Centers for Disease Control and Prevention, an arm of the Department of Health and Human Services. As with any medical issue, there are heterodox views. One heterodox scientist is Peter H. Duesberg, a professor of molecular and cell biology at the University of California, Berkely. Duesberg was a pioneer in cancer-gene research, and was the first to map the genetic structure of retroviruses (of which HIV is one). As a member of the National Academy of Sciences, he is well-qualified to dissent. Duesberg maintains that HIV may not be the cause of AIDS.[4] He maintains that the combination of prolonged malnutrition with heavy drug use, including alcohol and antibiotics as well as "recreational drugs" like heroin and cocaine, can provoke an immune system collapse. He points to the cases of AIDS patients who do not have HIV antibodies in their blood and asks: how can you be so sure HIV is the cause of AIDS? How do you explain these cases? So confident is Duesberg of his hypothesis, that he even offered to inject himself with HIV in front of a national press conference. As far as I know, by press time for this edition, nobody had taken him up on his offer.

Historically, of course, heterodox medical opinions have a way of being vindicated, or partly vindicated, in time. Remember Pasteur and Lister? They were real medical heretics in their day. And in our day, the trend continues. Don't forget that breastfeeding had practically disappeared among middle class America by the 1950's. The doctors who first began encouraging breastfeeding were unorthodox for their time, but in time, official medical opinion followed. Nowadays, every pediatrician will acknowledge that breast is best, and then recommend which formula to use. What that shows me is that people need to take more responsibility for their own, and their children's, health. The doctor will tell you breast is best, but if you're going back to work and want a formula, the doctor is not going to try to get you to re-evaluate what's best for your baby.

I'm old enough to remember back to when the American Medical Association was not willing to acknowledge a link between dietary fiber and colon disease, or between fat and breast cancer. Both connections are pretty standard doctrine today — but again, whether the information can help people depends on how responsible they are at taking care of themselves. I remember when the first reports began coming out that cigarette smoking was unhealthy, it was respectable to question that research. Few beyond the tobacco lobby are willing to question the mountains of research since then—but does that information make people stop smoking?

By raising questions that science hadn't answered yet, Duesberg did a great service to humanity. Subsequent research is focusing on his charges, and finding some of them valid. Another scientist, Robert Root-Bernstein, raised many of the same questions as Duesberg in his book, *Re-thinking AIDS,* a year later, and received more respectful treatment from his collegues.

So let us keep an open mind on whether HIV is the only cause of AIDS, or whether it is lifestyle choices that dispose a person who has come down with that disease. Who knows but what HIV may be a result as well as a cause of immune system breakdown?

CAN AIDS BE PREVENTED?

It's easy to avoid AIDS! Remain a virgin, marry a virgin, and be faithful to each other. Then, unless one of you has the misfortune to receive an unscreened blood transfusion, you should be quite safe from any danger of AIDS or any other STD.

For the individual man or woman, it is easy to avoid AIDS. Practice chastity. Practice pre-marital abstinence. Virtue is certainly its own reward when it comes to avoiding AIDS.

But what about the larger question? Can the AIDS epidemic be halted? Probably not—unless and until our society is willing to roll back the sexual revolution.

A lot of well-meaning people will spend a lot of time, energy, and money trying, however. When basketball player Magic Johnson announced that he had AIDS, and that he should have used a condom while fornicating with thousands of women, the national response was to make Johnson a hero, and to elevate condoms to the level of a national symbol. The national so-called "AIDS education" that has followed suit is despicable in its deceptiveness. If your children attend public school, what they are taught will be colored by this party line; it cannot but follow it.

Since it is so easy to avoid AIDS, this epidemic could have been a non-starter. A national campaign that meant business on two fronts could have stopped the thing in its tracks. By "national campaign", I mean the coordinated single-minded effort of the main institutions of society: the schools, the churches, the law, the family, and the propaganda organs known as mass media, with a clear, common purpose to prevent fornication and illegal drug usage. If every school had begun telling kids that sex was for marriage; if every church had begun telling the same thing; if laws had been changed so that drug users would be punished, as well as drug sellers; if the message in movies, and the constant theme on television had been "save sex for marriage, don't do drugs", it would have made a difference. You bet it would have. That's the kind of campaign that was carried out against the Germans and the Japanese before this country entered World War II, and while we were in the war. Even to this day, it's not respectable to say anything nice about our antagonists in that war.

But that was war! Of course we had to propagandize, you say, we had to get the country of one mind, to support the war effort, you say.

And this isn't war?

If it is war, the sexual revolution is beating common sense to shreds. When the AIDS epidemic began, what happened? The schools did not tell kids that homosexual behavior and sharing drug needles would kill them. Instead, teachers began handing out condoms and bureaucrats began planning curriculum programs that would systematically remove any intuitive or inherited dislike of overt homosexuality. Some churches started handing out condoms. The ones that already countenance homosexuality continued to do so, without asking a question. More were silent. The law was changed to give more privileges to homosexuals and other alternative life styles. And the mass media made Johnson into a saint for advocating condoms, incidentally failing to publicize his later remark that "abstinence is best."

Since then, homosexuality gains more acceptance, and more legal and political status daily. Morality, the sister of common sense, is re-defined as the major deviance in modern society. The homosexual movement wants homosexual acts to be accepted as a normal variant of human behavior; the goal of that movement is for homosexuality to be a legitimate, socially-accepted, lifestyle.

In order for those goals to be achieved, certain tenets of ideology have to be followed. You've heard them all. They go something like this:

Sex in any form is good.

Homosexual orientation is not a matter of choice.

Homosexual orientation is not changeable.

Children need to be liberated from the prejudices of their parents.

The age of consent should be lowered.

"Coming out" is a major life passage, a liberating experience.

Homosexuality itself has not moral implications.

Homophobia (opposing the homosexual ideology) is morally reprehensible.[5]

You can find these ideological premises underlying most of what is said by liberals today in their pronouncements on AIDS or gay rights. If you want to really receive death threats, try saying in public that homosexual orientation is reversible! There are, in fact, many ministries throughout the world to homosexuals who want to get out of the gay lifestyle.[6]

It is, after all, the Christian position to hate the sin but love the sinner. But oh, the censorship exerted to keep hidden any word of the successful therapies and ministries that rescue people from the lust of rampant homosexual practice.

So, I'm sorry. I may sound cynical, but I think I'm being honest. As I see it, our nation does not have the will to save itself from moral decay, or from AIDS. Absent a major outpouring of God's grace, of course.

WHAT COULD WE DO?

If God is merciful, and wants to save our nation, there are steps that could be taken to control the epidemic. The first would be partner notification and contact tracing. This is the first step in getting a sick person proper treatment, and an indispensable step in limiting the spread of the disease among the general poulation. People with terminal illnesses deserve to know they are going to die, in my opinion, and other people need to know if they have been exposed to a deadly disease.

It was, by law, standard practice with syphilis and gonorrhea, beginning long before antibiotics were readily available for treatment, and continuing today. It was a logical step to take as soon as enough was known about AIDS to recommend it. But the gay lobby swung into its most self-righteous high gear. "You can't do that!" they screamed. "It will violate our privacy to tell anybody we have AIDS!" A free translation of that might be "If people know I have AIDS, they might not be willing to have sex with me." And, since it is the politically protected minority, the wishes of the gay lobby were respected.

Today, a doctor recommending common sense has to tread very carefully in the professional journals: "I believe that, on balance, systematic tracing and notification of the sexual partners of HIV-infected persons and screening of pregnant women, newborns, hospitalized patients, and health care professionals are warranted," said one doctor timidly in the pages of *The New England Journal of Medicine*.[7]

Why can't marriage applications be accompanied by HIV testing? If officialdom wanted to cooperate (as they clearly did *not* in the one state that temporarily tried that), that could work smoothly and well. Under the leadership of Dr. Robert Redfield, MD, the Army contacts and tests partners of Army personnel found to be HIV-positive. Some already have the virus, of course, but those who don't are able to avoid contracting it. Knowledge is better than ignorance.

But better by far than any sexually transmitted disease is virtue.

Chapter 7

PARENTS' MANIFESTO

A
t this point, you may think I'm going on at greater length than necessary about the need for holiness within the home. Are today's young people really in such dire straits? Is it really necessary to be self-conscious about trying to create a Christian culture in the home? Aren't most people really doing pretty well, and aren't most teens really being raised pretty much okay? Oh, there's a little sexual experimentation, sure, but that's nothing new, even if it's not good. Aren't I being a little excessive in saying that we practically have to become fanatical about the upbringing of our kids?

Well, no, I'm not being fanatical. What I am doing is urging you to scrutinize carefully how much of a priority your child is in your life. For my part, I believe that one of the first things the Lord is going to demand of me when I get to heaven is an accounting of how I cared for the souls entrusted to my care. And I know that, when I face that judgment, most of the excuses that may sound so convincing to me today will be worthless then.

As I sit here typing these words and my children begin a heated argument at the other end of the house, it's tempting to pretend not to hear it. But I know the Lord is not going to judge me on whether I met my deadlines on time, but on whether I taught my children kindness. And this very moment might be the opportunity needed to teach that kindness. So I have to make myself willing to intervene. Then I have the prudential judgment to make: is this an argument in which I ought to intervene, or is it one they should be allowed to settle by themselves?

So no, I am not trying to make you a fanatic. I am trying to explain how little things add up in the rearing of children, in the developing of values, in the forming of the will. And enough little things add up to virtuous children, able to be sexually chaste, while an insufficiency of little things leads to children who become statistics of sexually transmitted disease and illegitimacy.

And no, by and large, most American kids are not doing fine. I know better. So do you if you think about it. How many teenagers do you know—not just personally, but including the families of your co-workers and friends? And how many of those teens have had problems with drugs, alcohol, school failure, attempted suicide, or sexual misconduct? And how does that number seem to compare to the number of your peers, in your teen years, who had problems with the same things? Unless you grew up in a particularly rough area, it's probably many more.

Nor is it just your impressions. Statistics will bear out that the well-being of American adolescents, particularly white, middle-class adolescents, is declining measurably. Peter Uhlenberg, a sociologist at the University of North Carolina, has documented the decline.[1]

We all know about the decline in SAT scores, a decline close to 10 percent over twenty years. Do we really believe that American college-bound youths are born with less intelligence than college-bound youths of twenty years earlier? Of course not. But we don't want to ask ourselves why, then, they perform so much more poorly. And it can't all be blamed on the decline of educational standards, either.

Between 1960 and 1980, the death rate by suicide for teenagers aged sixteen and seventeen increased by 140 percent. You can reassure yourself that the actual numbers are not that high if you want to, but if you're honest, you'll ask yourself why the increase. And between 1972 and 1979, the proportion of sixteen and seventeen-year-olds using alcohol increased 56 percent. The number of those using drugs increased 139 percent in the same period. You can say that's just the ripple effect of the 1960s, and you'd be correct, of course. But then ask yourself why that ripple was felt so strongly ten years later. What was missing in the lives of the teens of the 70s that made them vulnerable?

During the two decades from 1960 to 1980, the proportion of youths aged sixteen and seventeen dying from homicide—that is, murder—increased 232 percent. So we live in a more violent society, you say. Arguable, but why is the violence directed toward sixteen-year-olds? The FBI says there are 600,000 child prostitutes roaming the streets of our nation.[2] You say kids always ran away from home. But that many? And how did they end up that way?

And don't try to reassure yourself by saying that's just the result of poverty. Nonsense. During the same two decades, real per capita social welfare expenditures on youth increased five-fold. By 1980 there were 206 federal programs administered by 20 agencies, all devoted to meeting the perceived needs of youth. Twenty years ago there weren't all the programs, and there weren't all the problems, either.

What is really happening? Uhlenberg and Eggebeen conclude that American parents are paying less and less attention to their children, allowing institutions and government programs to do what parents used to do. Consequently, children are growing up with less and less love and personal attention from their parents. And material benefits do not compensate for personal attention. With half the mothers in the country working, when the kids have a fight, who is there to interrupt it and teach them how to turn away a wrathful word? And then when they get to be eighteen years old and the brother alienated by years of fighting is no friend, the loneliness becomes unbearable and suicide is contemplated.

THE FAMILY IN TECHNOLOGICAL SOCIETY

We have the experience of living on the front end of a new society, a technological society. Our parents ushered in this society, but they themselves had been formed in a much more traditional one. We have grown up in an increasingly technological society and are not even aware of how it has shaped us.

Where the family is concerned, the main characteristic of a modern technological society is that it removes functions from the family. It's all done with the best of intentions, perhaps, but the responsibilities are effectively removed nonetheless. The Constitution of our nation reflects the conscious sentiments of our Founding Fathers: individualism was what mattered, not family, not community. The individual was deemed the basic unit of society. How foolish this is. Individuals are no better than their formation, and who forms them? The family. The family is the basic unit of society.

The Founding Fathers made some assumptions that modern society has chosen to ignore. They assumed, for instance, that an attitude of private virtue would govern private behavior. They may not have spoken of the family, but they assumed it would be performing its functions and doing its job. And that job primarily consisted of forming the future generations to be strong and virtuous. It was an assumption that cannot be made today.

Yet the consequences of our abandoning that assumption are upon us. Either we will have private virtue and public freedom, or we will have private vice and, sooner or later, a police state. Everything we do affects other people, either for the good or for the ill, whether we intend it or not. No man is an island, as the poet John Donne said.

Consider the draconian measures being employed in other countries to cope with the AIDS epidemic. Foreigners living in Moscow for more than three months may be subject to a mandatory AIDS test.[3] In China, foreign students are given a blood test on arrival and deported if they are found to be HIV positive. In Sri Lanka, visitors with AIDS or HIV positive tests are deported, no matter how briefly they were planning to stay.[4] Nor are these examples the end of what the world will soon see as it attempts to protect itself from the consequences of a few people's private indulgences.

Some estimates have the cost to society of the sexually transmitted disease epidemic and the unwed parent epidemic as running at $30 billion a year, in the U.S. alone. How long will American taxpayers be able to pay for it? Already the state of Wisconsin has passed a law mandating that parents of minors who bear children are responsible financially and legally for those children. Some argue that the law will be an incentive to abortions, and perhaps it will. But on the other hand, if people are irresponsible enough to expect the taxpayers of Wisconsin to pay for their immorality, it is eminently understandable that the taxpayers of Wisconsin seek to defend themselves against the consequences of those people's indulgences. Such a law as this would not be necessary in a traditional society; in such a society, parents of girls who "got into trouble" would know that they had to make arrangements for the results of the trouble, and they would do so. But the parents in a traditional society were also more watchful over their children than are their cohorts in our modern, technological society.

In a traditional society, the family had many functions and worked to perform them. At birth, it was the family who provided care to the infant and kept it alive. In sickness, it was the family who cared for the ill, and fortunate was the family that had a wise granny around who knew the secrets of herbs and oils to cure the ailments of mankind. The family also cared for that granny and gave her a place by the fire on cold winter nights.

It was the family that taught the child everything he knew, from his prayers to his livelihood. Children grew up satisfied to be in the same craft as their fathers, proud to follow in their father's or mother's footsteps. Wealth was something that passed through the family, and being disinherited was a serious consequence for serious actions, for it meant an end to prospects for material advancement in life. On the other hand, if one contributed one's might and loyalty to the family and helped its situation improve, one knew that one would be a beneficiary later on.

But even more important was the task the family performed of providing a sense of personal worth to its members. One's status in a traditional society came from who one was, what family one belonged to. By contrast, today a person's status comes from what one accomplishes. While the former arrangement may have limited some horizons, the latter renders every person vulnerable to insecurity. Under the traditional arrangement, a person could relax because he knew his value. Under the modern arrangement, there is no limit to the pressure one can put on oneself to achieve more and more things. No wonder the workaholic is the typical man and woman of the modern world.[5]

Besides providing identity, the family in a traditional society greased the wheels of social contact for everybody. By being in a family, a person inherited relationship networks and friendship universes. A girl didn't need to fabricate reasons to get home from a date at a sensible hour. She knew, and so did her swain, that her father would be waiting and watching. Actually, she wouldn't be alone to begin with, but would more than likely be chaperoned—her mother would have seen to that.

Compare these functions with the way our modern society discharges them. A booming senior care industry provides day care or inpatient care for elderly grannies, as another booming industry provides day care for infants and children. Health care is so technologically oriented that the question of what's good for the human being at the other end of the machines sometimes becomes a subject of major debate.

Government provides education, and parents think they're being heroic if they attend PTA meetings to keep track of their children's learning. Government even provides breakfast, thus removing that simple discipline from the family's list of jobs. And we don't expect our children to follow us in our work anymore. Rare and delightful is the business that adds "and Son" to its name as Junior grows up. Rarer still is the business that remains a family one for longer than the founder's generation.

Thanks to inheritance taxes, few of us stand to be materially improved significantly by the demise of our relatives. Organized envy as a political cause has seen to that. And not only do we live in perpetual uncertainty about whether we are "adequate," but legitimate dependency has become something to be feared instead of the honor it is in God's plan. Many a young mother has been driven to depression simply because she couldn't stand the thought of being dependent on her husband, whereas the greatest honor her husband could have would be to provide for her and their children.

Far from providing us with networks of friends who would look out for us and on whom we could depend in need, modern society revels in its independence, and popular songs chide us to "mind your own business and don't be minding mine."

The picture is not all bleak, however. There is one area in which function is returning to the family in the modern world. In principle, it's a function that never left the family, but in practice, at least over the past couple of generations in the affluent Western world, it's a function that had been ceded to institutions. I speak of the religious and moral education of children. We would all agree that it is primarily the family's job, to be undertaken with guidance and assistance from the Church. But in practice, have we not depended on institutions to do it for us? How many parents over the past several decades have asked in frustration, "What are they teaching you in that school anyway?" but have continued to allow their children to go to "that school"?

We parents are responsible for the values formation of our children just as surely as parents were in the days of the early church, when Christian families in Antioch or Philippi knew they had to be careful and guard the treasure of faith they had received. Martin Luther was the first prominent Christian to urge the secular government to take responsibility for education. In fact, he spoke vigorously against parents' educating their children at home. It was not his intention to transfer moral and spiritual training from home to government; his concern was for book learning, and he didn't trust parents to teach their children to read. But the precedent he created took on a life of its own long after. It was the Prussian government in the nineteenth century that conceived the notion that the state should teach morality as well as everything else, a dangerous idea imported to the United States by Horace Mann and only now reaching full fruition in public schools.

As the experiences of many parents both Catholic and Protestant in taking control of their children's education demonstrate, today Christians cannot view each other as "the enemy." Christians must view each other as allies. The enemies are the secular value agnostics and moral consequentialists and the trends of our modern, technological society that would remove more and more functions from the family, replacing them with institutions.[6]

It can be argued that the learning that goes on in your home, in the few years in which your child is there, is more vital than it has been for any children in Western civilization for hundreds of years. If your child does not absorb now, in your home, the emotional climate and values that will enable him to survive, both literally and emotionally, in this corrupt world, he will be highly unlikely to pick up those values anywhere else. And the stakes are higher than ever before. The numerous deadly threats arrayed against the free democratic way of life cannot be met except by citizens who are strong and moral. The future of the world as we know it is at stake.

But parents have always had an awesome weight of responsibility on their shoulders. While all of us decide our own relationship with the Lord, much of our ability to build that relationship in practice depends on what we learned from our parents. It is downright frightening to think of what you are taking on with the rearing of a child, and it's probably good that most of us don't think about it before we have a child or much of the world's population would never be born!

SOME BASIC PRINCIPLES OF PARENTING

The first thing we need to understand is that children will do as we do, not as we say. They may intellectually understand what we say and even come to see the wisdom of it in their own maturity, but in the meanwhile, they will be doing what they saw us do.

Does Mom obey Dad? This can take many forms and have lots of subtle ramifications. If she questions his decisions in front of the children, or if she doesn't enforce his rules when he's not around, she's inviting the children to disobey her, because that is what they see her doing. Does Mom complain about Dad's shortcomings, or indicate her dissatisfaction because he doesn't earn more or can't fix a broken light switch? If so, despite her lavish praise of him on his birthday, the children will feel free to look for more shortcomings. They will look for hers as well.

Does Dad respect Mom? Does he respect all women? If he makes certain jokes and casts glances in certain directions when Mom is not around, he's not respecting her. And his children will get the message that the glances and jokes and snickers are all right as long as the wife doesn't see them. Does Dad help around the house and thank Mom for her housekeeping and cooking, expressing genuine gratitude for her struggles in doing things for the family? If he does, he is teaching his children respect for women. If he doesn't, he is teaching his sons that they can take for granted the labors of their wives, and teaching his daughters that efforts expended on behalf of a home are not important.

However you treat your spouse is how your child will treat you. It boils down to that. That's why the best gift you can give your child is to love your spouse. It's also a pretty good gift to give yourself, because it saves you a lot of hassles down the road. Children read mutual love between parents as cross-endorsement of teaching. It's an effective way of letting the children know that Mom and Dad are of one mind. The kids instinctively know whether Mom and Dad are likely to agree on how to handle them and how far they can go with naughtiness. Knowing that they couldn't get too far at age seven has a marvelous impact on minimizing trouble at age seventeen.

Parents need to realize that they are the first and most important standard-setters for their children. What cartoons a parent allows to be watched, what music a parent tunes in on the radio—these small things, usually done with no thought, are establishing a basis for the child's sensibilities for life.

A parent must not be afraid to vocalize moral opinions in front of children. Doing so helps them learn to think as you do. For instance, mothers going about routine chores can teach young children a lot about what sort of behavior is acceptable later on. At the park with a three-year-old, point out immodestly dressed people and say why that's not a proper way to dress. This is not lacking in charity: you aren't making a personal judgement about that unknown person. It is, actually, a form of charity, because it is training your child to have appropriate standards for his own later years. Be sure not to ridicule other people's bodies (which they cannot change), however, lest you inadvertently produce a preoccupation with physical appearance.

If you take your child to a movie and a couple sits in front of you necking all the while, don't let it go unobserved. If you see a couple cuddling each other in public, say something about it to your child. Say, for instance, that you certainly hope the people are married since they're cuddling that close. Tell your child it's obvious those two people want to be alone, so why are they sitting out there where all the world can see them? A three-year-old, on hearing that kind of observation, implicitly understands that physical intimacy is proper in marriage and improper outside it, and that privacy is important.

Standards of proper appearance and actions can be cultivated without conveying any sense that the body itself is not good. For instance, don't overreact to nudity in art. If a picture of Venus de Milo or another nude appears in a book you're showing your child, or on the wall of a museum you're visiting, calmly observe that the human body is a beautiful work of art, since it is the temple of the Holy Spirit, and that some artists have tried to give glory to God by capturing that beauty in art. Then go on to another picture, mentioning that a person's body is really pretty private, and that you'd just as soon not look at somebody else's body since you're not a doctor and don't have to. During the latency period, this is enough. If you have children past age eleven, you may want to pre-view the art books and be more selective in what you leave lying around, since now interest is growing in the opposite gender.

The danger in overreacting is that it hints to a child that there's something there you don't want him to see, which will only provoke curiosity. Or it suggests there's something there that's dirty or bad, neither of which is correct, and either of which would be a corruption of a godly concept of the human body.

Similarly, it's not good to overreact to accidental nudity in the home. Take reasonable precautions, of course. Keep doors closed, and so on. But if little Sam forgets to knock and opens the bathroom door at the wrong time, don't scream and scold as if he had set the house on fire. Chances are, he wasn't paying any attention to you anyway and won't remember it at all. But if you make an enormous fuss about it, he'll try hard to remember what it was he saw that you obviously didn't want him to see.

Different things are appropriate for different ages. A four-year-old running around the house naked after his bath should feel he is being naughty (which is why he is so gleeful when he does it), but not that the world should end. He should not, of course, normally get the opportunity to be a junior streaker. Within a couple of years, the desire to run around naked will disappear. By age eight, a child is likely to be embarrassed by pictures of himself as a naked baby, and that embarrassment is part of God's plan of modesty. If a child wants his naked picture taken out of the family photo album, comply with the request. The impulse to modesty should be encouraged, and protecting the child's developing sense of his own dignity is more important than holding onto a "cute" picture.

Around then might be a good time to tell the story of Noah's nakedness and to stress how respectful it was of his sons to cover him up while walking backward. When children are very young, don't mention the alcohol factor in the story, since the point you're making is about the privacy of the body. Later on, it's worth mentioning. By age eight, when natural modesty has set in, the point can be made that drinking too much alcohol can cause a person to embarrass himself.

There's nothing wrong with bathing very young children together, even if they are of opposite sexes, because you can use the opportunity to teach (and if you're the mother of two or more very young children, you need every minute you can squeeze from your day!) Children should know the proper names for all body parts and should not feel embarrassment over any name or any part. Use proper terminology from the very beginning. There is no benefit to the child in having to learn a new vocabulary later on. Besides, one of the ways in which we show respect is by using correct names, and respect for our own and other people's bodies is something that must be learned early on. Questions will come up at bathtime about the functions of different parts of the body, and they should be answered simply and honestly.

Bathtime is also a good opportunity to bring up the delicate but very important subject of touching. Our world today is such that before going to school for the first time, a child, for his own protection, should understand what kinds of touches, and by whom, are appropriate. A young child should understand, too, that if anybody tries to touch in a wrong way, he or she should object loudly and immediately and tell parents as soon as possible.

If another baby comes along and Mom is nursing, realize what a favor you are doing your older child by taking a relaxed attitude toward it. If the subject is handled straightforwardly, his first image of the female breast will be that it's a source of nourishment to a child, which is as God intended. How much more desirable it is for that to be a boy's first knowledge of the breast, rather than for him to view it only as an object of lust with other boys viewing girlie pictures at a later age. A wise mother can have beautiful conversations with an older child as she nurses an infant. When the situation of the other boys and the girlie pictures occurs, as it inevitably will, the fortunate son will remember that there is more to it than that, and he may be more able to resist the flow of peer conversation.

Of course, Mom will cover herself modestly, but the baby is going to move, or Mom may have to make a sudden movement, and the older child may get a glimpse of more than Mom had planned. Not to worry; no harm has been done in that brief moment. An innate shyness will usually limit staring at Mommy, though staring at Aunt Susie nursing could come more naturally. At some age, it probably will be necessary to explain that we don't stare at other people's bodies. This usually comes when a handicapped person is first noticed by the child. But overemphasizing such things can create an unhealthy preoccupation with the body, as well as give wrong ideas about the body and lay a foundation for real hangups later on.

How parents react to natural curiosity about the body and its functions sets a crucially important standard for how curiosity about other things will be handled. A child's curiosity about all things is natural and healthy and should always be encouraged. It is a key to intellectual growth. Whatever you do, don't discourage it.

When a three-year-old asks, "Where was I before I was born?" he's voicing a fleeting thought. He'll forget your answer, be sure of that. But he will remember your attitude. If your attitude is relaxed and encouraging, he will ask the question again and again, and each time your answer will get a little more adult. Parents sometimes unwittingly discourage curiosity, with the result that children get the impression that certain types of questions won't be welcomed favorably by parents. That doesn't stop the curiosity; it merely re-routes it away from home and onto the street.

Regard the curiosity of a child as a great opportunity to satisfy the thirst for information while instilling values. "How come Johnny's mom and dad are divorced?" can lead to a good discussion about the permanence of marriage. "Now that Mittens has had her kittens, how come the daddy hasn't come to look at them?" can lead to a discussion about differences between people and animals, and to instruction on the responsibilities of human fatherhood. Load up these conversations with content. Even if only a fraction of it seems to be retained, you don't know what might be remembered later. And you'll never have such attention from your child again.

"What's an abortion?" offers a chance to instill a fundamental respect for all human life. I did my level best to keep my children from being aware of abortion, but I only managed to protect them until about age seven. It wasn't until I was in high school that I even knew such a thing existed. What a comment on the accelerated pace of moral and cultural decay just in my lifetime! And when the question came at seven, I was as vague as I could be. "Abortion is killing a baby before it's born," I said. That gives pause, since children usually don't think of themselves as being alive before they're born (unless they've been old enough to pay attention to a subsequent pregnancy of Mom's).

Michael, being of a mechanical bent, asked practical questions: "How do they do it?" And there was my vagueness. The last thing I wanted was mental images in their minds that would frighten them. "Oh, they use some kind of drugs, I think," I said nebulously, and that was good enough for then. Over the subsequent years, the same question came back, and gradually, as they seemed able to handle it, I had to give more adequate answers. I say "had to" because I wanted to keep the channels of communication open. If I had clammed up and refused to answer that question, they would have been reticent about the next question they had. My "reward" for my openness came when Michael bopped into the kitchen one afternoon to ask what bisexuality was and, when I told him, followed up by asking, "Why would anybody want to be like that?"

Some parents might not consider that it's a "reward", and it's a good thing I'm not squeamish. But I count it a triumph that Michael asked me that question. Who else would I have liked him to ask? Who else but his father (at work and unavailable when the thought was in Mike's mind) or our pastor (whom he would never think of asking, for shyness and lack of opportunity)? Such is the indispensable role of mother in forming attitudes and values.

CREATING EMOTIONAL CLIMATE

I hope what I've written gives you a fresh appreciation for the mother's role in the emotional climate of the home. This is what the career-oriented feminist ideology simply does not understand. Yes, a mother can work at a demanding job twelve or more hours a day, race home and get dinner on the table, and do the grocery shopping. If she takes lots of vitamins, she just might have the raw physical stamina to do it. But what about the emotional accomplishments? Will she have the energy left over the attention span, or the simple raw information about what's going on between the kids, who's studying what in school, and whose friends are talking about what these days to enable her to tailor her remarks to their needs? That's far less likely.

Even if all the questions somehow get asked and all the right answers are given, the child needs something else: motivation to follow the teaching conveyed in those answers. Having the moral teaching, by itself, cannot motivate or enable a person to resist temptation. In human terms, the ability to practice morality depends a lot on a person's emotional stability. And where does emotional stability come from? The emotional climate surrounding one while growing up, the self-esteem one absorbs from that climate. A prerequisite to moral practice, but especially to sexual abstinence in an age of indulgence, is self-control. But self-control cannot grow unless there is self-confidence and self-respect.

Thinkers about moral philosophy through the ages have observed that caring about others precedes moral thinking. But one's heart cannot really and truly care for another unless one first knows the care of others. Yes, even if no human being ever cared for you, once the Holy Spirit acts in your heart, you will know God's love and care for you. Then, through His power, you will be a changed person. And of course we pray that that will happen to all the people in the world, those who have known human love and those who have not. But even as we pray, it is our responsibility before God to do everything we can to insure that for our children, the knowledge of being loved and cared for will come through our efforts.

How can parents tailor their efforts to maximum effectiveness? For this, some knowledge can be helpful. There are certain trends, certain patterns, in the stages of a child's development that a parent can be expecting and ready to meet. We'll consider those stages in the next chapter.

Chapter 8

PUTTING
THE VALUES BACK

In this chapter, we'll look at what values can best be instilled at what stages in a child's development, as well as how to do it. And the beginning place has to be the development of self-control, which is the foundation on which all other values must be built. Before children can become moral, they need to care about other people. Then they need to care about the effects of their actions on other people. To do any of this requires, first and foremost, self-control.

Until almost adolescence, some children cannot truly comprehend that events that will take place days hence can be caused by what they do today. Oh, they understand it on one level—they could answer a question correctly on a reading comprehension test—but when it comes to applying the principle in their own lives, the reality of it somehow escapes them. It can be frustrating for parents, who know the kid is smart but wonder why he's so dumb.

Even slower to come, particularly in boys, is empathy for others. My pet theory is that this is because boys are treated rougher from the beginning and are more likely than girls to be the butt of jokes (harmless and well-meaning, their perpetrators say) and other ridicule. Intended perhaps to give them the "tough skin" boys are said to need, one effect of this treatment is to numb the child's own sensitivity to pain. In the process, of course, it also dulls his sensitivity to anybody else's. Then parents and grandparents wonder why boys are so unable to sympathize with another person.

There's also neurological evidence to explain the difference. The bridge between the left and right spheres is bigger in women. In other words, women can transfer back and forth from information to feeling to communication a whole lot easier than men can, just on the basis of biological endowment. Compared to women, men have deficient ability to communicate their perceptions, in other words. They're dumb when it comes to emotions. This information is nothing new; recently, even feminist authors have written books on the subject. My husband's reaction was probably typical of the tradition-oriented man. When I explained this neurological difference between men and women to him, he sighed a happy sigh, sank back another inch into his easy chair, and said, "Ah, good. Then it's a hardware problem." I could see him exonerating himself for certain shortcomings, so I hastened to assure him that software had been invented which could overcome the tendency, and that it is called divine grace!

BASIC STAGES

Certain virtues are more easily taught at certain stages of development. David Isaacs, a professor of education at the University of Navarre, has written an insightful book called *Character Building,* the fruit of years of study of the moral development of children.[1] According to Isaacs, up to age seven, the virtues of obedience, sincerity, and order are the most essential to develop, and the ones most easily developed. From ages eight through twelve, the virtues to stress are fortitude (which includes perseverance, industriousness, and patience), justice (which includes responsibility), and charity (which includes generosity). As the child approaches puberty, Isaacs notes, it is desirable to develop the will so as to strengthen the character in preparation for the coming challenges.

For the early teen years, thirteen to fifteen, Isaacs emphasizes the virtues of temperance—modesty and moderation—and those that promote sociability: friendship and respect. By this time, a young person should be capable of being interested in the good of other people in a practical way. In the late teen years, Isaacs maintains, developing virtues requires thoughtfulness, and learning how to think before acting is the major task of ages sixteen through eighteen. (No wonder I got frustrated when my twelve-year-old couldn't do it!) The virtues that facilitate thinking before acting include prudence, flexibility, loyalty, audacity, humility, understanding, and optimism. Optimism, by the way, means making an effort of the will to look at things positively, seeking the best in others.

The years that a young person first becomes capable of modesty and moderation happen to be the same years of incredibly rapid physiological changes: growth, weight gain, puberty, menarche. All these changes conspire to put the young man or woman into a highly narcissistic phase of development, which on the one hand makes modesty and moderation and sociability the more difficult, but on the other hand makes precisely those virtues more necessary and timely. The later stage coincides with what doctors call middle adolescence, which is characterized by greater autonomy from parents and considerable dependence on peers. According to medical experts, the ages between fourteen and eighteen are the ones when teenagers are most likely to acquire sexually transmitted diseases or become pregnant[2]—in other words, the years of maximum premarital sexual activity. But precisely because the peer dependency is strong and the separation from parents is great, the need for thinking before acting is all the more important.

SHOULD CHILDREN BE TRAINED?

You're going to hear some people say that moral training of children is a surefire formula for disaster. Popular journalists blame strict upbringings for the downfall of the mighty. Politician Gary Hart, for example, had been raised a strict Christian, and when his extramarital shenanigans became world news, Gail Sheehy in the tres chic *Vanity Fair* magazine blamed his downfall on his Christian upbringing:

> People raised in such strict Fundamentalist families never experience the turbulence common to normal adolescence. And since the stage of rebellion and identity formation is not allowed, breakaways like Hart often behave for years like belated teenagers. Rebellious, angry, and irresponsible as adults, they . . . are compelled to break rules and backslide toward Satan.[3]

Not that Sheehy's attack is unique. Psychologists of the secularist mold have for long blamed "strict fundamentalist" upbringings for what they regard as "unhealthy" sentiments like guilt. Almost fifty years ago, a standard textbook on the psychology of adolescence included this passage:

> Especially in evangelical circles . . . do we find an extreme emphasis placed upon the sins of the adolescent. This emphasis upon the necessity for the conviction of having sinned develops an imaginary sense of sin and a group of morbid fears.[4]

To be sure, fire and brimstone can be overdone and can produce a backlash. Constant, ineffective harping on guilt can indeed produce some morbid fears and unhealthy mindsets. But that is not true Christianity! Christianity is not unrelieved guilt. Following Christ includes recognizing guilt and repenting for it. And after the repentance comes the joyful release of being forgiven and having the freedom, indeed the obligation, to forget the sin, wipe the slate clean, and start again on the journey of union with Christ. That is the wonderful thing about the mystery of forgiveness. As deep as the repentance is, so high is the joy of forgiveness. Secular mental health professionals and chic writers who perhaps have never experienced this cannot understand it.

And as for the remark that Christian youths do not experience the turbulence of adolescence, don't Christian parents just wish! Of course Christian young people go through the normal stages of experimenting with different identities trying on different roles, and pushing the limits of parental authority. Sometimes I think Satan goes after the children of committed parents with a particular vengeance. Wouldn't it be grand if Christian youth were formed in virtue before adolescence and continued to be formed in virtue during the turbulence of adolescence, so that as the forces of turbulence arose, they were met with internal restraint, as well as external restraint from parents when necessary.

Each child is different. Any mother can tell you that from the moment her babies drew their first breath, they had distinct personalities, and she could discern that she had to handle each one a little differently. Because of these differences, both subtle and great, a parent has to be constantly on his or her toes, monitoring their development. What might have worked as a discipline strategy with one child at a certain age might be the wrong thing on another child at the same age. Unless the mother has been very attentive, she may not know that. And then a father may impose a discipline that breaks the spirit rather than challenges it. This is a danger, of course. Ill-considered instruction can produce a backlash. That's why parents must pray constantly for discernment and guidance: because parental sensitivity is the best protection against this extreme.

As children get older, they need breathing room, space to go through the individuating process of adolescence. That's a valid need. A mother who is unable to relax can sometimes not realize when to let up the pressure. When a parent gets locked into a half nelson in a contest of wills with a child, it is hard to know when to let up or, indeed, to be able to let up, even if the parent realizes this is counterproductive. Mothers frequently encounter this with one particular child. They seem to tangle every mealtime, day after day after day, over what seems to be insignificant. If this kind of tension goes on too long, it can certainly cause a backlash. The youth in question will hear nothing and feel himself victimized and persecuted, losing his desire to please his parents. Home and all it represents will become a source of pain to him.

For times like this, God created two parents. Usually, there are sins on both sides that need to be recognized and confessed (to God and to each other), so a new start can be made. But neither the mother nor the child in question can see objectively enough to take such measures. A father, however, can call time out and, by exercising his authority over both his wife and his child, create a cooling-off period during which he can get to the bottom of the problem, as well as inspire his wife to get hold of herself. When it's the father who has gotten locked in the contest and it's clear that it's pure stubbornness on both sides that is keeping the situation deadlocked, the mother should speak privately to her husband and point out to him how he needs to let up. It's not only children who lapse in self-control, remember. We adults are prone to the same failings.

Our children need not only to know what is right, but they must also want to do what is right and have the willpower to do it in order to be fully moral. Time and maturity are needed to achieve these different plateaus. For all Christians, it is the continual struggle to follow Christ. And self-control is at the very foundation of it. All of us must be masters of ourselves before we can be servants of others. So learning self-control is the first task of a Christian. How to learn it? As Dr. James Dobson has so wisely pointed out in *The Strong-Willed Child,* self-control grows from being submissive to parental control. It cannot grow out of chaos. It does not appear spontaneously like a mushroom after a rainstorm.

TEACH TO THE INTELLECT

In motivating growing children to want to do what is right, they must first understand what *is* right. This requires intellectual effort. And the first stages of teaching sexual morality to the intellect come when the child begins to think about matters related to sexuality.

Questions about marriage and family begin well before age four. Four-year-olds are quite observant of differences between men and women.

They want to know about marriage and babies and all such things.[5] Five-year-olds are curious, too, but not with the same intensity as six-year-olds. Six-year-olds see themselves as the center of the universe, which may be why mothers remember age six as a year of their kids' constant fighting with other children. In boys, this is the peak age for bathroom jokes.

By six, children have figured out that they will marry a person of the opposite sex, though sexual distinctions are not completely clear. When my son Michael was six, we were expecting a new baby. The boys naturally wanted it to be a boy, but Mommy very much wanted a girl. Michael, showing the instincts of agreeableness that often make second children a joy, proposed a compromise: "How about if the baby is half boy and half girl?" Mike's eighteen-month-older brother, Pearse, ridiculed this suggestion, because by age seven the distinction between the genders is clearly understood, and Pearse was eager to flaunt his knowledge.

Seven-year-olds are aware of sexual differences and are beginning to have same-sex play patterns in school. It is a delightful year of maturing into family membership, since a child can now understand that his family is unique and special. If Mom has a new baby at this age, the interest of a seven-year-old in the whole process will be acute. I had known that Pearse and Michael were interested in how this new baby was going to come, and since the hospital offered sibling tours in advance, I arranged one for them. A delightful grandmotherly nurse took us all around, and showed us incubators and other equipment so that when they came later to visit the new baby, they wouldn't be alarmed at the chrome and plastic everywhere.

At the end of the tour came something I hadn't expected. The nurse asked the boys if they wondered how the baby was going to get out of Mommy. They both nodded vigorously. She sat down with a hand-made rag doll and explained things in a straightforward but simple manner, concluding by pulling a baby rag doll out from between the mother doll's legs. I was gasping for air at this point, wondering whether to be angry or what; I had had no idea this kind of sex education was part of the hospital tour. But then I looked at the boys' faces, and I lost my anger. The intense interest and comprehension they showed told me that this demonstration was answering questions they had been harboring secretly. I realized I had been remiss in not picking up on their curiosity sooner. The nurse asked them whether they had any other questions. The boys looked shyly at each other, and finally Mike ventured a question. Then I held my breath waiting for Pearse to ask how the baby got in there in the first place, but he didn't. On the way home, I asked them if they had more questions, which they did, and which we talked about as they applied the miniature-sized Pamper to the teddy bear in the car. But the question of how the baby got inside the mommy did not emerge.

When I was preparing the second edition of this book, I asked the boys what they remembered of that tour. Michael, who had asked the question, did not remember ever having the tour. Pearse remembered it as being very interesting, and he remembered the anatomically-correct doll as helping him understand something he had only heard about before. I asked him whether he had wondered how the baby got in there in the first place. No, he told me, that thought didn't occur to him for a couple more years. Somewhere along the line, he said, long before that tour, when he had asked me how babies were made, I had told him something that left him with the impression that mommy and daddy sleeping together put a baby inside mommy. I didn't even recollect any such conversation, but it had satisfied his curiousity for a long time. He took the phrase "sleeping together" quite literally, and, at age seven, it never occurred to him that there was anything more to it than that. And that is the beauty of innocence.

According to renowned developmental psychologists Arnold Gesell and Frances Ilg, a seven-year-old girl may have asked how babies are made, but a seven-year-old boy would be unlikely to think of it. Certainly by eight, a girl is very interested in how Daddy planted the seed, though boys still aren't as inquisitive. It was two years before Pearse found out that part of God's plan, and after that his inquisitiveness subsided until it was artificially aroused by Toby. After Toby's departure, I might mention, Pearse's interest subsided again. And when another new baby was on the way, his occasional questions all concerned the baby's development. I was pleased to spot some emerging empathy when he repeatedly expressed sympathy that the poor baby was so crowded in there, and how boring it must be!

By nine years of age, girls and boys will naturally segregate themselves completely, socially, not to mingle again until adolescent girls begin paying attention to older boys. The years between nine and eleven are wonderful: it's a time of stability and steady growth, without the peaks and valleys of the first four years of rapid growth and the six or so that commence with age twelve. The ability to reason is pretty well established, and if the emotional climate has been satisfactory, there is a desire to please parents and authorities. Right and wrong are perceived as pretty absolute during this time, too, so it's an opportune period for talking in those terms. Later maturity will bring questioning, to be sure, but principles embraced at this age will command some loyalty later, even if it is hidden.

Enjoy the stage while it lasts: the next one, the pre-adolescent stage, is totally narcissistic and seeks to please no one but self—unless a strong conscience has been formed during the years of quiet and the child is consciously capable of rising above natural inclinations. And by twelve or thirteen, the desire to be part of "the group" is strong. If good taste and the ability to make critical judgments have been established earlier, an appeal to the intellect can help a youngster to mitigate his natural susceptibility to peer-groups influence, which is often harmful.

By age thirteen, for sure in a public school, a Christian youth will have been challenged and will have had to defend his or her values. If a girl says, "I won't sleep with anybody because God forbids it," she will be laughed at. Furthermore, she is vulnerable to being told that she is simply following unquestioningly what she has been told by the adult generation—a charge no teen wants to have to confront.

But if she can say, "I won't sleep around because I don't want to get a disease that will make me have pain for the rest of my life," she wins herself an opportunity to argue her point of view. She might even gain her peers' respect and change somebody else's mind. Arguments can, of course, wear her down, and temptation can be strong, which is why faith must *underlie* the decisions. Even if she can't argue well, if worst comes to worst, she'll simply refuse to do what she knows to be wrong because her faith is strong and she is capable of being stubborn.

Kids need intellectual arguments to defend their virtue. They need their parents to provide these arguments. What often happens instead is that parents shield kids from information that might become useful ammunition to them, mistakenly thinking they are protecting their innocence.

I remember one Sunday morning when I was in high school, my father took the magazine insert out of the Sunday paper and threw it away. I happened to hear a hushed discussion between him and Mother to the effect that they didn't want the kids to see it. Well, naturally, the first opportunity I got, I went to the trash can and grabbed the article. It was on teenage pregnancy. As far as my parents were aware, I didn't know anything about how babies got made, and I guess they didn't want to harm my innocence. They figured they were protecting me. Well, I read that article, and I couldn't tell you today what it said, but I do remember one strong impression from it. I thought to myself, *Aren't those girls dumb, ruining their whole future?* If my parents were afraid of corrupting me and my sister, they didn't realize how high our standards already were. Far from being influenced in a lax direction by reading such a thing, we were more likely to err in a self-righteous one.

Now that we live in a post-AIDS crisis world, talk of condoms and such have become commonplace news items. A youngster hearing even just the headlines cannot hang on to much innocence any more. Caroline was five when she first noticed a news item on the car radio. I was trying to get a weather forecast, and had left the dial on an all-news station. This particular item was about a shooting at a grocery store. I wasn't even listening to it, when her voice startled me with its fear: "Mommy, how could somebody kill somebody at a grocery store?" I was able to reassure her, I hope, and we said a prayer for the people involved, right then and there in the car. But while I was pleased she was paying attention to her environment, another part of me was sad, because I know more loaded questions will soon be following unpredictably, and I'll have to answer them, and little by little, her innocence will evaporate. Hopefully, of course, it will be replaced with the kernels of wisdom . . . if, rather than evasive answers, I can give value-full answers.

"Mom, what's AIDS?"

"AIDS is a terrible disease. There's no cure for it."

"How do people get it?"

"Usually by being sexually immoral with people they're not married to," was the simple answer I gave my eleven-year-old when the headlines first began. "By breaking laws," is another answer, since both intravenous drug usage and promiscuity are technically against laws. Leave matters there if there's no follow-up question.

"But don't only gays get it?" There's something else you can't pretend doesn't exist. My eldest was in third grade when he first called his brother "gay," because that was the current word for anything unusual. That required some immediate instruction, you can be sure.

"Mostly, but people who go to bed with lots of other people never know what diseases those other people may have picked up along the line."

At this point a liberal would screech, "You're instilling fear in the child!" Fear is a negative thing, yes. But there is such a thing as good fear. Good fear protects a person, restraining him from doing something that could be dangerous. The consequences of non-marital sexual activity are so dire that they deserve the respect and, indeed, the fear of our young people. One of the things wrong with the Planned Parenthood mentality is that it eliminates good fear.

Older children should not be kept ignorant of the dangers of sexually transmitted diseases. They ought to know the gory details. Such things can be vivid in adolescent imagination, and in a moment of weakness, fear of such a consequence may be more real than all the teaching and good intentions of a lifetime. When new research is publicized about sexually transmitted diseases, don't ignore it. Find ways to bring up the new findings with your adolescent. In just a couple of sentences, you can convey information that could protect him for life.

Girls particularly should know the effects of teenage pregnancy. Before they're of an age when such discussions might be taken personally (*What does Mom think I'm doing, that she's talking to me about this?*), children should know that anyone who has a child is obligated to support that child its whole life long or else find a good home for it through adoption. They should know that every act of sexual intercourse is an invitation for God to make a baby, even if contraceptives are used. From her first understanding of herself as a potential mother, a girl should sense an obligation to her future unborn (and unimagined) children. It's not inappropriate to tell a ten-year-old in passing, "Eat a good diet, not junk food, because you're storing vitamins for the children you will have later."

Further, while no one wants to discourage motherhood, mothers should not shrink from letting their children know that it's not an easy job. Some sort of unrealistic aura surrounds the notion of teen motherhood these days; girls have the idea that babies are always cute and gooing and cooing, and immature girls have what doctors call "magical thinking." They somehow have the idea that even if they've babysat for difficult babies, their own babies will be sweet and pretty, will sleep all night long, and will be no trouble to take care of. The same tendency to magical thinking is also to blame in many cases of teen pregnancy: the girl was "sure" it "couldn't happen to me."

Girls should also be aware of the danger of psychological damage to them by boys to whom sex is a casual thing. In one of Planned Parenthood's own studies, 70 percent of male teenagers said it was "OK to tell a girl you love her so that you can have sex with her."[6] Most girls wouldn't dream of having intercourse with a boy unless they thought he loved them, but they are so trusting that they fall for the lines earnestly delivered by ardent boys. To a boy, sexual intercourse is a physical experience; to a girl, it's a major emotional experience. This fact of nature leaves girls much more vulnerable to exploitation. One study found that girls were twelve times as likely as boys to report feeling guilty after the first episode of intercourse.[7] They are tricked, and then they feel rotten afterward. This is supposed to be fun? Girls shouldn't have to wait until the heartbreak of being used to develop some self-protective cynicism. We're talking here about self-respect, knowing that one is worth more than a few moments' pleasure to some headstrong boy.

Boys should be aware of the harm that pornography can do them. This is what's really wrong with pornography: the harmful effect on the viewer. It's well known that exposure to pornography at young ages leaves permanent marks in the mind, and these marks can be real barriers to happiness in later life. The harm is particularly severe if the viewing of pornography is connected with sexual gratification. Mental images cannot be erased; they return to haunt a person again and again. Even men who have met the Lord and reformed their lives are still tormented by images from pornography that come uninvited to their minds when they least expect it.

And if just looking at pictures of different women does that much damage, how much more harm does actually experiencing different women create? To a teenager full of demanding hormones, it may be asking too much to project ten years into the future and imagine marriage with a wonderful woman. But a boy, too, should have self-respect and an intellectual understanding of his obligation to a future (if unimagined) wife. These will help him to protect himself against powerful temptations that could damage his future.

Teenagers are sometimes very idealistic. Kids can understand that the entire nation pays the price of their indulgences and mistakes. It doesn't help America's economy when our foreign trading partners read on the front cover of our national magazines that drugs are the number one problem in the American workplace. But why do people take drugs? To overcome the pain of having been used and exploited, for one thing. To overcome the pain of other human relationships' having failed. Drug use is a sign of failure, and young people can understand this long before the peer culture begins to urge it on them. In protecting their self-respect and preserving their virtue, they are making a stronger America. That is an exciting challenge to an idealistic youth.

TEACHING TO FAITH

God made sex and saw it was good. But He did lay down certain rules for its exercise. There are intrinsic rights and wrongs to certain actions; it's not just the context that defines the morality.

Before examining particular Scriptures that give particular instruction on the use of sexual powers, be aware of two pitfalls of moral thinking. They are the twin traps of condoning unrighteousness and condoning self-righteousness. Neither is approved by the Lord. Yet both are easily fallen into. It's the most natural thing in the world to feel self-conceit if one practices sexual virtue: *Thank God I'm not like the rest of men, unable to control my passions,* the little voice of pride whispers inside us. It grows into smugness, so that before long our witness is worth little, because our self-righteousness is so overpowering. Then, being human, we may fall. Our self-respect may be destroyed, because not only are we guilty of the sin itself, but we're also disappointed in ourselves. And then, if the sin continues, we may take refuge in the opposite trap and find excuses to condone our sin: *Well, I really love him/her. . . . By being kind now, maybe I can lead him/her to the Lord later. . . . God is merciful; He knows the pressure I've been under. . . . I didn't mean to hurt anybody.*

The Word of God, however, leaves no opening for excuses: "Do you not know that the unrighteous will not inherit the kingdom of God? Do not be deceived. Neither fornicators, nor idolaters, nor adulterers, nor homosexuals, nor sodomites. . . ." (1 Cor. 6:9). And the instruction to us when we sin is equally clear: "Let the wicked forsake his way, and the unrighteous man his thoughts; let him return to the Lord, and He will have mercy on him; and to our God, for He will abundantly pardon" (Isa. 55:7).

To those who indulge in self-righteousness, the Lord spoke equally severely: the parable of the Pharisee and the publican was directed "to some who trusted in themselves that they were righteous." The whole parable speaks daggers to a self-satisfied heart: "For everyone who exalts himself will be abased, and he who humbles himself will be exalted" (Luke 18: 9–14).

And hardly a passage in Scripture is more frightening than the imprecations against the scribes and Pharisees for their hypocrisy:

Woe to you, scribes and Pharisees, hypocrites! For you are like whitewashed tombs which indeed appear beautiful outwardly, but inside are full of dead men's bones and all uncleanness. Even so you also outwardly appear righteous to men, but inside you are full of hypocrisy and lawlessness. (Matt. 23:27–28)

It is an accusation before which we all should quake.

The sexual faculty goes all the way back to the Creation in Genesis 1:26–27: "Then God said, 'Let Us make man in Our image, according to Our likeness.' So God created man in His own image; in the image of God He created him; male and female He created them." The sexual faculty was no accident, no afterthought, no result of the Fall. It was there from the beginning, part of the image and likeness of God. Nor was it incidental to man's job: "Then God blessed them, and God said to them, 'Be fruitful and multiply; fill the earth and subdue it'" (Gen. 1:28). And having created them and told them what they were to do, "God saw everything that He had made, and indeed it was very good" (Gen. 1:31).

Then came the temptation and Fall. And the first thing that happened after Adam ate the forbidden fruit? "Then the eyes of both of them were opened, and they knew that they were naked" (Gen. 3:7). Shame had entered the world as a result of sin, but not as the result of *sexual* sin. Eating the fruit was not a sexual act. Other consequences of the sin were sexual, however: "In pain you shall bring forth children" (Gen. 3:16) is a consequence that has an impact on sexuality. The curse that followed, that Eve's husband "shall rule over you," is not as feminists portray it. Adam already had authority over Eve; it was his failure to exercise his authority and refuse her cajoling to eat the fruit that caused the sin. What was being changed with this curse was the manner of the husband's authority: and indeed, many a woman whose husband "lords it over her" has experienced that curse.

The heart of man is hard, and the lusts of the flesh are strong, and it is a constant, intense struggle for people to learn the ways of the Lord. "How can a young man cleanse his way? By taking heed according to Your word" (Ps. 119:9). Over and over again, the emphasis is the same: "Teach me, O Lord, the way of Your statutes, and I shall keep it to the end" (Ps. 119:33). "How sweet are Your words to my taste, sweeter than honey to my mouth!" (Ps. 119:103).

But the words of the Lord aren't always easy to hear, and the way of His statutes isn't comfortable to follow. "Whoever commits adultery with a woman . . . destroys his own soul" (Prov. 6:32) does not leave much gray area for rationalizations about "My wife doesn't understand me" and "I was so lonesome," just as 1 Corinthians 6:9, above, does not leave much room for squirming excuses like "We didn't intend to go all the way" or "I couldn't help myself." The Word is very clear: neither adulterers nor fornicators will inherit the kingdom of God. Period.

This is hard teaching! The faint-hearted may complain, "Why do I have to live such a straight and narrow life?" "He who commits sexual immorality sins against his own body," Paul taught in 1 Corinthians 6:18. And isn't that borne out today in the millions of cases of sexually transmitted diseases? Who has suffered from the promiscuity? The ones who set out to "enjoy" it and have inflicted disease upon their own bodies. But Paul wasn't even talking about this kind of physical harm to the body. He had something else in mind: "Do you not know that your body is the temple of the Holy Spirit who is in you, whom you have from God, and you are not your own? For you were bought at a price; therefore glorify God in your body and in your spirit, which are God's" (1 Cor. 6:19–20).

Our bodies are not our own. They belong to God. We need God's permission to do anything with them. This is the radical Christian stance on sexuality: it does not exist merely to aid and abet in the pursuit of pleasure, but primarily to glorify God. This is why we cannot buy into the "If it feels good, do it" mindset. Our mindset, rather, must be, "If it glorifies God, do it." And only in faithful, fruitful Christian marriage do we find what glorifies God.

WHAT TO TEACH

What glorifies God is monogamous, heterosexual activity within permanent, exclusive marriage. That is the norm. Everything else is to be measured against this. That's the first thing to teach our children. Adhering to that norm is the only formula for achieving sexual happiness on this earth.

When we're masters of our bodies, our bodies are glorifying God. When we are slaves of our passions, we're shaming Him who bought us at a great price. "While they promise them liberty, they themselves are slaves of corruption; for by whom a person is overcome, by him also he is brought into bondage" (2 Pet. 2:19). It isn't freedom to be owned by our flesh. But the message of the modern culture says it is.

SELF-CONTROL IS EXPECTED

The modern philosophy of consequentialism, or situation ethics, preaches that acts must be considered "in context" to decide whether they're right or wrong. A baby, even one that's been born alive, can be killed if it's the "loving" thing to do: if it will save the family the hardship of dealing with a handicap, if it will save the child the supposed misery of growing up with less than "full potential" (whatever that may be). Adultery is a "loving" thing to do if it makes the two persons feel better for a day. And fornication, why, that relieves sexual tension that might make a teenager crabby, so in that context, of course it's "right." These are simplistic examples, of course, but the contrast should be clear: in all the world's standards of sexual and other morality, the consequences of the action are considered part of its morality. But for a Christian, this is a perilous road to walk, for only God controls consequences. *He expects us to control our actions.*

Many people don't even know they can control their sexual urges. Thousands of teenagers genuinely believe they "have" to have sex or they will become mentally ill and "repressed." This, of course, is a strong but seldom-stated premise of the sex education mentality: that teenagers are going to have sex anyway and there's nothing wrong with it, since they're only doing what they can't help. In other words, what they consider inevitable, Christians consider sin. Their attitude would treat young people as animals, controlled by their instincts and passions; our attitude treats them as redeemed men and women who are capable of holding themselves to a higher standard.

We know Christ died on the cross so that we might have the power to resist the temptation to act like animals. We know God will hold us accountable for our actions. Would He have given us laws but not the means to obey them?

Contrast that invigorating challenge with the attitude of our society. Modern culture expects us to yield to all our desires, sexual as well as otherwise. Grocery stores earn millions of dollars a year because they plan attractive layouts to snare a shopper into impulse buying. Colleges allow students to have refrigerators in their dormitory rooms because they have succumbed to the students' arguments that it is too difficult to walk down to the lobby to buy a soft drink from a machine. Cartoons that our children absorb from the time they can read portray characters eating everything in sight and then saying sweetly, "I couldn't help it." Then the children quote that to their parents when they're caught doing something they shouldn't.

Our society is predicated on indulgence. The Christian world view is predicated on self-denial for the sake of the Kingdom. But don't misunderstand this to mean the Christian world view allows only for slogging through life in sackcloth and ashes. In fact, most of the Christian perspective is positive, hopeful, and joyful, as we'll see in the next chapter.

Chapter 9

FIVE BASIC CONCEPTS

My husband and I have identified five basic concepts of Christian family life that we are instilling in our children. These beliefs are foundational to creating a Christian culture in the home.

GOD HAS A PLAN

Lots of religions believe in the existence of a God. But only one religion, Christianity, believes that God cares about each individual and is involved in every person's life.

We know that God watches each one of us. He watches each little sparrow and cares about each of them, too, but we are of far more value to Him. He comes to our aid when we call upon Him. Most of all, He has a plan for our lives. He thought of us from all eternity, created us out of nothing, and knit us together in our mother's womb. He doesn't go to all that trouble just to set us loose on the earth and forget us. He knows the color of our eyes and hair, how tall we will grow to be, and the state of our health. He decided whether we'd be male or female. He made us just the way He wanted us in every respect. Therefore, we should be satisfied with our natural endowments, whatever they may be. Best of all, He has adopted us as His children, because He wants to share His kingdom with us in the next world.

He has a plan for us that will get us to His Kingdom. We can follow the plan or foil it by insisting on our own plans. But we'll be a whole lot happier if we just follow His plan. In order to know His plan, we do have to communicate with Him, but He's waiting to hear from us in order to share Himself with us. This is why prayer is so important—it's that communication. Meaningful, daily prayer keeps those lines of communication open.

God has given us a basic set of commandments: Love Me, and love one another. Everything else flows from that. He's also given each of us lots of different talents and gifts, which he wants us to use to help one another and to show forth His glory. He doesn't like us to hide our talents and let them go to waste; He wants us to use them. And the most important way we can use them is to lead other people to Him.

It's not His fault that Adam broke the rules of the garden of paradise. He made Adam to be eternally with Him in paradise, but Adam wasn't satisfied. He wanted more. He wanted to do things his way. Just like us. So Adam and we suffer the consequences of his dissatisfaction with God's plan. One of those consequences is that sin has a grip on our fallen natures: it's easier to do things our way rather than God's way; it's easier to be angry than to be patient; it's easier to feel sorry for ourselves than to help someone else; it's easier to indulge our senses than to discipline our bodily appetites.

The Lord knew how difficult it would be. But He always required His people to follow him. Two thousand years ago it became a lot easier to follow Him than it had been before. At that time, His Son, Jesus, suffered shame and pain and death on a cross so that we who believe in Him would be released from enslavement to sin and freed to obey Him. All we have to do is ask for His help.

CREATION IS GOOD

A second foundational concept is that creation and everything in it is good, because God made it. When God made Lucifer, he was good. It was Lucifer who decided to become evil, not God who made him so. God allows Lucifer to be evil for the same reason He allows us to be evil: because when we choose freely to follow Him, our submission to Him is an act of love. Sure, God could have made a world in which nobody had any choice except to be good. But there wouldn't have been much freedom in that world, and how would we have been able to show our love?

All bodily functions are good. The eyes were made to see; the nose to smell; the feet to walk; the mouth to chew; the stomach to digest; the intestines to eliminate; and the sexual organs to express marital love and to reproduce. The sexual organs and the capacity to reproduce are good, in and of themselves. How we use those organs and that capacity determines whether we please or anger God.

Why did He create sexuality? Because it was not good for man to be alone. A second gender was created when God wanted Adam to have one of his own kind to help him. When children become adults now, they begin looking for one of their own kind, of the other gender, to help them. It's clear that the sexual faculty was given to be used not for solitary pleasure, but in conjunction with a partner. The focus on another person in all sexual behavior is a fundamental truth.

Sexual loves bind us to a spouse and makes us parents. "Therefore a man shall leave his father and mother and be joined to his wife, and they shall become one flesh" (Gen. 2:24). Later, the apostle Paul made it explicit: "Because of sexual immorality, let each man have his own wife, and let each woman have her own husband" (1 Cor. 7:2). Marriage, in other words, is to protect us from sexual immorality, from sexual sin. If after marriage a person lives in promiscuity, what was the purpose for getting married? That person is only making his guilt worse.

That's why getting married is not a license to sexual indulgence. It's a license to devote yourself to another person—and to the children who may result. How can two become one flesh except by commingling their flesh? And the result of that commingling is sometimes a child. Thus, the sexual faculty is not only at the root of marriage, but also at the very root of the family. It cannot be separated from either, just as we cannot be separated from the creative, self-giving love of God.

Marriage is a call to generosity in every way. "The wife does not have authority over her own body, but the husband does. And likewise the husband does not have authority over his own body, but the wife does" (1 Cor. 7:4). Husband and wife are to be available to each other and are not to deny each other except by mutual consent for brief periods of time. And just as we are called to be generous in sharing ourselves with our spouses, by implication, they are called to be unselfish and sensitive in asking.

The sexual act is an exchange of gifts, of the gift of self. It's an offer and an acceptance, a pledge of permanent trust and care. It's a sharing of the power to give life. This isn't a symbolic sharing, but a real sharing of sexuality and its life-giving power. After the act, the woman contains in her body the man's seed, his promise of tomorrow with her, loving her and caring for her, and for the fruit of that seed, if God gives life to it.

Having children in today's world is an act of witness, an act that in and of itself displays trust in God. It may mean economic hardship. It may mean frustration of materialistic ambitions. Maybe we'll never catch up with the Joneses, let alone get ahead of them. But by rejoicing in children, we are giving witness to a world that has forgotten the generosity and love of God and is lost in its own selfishness, needing desperately the example of self-giving Christians.

In light of this noble purpose, it's obvious why certain uses of the sexual function are wrong. Anything outside of chaste, faithful marriage does not represent a lifetime commitment to one's partner. Nor does it represent the pledge to give love and care to the child with which God may choose to bless the sexual union. If God is going to send a gift, the least we can do is be prepared to receive it. And since the second of the great commandments is to love one another, it's obvious why merely using another person for one's own sexual gratification isn't right, either. That isn't love; it's exploitation.

CREATION BELONGS TO GOD

Third, the power to create new life belongs to God. Not all Christian couples will be fertile. Marriage implies no "right" to children. They are a gift direct from the Creator. Thus, all human life, even if conceived illegitimately, is to be honored.

Science has brought us so far that sometimes we think we're entitled to any physical change we want. Relief from a sneeze? Take this pill. Relief from fatigue? Take these pills. A problem with this organ? Have this surgery. It's an easy step to tinkering with the reproductive capacity. Trouble conceiving? Use a test tube. Hire a surrogate.

I know that the pain of barrenness is terrible for those who want children. It drives even Christian couples to desperate measures. Further, a technique like in vitro fertilization uses a husband and wife's own sperm and egg, and fertilized eggs are then implanted in the mother, all of which makes the process less objectionable than other methods. Of course, this technique has a high failure rate, too, which means God is still in ultimate control. But even so, there's an underlying problem with things like in vitro fertilization and its related high-tech cousins. They attempt to give the task of creation to man, not to God. Hence, they are questionable for Christians, because Christians want to do things God's way, not their own. God is the master of creation, not man. And the hiring of surrogate mothers is another form of paying for the use of a woman's body. In the Old Testament, concubines were permitted for such purposes, but the New Covenant changed that.

CHILDREN ARE A BLESSING FROM THE LORD

Fourth, though it's easy to lose sight of the fact, children are a blessing from the Lord. So pervasive in our society are high material expectations and a desire for "freedom" that, even among Christians, a large family is the exception rather than the rule. A careful, two-children family is almost the norm. And while it's commendable, of course, to be responsible in caring for one's children, there are lines that careful responsibility can slip across into subtle materialism. Giving children the best may be taken to mean dinners out a couple times a week for the family and never wearing secondhand clothes. If taking vacations is a reason to avoid another child, a couple would do well to ask themselves whether trips are really more meaningful to a child than another sibling would be.

It's not unheard of for a pregnant woman to be asked in a friendly voice, "And is this your first?" If the answer comes back, "No, this is my fourth," the questioner's smile may disappear as a frown takes its place. "Well, how many more do you intend to have?" may be the next question, with an edge in it. As if it mattered to the questioner! Whatever reasons may underlie that edge, as a mother who has given birth to five children, I'm here to tell you that that kind of conversation is unworthy of a Christian. Not only is it unkind (pregnancy is no fun, no matter how welcomed it may be, and a pregnant woman needs criticism from strangers like she needs a case of the German measles), but it is also, plainly, unscriptural.

Everyone knows the God of the Old Testament expected children to support their aged parents, an expectation that has never been withdrawn. This is no light obligation. But implicit in that expectation is an earlier obligation on the part of the parents to have children. In the days of the Patriarchs, and still today in much of the world, wars and famines and plagues may diminish the number of children surviving to support parents in their old age to well below the number originally born. Fertility was a way in which God demonstrated His power over the devouring forces of death.

One of the blessings of Abram was the promise that his descendants would be "as the dust of the earth; so that if a man could number the dust of the earth, then your descendants also could be numbered" (Gen. 13:16). And again in Genesis 15:5, the Lord promised Abram numerous progeny. He took him outside to look at the skies: "Look now toward heaven, and count the stars if you are able to number them. . . . So shall your descendants be." Clearly, God was intending to bless Abram by giving him and his children fertility. I know of nowhere in the Bible that God declared that no longer a blessing. In our affluent, urban Western world with its advanced health care and social welfare programs, children don't seem to be the same practical necessity they were in Abram's time, but their utility in the family economy is only a small part of why they're a blessing.

When you come right down to it, most reasons for intentional sterility end up being forms of selfishness. A focus on self, even an unintended or unconscious one, is used to justify all kinds of evil. In a marriage, it can be particularly vicious. If the act of love does not contain any exchange of life-giving power, it also does not contain the ultimate giving of self on the part of either spouse. And without the promise of self-donation and self-sacrifice, the act can easily degenerate into a mere exercise in the release of tension. A wife can become no more than a tool for her husband's sexual release; what he does with her, he could do with anybody, since ultimately he is not giving anything of himself in the act. The bitter feminist complaint about marriage, that it makes every wife a prostitute, has some validity if all the marriage ever practiced was sterilized intercourse.

What did Jesus say about children? Did He avoid them? When people brought their children to Him, the apostles, practical souls that they were, rebuked the parents. Can't you just imagine them efficiently scolding the parents: "Listen, He's a busy man, He doesn't have time to play with babies. Can't you keep them more quiet? We're trying to listen. That child is too young to get any good out of prayer. You should have left him home." But what did Jesus do? Matthew 19:13–15 tells us that Jesus rebuked the apostles for trying to "protect" Him from the children. "Let the little children come to Me," He said, and then He laid hands on them after telling the apostles that "of such is the kingdom of heaven."

I've always liked the older translation that had Jesus' words as *"Suffer the little children to come to me."* I enjoy the unintended pun there. Children, as any parent knows, can be a cross. Some days you do suffer your children rather than enjoy them. And parenthood gets its profundity from the amount of suffering parents do for their children. The kind of days your mother warned you about can come steadily for years. But the difficulties that sometimes accompany them don't make children any the less precious in the eyes of God, nor should they in ours. After all, avoiding the cross is not what Christians are called to do.

Fortunately, the way we're designed, begetting children comes naturally and pleasantly to us. Our technological society, however, has made us so oriented toward controlling our environment that we assume our fertility is one more thing to be controlled. So automatic is that premise that it has almost become a reflex. Only too late do some people realize that, as C. S. Lewis so succinctly put it, "man and wife are one flesh; one flesh must not and cannot live to itself any more than the single individual."[1] But since you're reading this book, chances are you're already a parent and you already know—in your bones even if you've never thought about it—that we are enriched by what sexual intercourse demands of us, namely, intimacy, as well as by what it gives to us, namely, our children.

Some people's intentional sterility is motivated by genuinely altruistic intentions, ideals that were propagandized massively in the 1970s, but which time has proved false. Chief among such ideals is the concern about overpopulation. Rarely has there been such a vivid demonstration of the old saying that "figures don't lie, but liars do figure" as in the campaign to frighten young people into avoiding having children for reasons of conscience. For almost a generation, everything from starving children to illiteracy to trade imbalances to war has been blamed on population growth. The notions that people are the problem and that population growth slows economic development die hard, but the fact is that such notions simply do not stand up under scrutiny. Dr. Julian Simon, one of the nation's foremost demographer-economists, has spent a lifetime studying growth and prosperity and their opposites. He has done the definitive refutation of the population bomb mentality.

Population control alarmists assume that there is a fixed pie of resources, and that the more people partake of the pie, the smaller everybody's piece will be. But the assumption is false; the resource base is not fixed. One hundred fifty years ago, whale oil was a vital commodity; people couldn't live without it. But nobody needs it today. Why? Once petroleum was discovered and its uses explored, it more than replaced whale oil. More jobs were created because of petroleum than would ever have been possible with whale oil. Simon tells the story that when a shortage of elephant tusks for ivory billiard balls was threatened in the nineteenth century, a prize was offered for a substitute. Somebody invented celluloid to serve as a replacement billiard ball—and in the process started the entire plastics industry![2] No matter what the shortage may be, human ingenuity can overcome it—and generally leave us better off as a result.

Most of the world's poverty comes, not from too many people, but from mismanagement of resources. The Ethiopian famine had the millions of casualties it did not because there were too many Ethiopians, but because the government was pursuing policies to suppress people unfriendly to its regime. The same was true in the Biafran famine of the previous decade, and the Somalian famine of the early 90s. The nations that have the most coercive population policies, such as China, also happen to be the nations with the most centralized economic systems. Rather than blaming their poverty on an economic system that discourages hard work and risk-taking, and teaches people to freeze rather than free their talents, the totalitarian countries attempt to blame their problems on babies. On the other hand, a nation such as Singapore, which was in economic circumstances similar to China's a few decades ago but today is thriving, has lots of economic freedom along with its large population. Result: economic growth and prosperity.

If we're going to appeal to social conscience, the real appeal nowadays should be to have more babies and have them fast. A great birth *dearth* looms in the immediate future of all Western democracies, and it's a graver danger to our future freedom and security than all the political arguments imaginable. Our grandchildren will be poor—there is no way to avoid it—and our nation will be scarcely defended militarily unless American women begin having 15 percent more babies per year immediately. Failing that, American women will follow the lead of many European women and simply not replace the current population, leaving a shrinking tax base to support an expanding welfare state.

WHAT ABOUT MASTURBATION?

Before we depart totally from this discussion of the purposes of the reproductive capacity, there are a couple of other areas in which the application of fundamental principles is important. One is the area of masturbation. Many people, including some Christian counselors, consider it a minor problem. However, in our desire to overcome the ludicrous and sometimes paranoid teaching that our parents' generation may have had, we should be careful not to go too far in the direction of permissiveness.

Understand first that I am not talking about a baby's playing with his genital organs. That is self-manipulation, but it's not masturbation. Only a physiologically mature person is capable of masturbation. Babies will explore every part of their bodies, and this is as it should be. They should not be afraid of or unfamiliar with any part of their bodies. The process of discovery should be a natural and easy one.

However, masturbation regularly pursued by teenagers or adults—that is, habitual and obsessive masturbation—is damaging to the person who is dependent upon it. It quickly becomes easier to focus on oneself than the challenge of focusing on another person. The readily available release can be addictive. It can spawn depression. It certainly accompanies loneliness and fosters isolation. It can be a means of avoiding reality, particularly what is in adolescence the very difficult but crucial reality of establishing relationships with the opposite sex.

When linked with pornography, as it frequently is, the habit of masturbation can set up a habit chain that is practically incompatible with Christian family life. Sexual habits are hard to break. If a person's first orgasmic experience comes with self-manipulation aided by pornography, and if that habit is repeated over the years, that will be the pattern the brain comes to expect to produce a sexual response, whether or not a spouse is present. If accumulation of sexual tension is repeatedly met with release obtained by masturbation *before* marriage, what is to stop the pattern from continuing *after* marriage or being reverted to during a time of stress in the marriage? In neither case is the marriage improved by the presence of the habit. Quite the contrary is true.

An even more stark danger exists. Just before puberty, boys go through a phase of strong attachment to a friend of the same sex. If, in the course of sex play, orgasm should be experienced in this relationship, it could have the psychological effect of freezing the desire at this stage. Perhaps this gives a clue why pederasts pursue young adolescent boys. It should be noted that masturbation, accompanied by fantasies about children (usually pornography-assisted), is a habit of almost all child molesters.

Masturbation is at best a sign of immaturity. At worst, it's a bad habit that can make a person its slave. One of the hallmarks of true maturity is the ability to defer gratification, and what is so opposite to deferred gratification as masturbation?

SIN HAS CONSEQUENCES

Our fifth foundational principle is that sin has consequences. Adolescents go through so many stages: the narcissistic phase, the "chum" stage, and so on. There is also the "magic thinking" stage, mentioned earlier. If I seem to be pessimistic in urging you to teach your pre-adolescent child about such gruesome things as homosexuality, it's because I am anticipating this stage of mid-adolescence.

Well before adolescence, children need to know that the wages of sin is death. They need to know it not only abstractly, but graphically as well. We adults would do well to remember it ourselves.

Most consequences of immorality are not final in this world. Sexually transmitted diseases, with the exception of AIDS, aren't usually fatal anymore, though the misery they produce may make their victims wish they were at times. But not all the consequences of sexual sin are suffered by the perpetrators. The consequences of divorce, for example, are most suffered by children. The consequences of abortion are suffered most by babies. The larger weakening of society that is a consequence of widespread sexual indulgence and immorality will bring suffering in its wake to millions of people yet to come. The Roman Empire was not the first, nor the last, to destroy itself through unbridled lasciviousness. But generations to come suffered the harm caused by the fall of that empire.

The physical pleasures of this world don't last, nor do they produce true happiness. This is the lesson of maturity. Happiness does not equal pleasure, though it may have a measure of pleasure in it. But what produces true, permanent happiness is the pursuit of what is good, for oneself and for others. The single-minded pursuit of pleasure produces, eventually, misery. Why? Because human nature was not designed for immediate gratification. The body demands it, true, but being truly human means the mind, the soul, is in control of the body. If the body is running the show, it is not humanity at its noblest. It is not mankind acting as the image and likeness of God. And since "the form of this world is passing away" (1 Cor. 7:31), knowing and living by the five basic principles in this chapter can enable us—and our children—to behave as befits a temple of the Holy Spirit.

Chapter 10

KEY TO SEXUAL RESPONSIBILITY: SELF-ESTEEM AND TEMPTATION

In this chapter, we will look closely at the motivations for doing right that we want to instill in our children. Having them act rightly isn't enough; we also want them to do it for the right reasons. Healthy self-esteem is a key ingredient, but it's not the whole story.

Ultimately, the best reason for saying no to premarital and extramarital sexual relationships is not that it avoids disease, disclosure, and embarrassment. Those are valid reasons, and they provide strong motivation. Young people should certainly know them. But there is a more spiritual reason. It's a motivation that nothing can ever shake, though it's not readily available to most young people.

The love of God is the ultimate motivation for doing right. A person motivated by love for the Creator will want to do right because he is a temple of the Holy Spirit, and he'll want to do right by his fellow human beings because that is pleasing to God. This kind of love is a mature love. It is the goal toward which youth should strive.

But the desire for this level of spiritual relationship with God, commendable as it is, is not sufficient to empower an adolescent to say no to temptation. For that matter, the desire for deep love of God is not sufficient to empower an adult to say no, either. The spirit may be willing, but the flesh can be very weak. This is an example of that time-honored saying.

By all means, the heart is the fundamental ingredient: the heart must want to be virtuous, must want to choose what is right. But doing right out of love for God requires more than a feeling. It means acting in a manner pleasing to God. One can sin and sin and sin and still claim to have warm, fuzzy feelings for God in one's heart. One can even deceive oneself into believing that this is love. But God will not be fooled.

An analogy would be loving a spouse. Sometimes you have the warm, fuzzy feelings, and they're delightful when they're there. But what makes a marriage great is that underlying the changeable feelings is the rock-hard commitment of permanent service and desire for the well-being of the spouse. We must raise our children so that they know that their lives are committed, rock-hard, to God, and that no matter what else, pleasing God should be the number one consideration in every thought, desire, word, or action. Moods come and go; feelings change; but being mindful of God's opinion of every action is the habit of a lifetime.

The habit can be taught intellectually, but it should also be reinforced emotionally. It's difficult to love somebody with whom you don't communicate. Prayer is communication with God, and children can learn to pray—if we teach them. Taking them to church every Sunday doesn't guarantee learning to pray. There is no substitute for personal prayer all through the day. If children observe their mother praying for a parking space as she drives around the block looking for one, they absorb the fact that God is real to Mom. If the car stalls on the shoulder of the interstate and the kids watch Dad start singing a hymn of praise to God, they can see his real, personal, immediate faith. That happened to us one night, and when we began praising God instead of cursing our luck, our son who was with us asked what there was to praise God for right then. But a police car pulled up behind us five minutes after we had finished praying, called a tow truck for us, and arranged for a call home to reassure everybody there. That experience of faith's being answered directly is an experience no one should deny to her children. When my older son is stamping his feet with impatience at his new contact lenses, I tell him to ask God to help it go in this time. And sometimes, when he asks, it may go in no matter how many times it hadn't before. Little things like this reinforce the intellectual knowledge that God is real, present, and involved in every moment of life.

A habit of depending on God, an awareness of His presence: these are valuable ammunition against temptation. But there's another key ingredient to successfully practicing sexual responsibility.

THE NEED FOR HEALTHY SELF-ESTEEM

Because we're human, we have emotional needs. And one emotional fact of life is that our expectations of ourselves are good predictors of our behavior. If you think you're too tired to be able to do your laundry, you will be. If a student thinks he's too dumb to get an A in geometry, be sure he won't get one. And if a girl really believes she's dumb and unattractive, she most likely will be, because that's how she'll treat herself. If a guy really believes he's not man enough to control his passions, he won't be able to control them. If a teenager thinks he has no future, he'll act as if he hasn't, and pretty soon he's ruined his chances of having one. The problem in all cases is a lack of sufficient belief in one's own ability, one's own worth—in other words, a lack of self-esteem.

Now, Christian self-esteem is not the same thing as secular, "me-first" philosophy. It's not self-love. It's not a single-minded focus on oneself. The "I'm OK, you're OK" type of secular self-esteem theories are appealing on the surface, but they're hollow, to say the least. Because they so exclusively focus on the self, they are positively dangerous. They don't recognize that we are made by God to live in harmony with other people according to certain objective laws. Just believing in one's own ability and worth, without any attention to God, is a source of dangerous individualism.

Where does a proper sense of self-esteem and respect come from? It grows out of the knowledge that we are loved. A Christian understands that he is of immeasurable value, intrinsically, when he recognizes that even if he had been the only person in the world, God would have loved him enough to send His Son to die on the cross, to redeem him alone. The love that makes us feel loved comes to us from the moment of birth, if not sooner. While the first adolescent years are critical to preserving or destroying self-esteem, the foundations for self-esteem are laid much earlier.

An inherent weakness in adolescent "love" is that it is not focused on the other person. Nor can it be—adolescents are by nature, because of their age, incapable of selflessness. It feels nice for a teenage girl to be told by an impassioned boyfriend that he "needs" her—but what he needs is support to his ego. Sex among adolescents is egocentric sex; it boosts the ego. Hence, the bragging among boys of their achievements, and among girls of their catches. An emotionally vulnerable adolescent who gets caught up in this relentless ego feeding frenzy very soon becomes used goods—and that is profoundly damaging to self-esteem. Knowing (whether one can articulate it or not) that she is used as a means of physical satisfaction, used in the deepest, most private, most personal way, by someone who has no real interest in her unique personhood, and has no commitment to the complete person she is—he's only interested in her body, and, actually, only in the part of that he can use for his own purpose—is enough to engender hatred of him when the heat of passion has passed. And seeing her own complicity with the act is enough to engender hatred of herself. And it happens all the time.

Physical passion alone can go a long way, but when a girl gets pregnant, and the boyfriend gets annoyed and tells her to get an abortion, reality often sets in like a lion. Her impulse is to, at some level, cherish the new life—and because she fancies that he loves her, she assumes he will cherish the new life within her. But in fact, he never loved her, and he certainly never wanted any part of her fertility. He was only interested in her as a means to gratify himself—and she let him use her. It is excruciatingly painful to realize one has been used so callously, and that one went along with it. The emotional consequences of abortion are often the same as the emotional consequences of adolescent sexual activity—it's just that, without the pregnancy, the girl wouldn't have stood still long enough to realize all the unsavory truths about the relationship.

The pregnancy makes her take stock of her life, and of the relationship. It is a time of incredible vulnerability. Feeling disgust for herself makes precious any real love she may have experienced in the past. And you can see how critical can be the outreach of a loving, honest crisis pregnancy worker. Genuine love, as distinguished from its counterfeit, is needed as never before. And, indeed, the record shows that the crisis of a pregnancy can be the incentive for getting life onto the right track.

But it is so, so much better for a young woman to know true love from childhood on, to have self-esteem founded on parents' love, and on the knowledge of God's love, than to be battered about the marketplace of adolescent sexuality.

ENEMIES OF SELF-ESTEEM

Cruelty is the first enemy of self-esteem. It doesn't need to be intentional cruelty, either. Parents do not intend to hurt a child's feelings, but criticism that includes comments like "Don't be such a chicken" has exactly that effect. Hurtful things that are going to be said in life, of course, but let them be by strangers, not in the shelter of the home! Home is supposed to be a safe harbor for the emotions. Likewise, a parent who is never pleased with the achievements of his child is laying no foundation for self-esteem. *If nothing I do makes my parents happy, the child may think, then I have no hope of ever pleasing anybody else. I must be pretty worthless.*

If the love given by a parent is hesitant or uncertain ("Well, he wasn't really planned. . . . He was such a difficult baby, I never could enjoy him. . . . When he was born, I had to quit working, and that's when the problems in the marriage began. . . . "), the child will sense something amiss in his relationship with the persons who should love him totally and unconditionally. He won't know that the fault is in his parent; he will assume there is something about him that is displeasing to his parents. If a parent or other relative compares one child to another, continually to one child's detriment, that child may believe his older brother is wonderful, pleasing, brilliant, clever, talented, and all sweetness and light, while he himself is stupid, second-rate, slow, and unlovable.

The cruelty of children to each other should never be underestimated, either. The arrogant tones of voice, name calling, and teasing that constantly go on among kids is not "normal," though we like to tell ourselves that to excuse ourselves for allowing it. At least, it should not be normal for a Christian child. Parents should not tolerate it. It does harm to a child's self-image, to say nothing of harm to the relationship between siblings. Kindness isn't inherent in children. Anyone who believes children are basically good should watch a bunch of fifth graders gather like vultures around the new kid in class and make his life miserable for a semester. Nor are peers any the less brutal as they get older. Child psychologist James Dobson laments the viciousness of junior high school peers on the self-images of one another and considers the destruction of self-esteem at that age to be one of the most treacherous experiences of growing up.

Our technological society is another enemy of self-esteem. If society tells us our value depends on what functions we perform or what our accomplishments are, the child who has nothing to boast about is indeed a non entity. The status symbols of adolescence are no less demanding than those of adulthood. If anything, they're more rigid. The lack of a designer label can cause real anguish to a thirteen-year-old. Is that as it should be? Of course not. But it's the basis upon which our materialistic, modern society bestows its esteem.

Gender stereotypes are another threat to self-esteem. "Another dumb woman driver" may seem like just a bad joke, but the attitude disguised in that casual insult is far from dead. And if enough expressions of attitudes like that are peppered through the mental food of a young life, the young mind is going to pick up the attitude. The dynamic works with snide remarks about either gender, of course.

The excessive valuation of physical beauty, a trait so noticeable in the youth culture, is not new. Dr. Dobson put it succinctly when he said, "The average American woman would rather have beauty than brains because the average American man sees better than he thinks." It's a wry way of stating a fearful truth. Woe unto the plain girl! This standard, shallow and superficial though it is, is perceived from the youngest age. Mothers, without thinking, instill it in their children. So do doting grand-mothers who, thinking to give a compliment, tell a girl how pretty she is or a boy how handsome he is. Playing to this false standard not only costs money, wastes time, and builds vanity as the years progress, but it can supplant the desire and opportunity to develop deeper, interior resources.

Failure is a great enemy of self-esteem. This means primarily one's own failures, but it also includes the failures of one's relatives or the family skeletons in the closet. Keeping family secrets imposes shame on a child, because a child cannot understand why things have to be kept secret. Fear, which prevents a person from doing something that might overcome an earlier sense of failure and from challenging his own limits, is an obvious enemy.

SOURCES OF SELF-ESTEEM

"Reality is God's greatest gift to mankind," Francis Schaeffer told me the only time I ever was privileged to meet him. It's a truth I have thought much about ever since. Proper self-love cannot be built upon lies. We are not great in and of ourselves; "not that we are sufficient of ourselves . . . but our sufficiency is from God" (2 Cor. 3:5). Our intrinsic value comes because we are adopted children of God. That's a fact, a reality. It's a reality a child ought to know.

This reality is easily obscured, easily overlooked, however. Do adults really believe it? How do adults react upon hearing of a new baby's being born? That is, in a child's-eye view, a crucial test of the truth of the teaching. A child will instinctively be delighted to hear of a new baby's being imminent or having arrived. To a child, any child is a good idea and is welcomed. This is particularly so if the child has been taught that Jesus loves children. Suppose then that Mom, on hearing that Mrs. Smith is having another baby, reacts negatively. A young child may not wonder consciously, *Why is it that if Jesus loves the new baby, Mommy thinks it's a terrible mistake?* But he'll approach the next Sunday school class with an element of skepticism that wasn't present before. An older child may wonder such things consciously and may extend the wonderment to include, *Well, if Mommy didn't think it was a good idea for Mrs. Smith to have a new baby, I wonder if she thought it was a good idea to have me?* Mom might think that her explanation of why it's not wise for Mrs. Smith to have another baby is adequate for a child, but the thoughts of childhood are deeper (and more self-centered) than most adults remember. Kids have subconscious lie detectors that operate at full power all the time.

We can learn that Jesus loves us as adults, but it's easier to be chaste for the love of God if we know it from childhood. If parents and family give a child a conflicting set of signals, it's harder to believe in God's love even if he hears it in a Sunday school or religion class. And it may take years of mistakes and suffering until he comes to the realization for himself.

The next source of self-esteem is loving our neighbors, serving others, and being focused outside ourselves. "He who loves God must love his brother also" (1 John 4:21). Household chores are most children's introduction to serving our neighbors. Children don't like to do chores; even less do they like to serve others. Least of all, I sometimes think, do they want their friends knowing they do chores for their Mom. Such a thing as that just isn't "cool." Parents frequently can't stand the hassle of making their children do even minimal chores. For sure, kids can make the doing of chores a matter of federal stature. But doing chores builds a sense of accomplishment; it also builds tangible competence. It is frequently a first introduction to obedience, and it eventually helps kids to come to a realization that others need our help.

There is something even more fundamental than doing chores that can build children's self-esteem. It can begin younger than chores can and produce more real benefit to others. I refer to prayer. Children can be intercessors. Their prayers matter to God.

How often, however, do we ask children to pray for the needs of others? We probably assume that since they can't understand the problem at hand, they can't pray about it. We're wrong, of course, but never mind for the moment the benefit we deny ourselves by not asking the intercession of children. Think about what we're denying the children. Talk about knowing you're important and needed. What is more important than talking to God on behalf of another person? What can do more to build the relationship between the heart of a little child and the heart of God than prayer? And what builds faith more than seeing a prayer answered? How can we deny our children that joy?

SELF-ESTEEM NEEDS COMPETENCE

Self-esteem, in more worldly terms, comes from competence. And the arena where most children test themselves and prove their competence is school. The challenges of difficult material to learn and remember, and the thrill of learning something they thought they never could, are real, tangible accomplishments for children. The algebra may be forgotten in time, but the sense of having been able to do something they didn't think they could remains forever, to their permanent benefit.

Nothing gives a boost to a child's opinion of himself—and of hard work—than to get a sixty-five the first quarter and then end the year with an eighty-five average. How ironic it is that when the education establishment became concerned about "student self-esteem," practically the first thing it did was to lower academic standards and shift the focus away from an achievement orientation to a vague social orientation. This denied many students the opportunity to improve their self-esteem through readily available, at-hand, real accomplishments.

Of course, not all students are, as teachers put it, academic material. Parents may have to be creative in subtle, imperceptible, and even anonymous ways—and absolutely, relentlessly persistent—in providing opportunities for their children to achieve. Some children sparkle all over with talents waiting to be developed. In others, one has to mine deeply.

Getting an A in math is no more worthy an accomplishment than fixing a splendid apple pie, and a family should greet either achievement with equal acclaim. Unfortunately, the A in math is more visibly connected to the prospect of worldly success, which parents are right to be concerned about. That connection makes it easier for parents to applaud the A. But a splendid apple pie can be an expression of love of a neighbor, and as such, accomplish a lot of good in the world, though its maker may never be famous or rich because of it. The materialistic, yuppie mindset is not conducive to building self-esteem in children whose talents lie in other than remunerative or potentially remunerative activities. Loving parents must be careful to avoid this trap. Successful baby-sitting, pleasure in sports, visiting old-folks' homes, growing a beautiful garden, sewing well, volunteering at a soup kitchen, fixing a bike or repairing a fence— these are all skills that justly ought to earn a child a sense of accomplishment and parental acclaim.

SELF-ESTEEM AND THE HOME ATMOSPHERE

The atmosphere of the home determines a great deal about a child's self-esteem. If the emotional climate is pleasant, steady, supportive, and accepting of all the members of the family, the development of self-esteem will occur pretty spontaneously, without a whole lot of conscious intervention by parents. Dr. Edward Sheridan stated it beautifully: "The dramatic things of life should not be happening in the home." Elsewhere, sources of fear and insecurity may abound. But if the home is the place of peace, acceptance, and love, a child is safe and has a good chance of thriving.

Growing children, no matter what their age, need time when their parents pay attention to them individually. It's hard to avoid spending time with little children. But as children get older and become more self-sufficient, their own schedules get crowded, and their interests move away from the home. Still, as parents, we need to know what they're thinking and what interests they're pursuing. We need to take enormous care not to let the channels of communication become clogged because of disuse. Tactics as simple as reading a junior high student's book reports can spark important conversations. There's no need for elaborately planned special events. Ten minutes here and fifteen minutes there a few times a week do a great deal to nurture a relationship.

There are especially two things that occur as barriers to communication between parents and children: lack of confidentiality, lack of context, and lack of interest.

If your daughter asks you a question about sex, or shares a worry about Daddy's job, or complains about something that happened at school, be sensitive to the fact that *she asked you.* She did not ask Dad. Presumably, if she wants Dad's input—and reaction—she will ask Dad. Maybe she just wanted to float the idea with you first. Maybe she's really asking the question for another reason, a reason you can't guess. If Dad comes to her tomorrow and says, "I understand from Mom that those stupid idiots at your school are forcing you to read filthy books, so I called your teacher today and gave her a piece of my mind," you may have just slammed the door of communication shut. You may have heard your last report about what goes on inside her school. And that is the opposite of what you want. *Your job is to treat your communication as confidential.* Maybe she doesn't want Dad to know what she's worrying about. And if there's no compelling need to bring Dad into the picture, you're worthy of the trust. And if you do feel there's a compelling need to involve Dad, tell her that you will have to tell Dad, and get her used to the idea before you do it.

I know a family in which one of the children was experimenting with drugs. A sibling knew about it, and week after week begged that kid to tell Dad. Finally, the wayward teen agreed to tell Dad if Dad promised not to tell Mom. The child did not want the emotional scene that he believed was inevitable if Mom found out. So in the middle of the night one night, Dad got awakened from sleep and called in whispers into another bedroom. "Dad, there's something we have to tell you, but you gotta promise you won't tell Mom," was how the conversation began. Of course, he promised. Several hours later, as everyone was winding down, he gently broached the subject that Mom would have to know. It took another long time to calm the child down, and they negotiated awhile about how much Mom needed to be told, and what, and why. He had to promise absolutely that Mom would not react. Then he had to wake up Mom early, and tell her, and spend the necessary time to let her react to his ears only, then to calm her down, and use every ounce of his persuasive abilities to make sure she did not react in front of the child. He didn't get much sleep that night, but his diplomacy kept his family together.

While it is good for parents to be of one mind with regard to child rearing, often they are of different temperaments. And children prefer one temperament to another. Some kids can open up to Mom, some to Dad. Some would rather tell bad news to one parent than the other. Be aware of these preferences, and respect them. The goal here is to keep communicating with the child. As adults, you and your spouse can communicate non-emotionally with one another about your the children and how you are going to handle problems—at least, you should be striving to, even if you're not completely there.

In the case I just related, the Dad was able to deal confidentially with his child. Because the worlds which adults inhabit are so different from the worlds kids inhabit, the codes of behavior can be very far apart. Especially if parents are older are they more likely to be unfamiliar with the prevailing mores of the youth environment. You just read a chapter telling you about how awful the youth culture is, and I stand by that. But if your child is living in some form of it—and every school is a youth culture—you have to know the context before you make a move. A personal story to demonstrate lack of context.

My first encounter with kids my own age of the opposite sex was in seventh grade. Prior to that, I had always been in all-girl schools with very high standards of decorum. Seventh grade boys are notoriously lacking in that, but I didn't know it. When a seventh-grade boy throws a spitball at a girl, it's a sign of friendly interest. I thought it was peculiar, and told my mother about it. My mother, alas, took great offense at this assault and battery, and, to my total astonishment, marched into the principal's office the next afternoon to demand justice. The principal came to the classroom with my mother, hauled the boys and me out of the class, and meted out some sort of punishment to the boys. My mother was pleased that she had upheld moral standards, but for the next two years no kid at that school would talk to me on the playground or anywhere else.

I resolved not to make the same mistake with my children. So when one of my sons was starting at a new school, and brought home complaints about how the other kids were picking fights with him, I kept my distance. "You're probably giving offense to them in some way," I told him, figuring that there was some code of unwritten boy-behavior of welcoming a new student. And he never made a friend at that school. Years later, after hearing from many other moms how rough the kids were allowed to treat each other at that school, I came to realize that my son was right to complain to me, and that I should have listened to him. I should have asked him if he wanted me to talk to the authorities. Maybe he would have said, "No, Mom, I can cope," which would have meant he was just looking for sympathy but was prepared to tough it out. But at least he would have known I cared, and that I believed in him. As it was, I think what he learned was that there's no point in talking to mom, which was, of course, both painful and harmful.

I had erred in the opposite direction from that which my mother erred in. From one extreme to the other. The antidote to each might have been for the moms in both cases to be talking to other moms. If my mother had talked to another mother, and said, "Is it normal in this part of the country for boys to throw spitballs?" she might have found out that it was perfectly normal behavior. That might have tempered her response. If I had talked to other moms in my son's school, I might have found out what were considered normal standards for that school, and that might have tempered my response.

This issue of confidentiality is particularly keen as children approach adolescence, and begin to value their privacy as part of normal development. The difficult part of respecting privacy is that privacy can be a screen to deceptiveness. It can be a tricky business knowing what your youths are up to without their realizing you know. This is why as a parent, you will be wise to treat all communication with other parents as confidential. "I know you smoked after school last Tuesday because Mrs. Goliath told me she saw you smoking while you were standing by her car with David" may give you the pleasure of presenting the irrefutable evidence to prove your accusation, but let me tell you, it will only drive the smoking further and further away from the neighborhood, and it will sow seeds of resentment against the parents of the world. It will feed the youth culture lie that "grownups are all in a conspiracy to deprive you of fun."

When I told my mom about the spitball incident, she could have told me, "I don't think it's nice to throw spitballs, and I wouldn't like any boy that did it. If you ignore it, it probably won't happen again." That would have been enough; at that tender stage of development, I would have been disgusted by spitballs. Kids start out wanting to adopt their parents' values—but if the cost becomes too great, they start to pick their own. And the cost can be very subjective. Embarassment in front of friends or teachers is very costly any time it occurs—so don't cause it unless the issue is one of pararmount moral importance. Spitballs aren't.

Lack of interest can render null and void everything I just said. If a parent doesn't pay attention to what's going on in the child's life, no amount of diplomacy or information is going to make much difference. Fathers, listen up.

A parent may well say, "Skateboarding means nothing to me, so why should I waste my time looking at a skateboarding magazine with my son?" I would ask in response, "What does your son mean to you?" And if he happens to be into skateboarding, right now, it's an interest you may be able to share with him. He may think he's pretty good at it. Maybe you know he's not. You don't have to tell him that. It's a given that he's fascinated with his hobby. You should take advantage of the opportunity to look at his magazines so you can help him sift out what's acceptable and what isn't about the "skate rat" phenomenon. You'll also get a sense of how his mind is working these days, what he admires in another man, and what his sense of his own talents and interests is. It can be an education for you about your almost-adolescent or adolescent boy. For him, it's a reassurance that you think he's worth your time.

From the time a child is small, he (or she, of course) should know because his parents tell him that he is precious, that he is loved whether he gets A's or F's on his report cards. He should know, because he will have heard it from the time he can remember, that he is special, that he has great potential, that he can be anything he wants to be when he grows up. He should know, because his parents tell him and act accordingly, that no matter what mistakes he makes or what trouble he gets into, his parents will help him if he just tells them. If he's broken their rules, they may have to discipline him, but they'll still love him, and they'll help him. Even if he's a slow learner, clumsy, inept on the ball field, forgets his homework and his mom's instructions, and stutters to boot so that other kids make fun of him—with all that support from loving parents, he'll know he still matters. As the poster says, "God made me, and He don't make junk." And when his neurological system settles itself down and he eventually finds some area where he can achieve and be proud of himself, he'll have some self-esteem.

All along, as children are growing up and are faced with decisions, hypothetical or real, parents can give guidance that builds esteem—or does the opposite. Suppose you have just heard that somebody has spent $150 on a pair of jeans. A parent might say, "I'm glad you're too smart to waste your money like that." Or a parent might warn in a dire tone of voice, "Don't you dare ever ask me to spend that kind of money on a pair of jeans!" Which response is going to make a child feel trusted? Which is going to make her feel like a financial burden? Either way, the message is gotten across that $150 on a pair or jeans is a waste of money. But one way conveys the idea along with a positive message about self-esteem, and the other way practically insults a sensitive, peer-oriented adolescent.

Or suppose the subject of a classmate who has gotten pregnant comes up at the dinner table. A mother can tell her daughter, "I'm glad you're too smart to do that. Let me know if you ever have trouble cooling off some fresh guy—I have a trick or two that might come in handy." Or she can say something like this: "What a disgrace! I tell you, if you ever get into that situation, just forget about coming home. I'd never live down the shame of it!" Which response is going to make the girl feel capable of resisting temptation? Which is going to incline her to think her parents believe in her? Which is going to make a girl more likely to adopt her mother's standards as her own? Yet which comment is going to be the first thought a parent has? Probably the second. Parents never stop needing self-control. "Think before you speak" is a good rule for all of us all our lives. Think what effect your thoughts might have on your children if you blurt them out without reflection.

COMPLIMENTS AND OBJECTIVITY

How many adults do you know who can't accept a compliment? When you offer one, they demur, saying, "Well, if I hadn't added that extra teaspoon of vanilla, it would have been better," or, "Aw, I didn't do much, really." These people usually don't have a good self-esteem, either, and they've spent their whole lives under that handicap. In some cases, we know we're not supposed to be prideful, so we figure that if we brush off the compliments of other people, we're helping to kill pride in our souls. Actually, the contrary is true. A sincere compliment, a wise friend once told me, is a gift. If we don't accept the gifts of our friends, we hurt their feelings. There's no spiritual gain to be gotten from refusing gifts from friends. If we did a good job on something, it's a lie to pretend we didn't. If we deserve credit, we should take it. And if we had help, by all means tell the person offering the compliment so the credit can be shared.

I have known parents who taught their children not to accept compliments. A little girl runs up to her mother and bubbles over how Grandfather just told her that her drawing of a horse was very good. "He just said that to make you feel good," the mother says. The pattern continues. In junior high school, an essay wins a compliment from the teacher. Says the mother, "The teacher just said that because you were voicing her own opinions." As this child grows up, she not only doesn't believe she can do anything well, but she also knows not to believe anything anybody tells her, because she has been taught everybody is insincere.

Of course, people can have ulterior motives in complimenting us. A little more cynicism in that regard, at least on the part of girls who are too quick to fall for the lines of opportunistic boyfriends, is not a bad idea at all. But between trusting everybody and trusting nobody lies a middle ground: the ground of objectivity. We all need to be able to see our faults as well as our strengths, and the younger we can learn, the happier we will be. The ability to be honest and objective about oneself, one's talents, and one's behavior is a consequence of both grace and teaching. It is certainly something everyone should strive to develop, but parents should particularly try to give this gift to their children.

A child needs to be able to see his defects. But in order to see his defects, he needs to have an idea—an ideal, if you will—to which he can compare himself. And I don't mean just an abstract ideal. I mean real examples. Books can provide some of these. I remember being prone to daydreaming as a child, and I loved the book *My Friend Flicka*. In that story, the protagonist, Ken, learns to overcome his habit of daydreaming. Ken was a real example for me. A few years later, I became fascinated with Irish history. The achievements of Daniel O'Connell, who won political power for a disenfranchised population, made a deep impression on me. Remembering O'Connell's impassioned pleas to his followers for no violence made me able to be objective about the organizing tactics of the anti-war agitators who came to my campus in the late 1960s. Having thrilled in late childhood to the proclamation of the Irish Republic of 1916, and having noted the prayer in that proclamation that no adherent to this noble cause would dishonor it with personal immorality, I was able to view objectively the immoral excesses on the college campuses for what they were.

Real, living people, of course, are the best examples of virtues. Usually their example is absorbed as if by osmosis, but an observant parent can articulate what the child is seeing. "Isn't Aunt Katie wonderful? You never hear her say an unkind word about anybody." Such a statement might help give form to the admiration the child feels for Aunt Katie without knowing why. "Don't you admire Aunt Sue's patience? I've never heard her raise her voice to those children." Without such help, it may be thirty years before Aunt Sue's nephew realizes why she seemed so nice. In the meantime, her example might have been more real an ideal for him to emulate.

We rarely get the opportunity to see others exercising sexual virtues, since sexuality is by nature very private. But children can be taught to look for certain things. Narratives of parental courtships are useful: "Mommy and I went with each other a year before we ever had a date just by ourselves." "Did you notice Angie and Mark at the picnic? Did you see them holding hands and looking at each other? They're getting married soon. But I was glad they stayed with the rest of the group and didn't wander off by themselves. They know that once they get married, they'll have all the time they want for each other, and now is the time to enjoy lots of other people."

The Navy has a custom of fitness reports every year or so on officers. These are character descriptions and records of accomplishment filled out by the supervising officer and kept in the central file as the basis for promotion decisions. I've often thought that a modified form of that custom would be helpful for a preadolescent if it could be done right. When a child becomes conscious of himself and capable of separating his thoughts and actions from his emotions, he usually becomes concerned with self-improvement as well. Having some objective but loving assessments of his strengths and weaknesses every six months could be very helpful. Of course, it would only work if there were a high level of trust between the child and the parent, and if the parent were capable himself or herself of total objectivity and did not allow his or her own emotions to cloud the assessment. If such objectivity and trust were present, the child would be fortunate indeed. The parent could become a real partner (rather than a nagger) in working to bring about changes of bad habits, a further self-awareness of weaknesses, and so on. Learning to conquer one's weaknesses is a difficult, lifelong battle. The struggle is more willingly joined, however, if one has explicit encouragement from a kind parent.

Thus, the real point is that the more explicit, articulate awareness of his strengths and weaknesses a child has, the better he will be able to cope with the trials and temptations of adolescence. And the best assistance one can have in fighting one's weakness is the knowledge that God is on the side of your changing for the better. "I will put a new spirit within them, and take the stony heart out of their flesh, and give them a heart of flesh, that they may walk in My statutes and keep My judgments and do them" (Ezek. 11:19–20).

TEMPTATION: THE BASIS OF A CONSUMER SOCIETY?

A good self-esteem helps us to resist temptation. But children also need special training. We live in a consumer society predicated upon the assumption that people can easily be made to succumb to temptation. Fortunes have been made in advertising, proving that people can be convinced to say yes to a certain product, even though they never heard of it before, don't need it, don't have room for it, and would never have thought of it without the ad or the sales pitch. Candidates get elected to public office on the strength of their superior advertising.

Children are taught to give in to their impulses. Grandmothers are encouraged to spoil their grandchildren. Women's magazines talk about the joys of grandmotherhood in precisely such terms. Parents who try to limit the gratification become ogres: "But Grandma always buys me candy when I go to the grocery store with her. You're mean because you won't." What mother has not winced under such a charge? Popular child-rearing manuals tell parents to reward good behavior. So children come to expect bribes, and when the bribes are no longer big enough to appeal to them, they whine.

Our devotion to self-gratification can be subtle. Asking a two-year-old on a regular basis what he would like for dinner is an everyday example. Already at age two, a child is being prepared to believe that if he doesn't like something, he shouldn't have to eat it. When Mom and Dad allow him to declare his meal "finished" without eating something he doesn't like, the lesson of self-gratification is reinforced. Slightly older kids convince Mom they "need" this or that beverage. Not that they "want" it, but that they "need" it. How often do you hear kids saying they're hungry between meals and need a snack? You offer them an apple. Suddenly they're not hungry. What they had in mind was chips or a candy bar, and they felt they had a right to that self-gratification.

Watching fast-food establishments proclaim on television that "you deserve a break today" gives us ideas about what else we deserve. When a sixteen-year-old boy tries to convince his girlfriend that he "needs" sexual intercourse, it's the logical conclusion of sixteen years of self-in-dulgence.

As a nation, not only do we have a staggering proportion of consumer debt, but we also have mountains of other problems caused by our unwill-ingness to deny ourselves gratification of the moment. How many people come tired to work in the morning for no better reason than that they stayed up to watch "The Late Late Show?" They'll tell you what a dumb movie it was and how many times before they've seen it, but they don't mind being slow-witted for their employers and out-of-sorts for their families the next day, because this kind of self-indulgent behavior is considered acceptable in our society.

Unless and until we can teach our children self-denial in simple things, we can't really expect them to practice self-denial in the back seat of a car—or in their girlfriend's house before her mom comes home from work.

THE FORGOTTEN VIRTUE OF MODERATION

Does anybody still remember the old-fashioned virtue of moderation? Fundamentally, moderation means not being emotionally attached to things of this world, particularly material things, and being able to control our desires for material things. It means distinguishing between what's necessary and what's nice, and opting to be content with what's neces-sary. Catering to whims is directly contrary to the virtue of moderation, whether in children or in adults. A little bit of a good thing is enough; there's no need to have as much of it as you can possibly absorb. If the pumpkin pie after Thanksgiving dinner is good, be content with one piece, even though you would like three with extra whipped cream. That's moderation.

The root of that old teaching was the wisdom that when your senses are satiated and over-satisfied, your spiritual capacity diminishes. If you make sure you're well fed and well indulged, chances are you're not very attentive to your spiritual well-being. Not that you have to be starving in order to pray, but a little less focus on the physical tends to encourage a little more focus on the spiritual. Adults are hard put to realize this; how much more difficult it is for young adults.

You can be poor and have no moderation, and you can be wealthy and have great moderation. The opposite is also true. It's not a matter of circumstances; it's a matter of your internal disposition. If you're content with what you have, are not emotionally attached to your creature comforts, and know which appetites you need to control, you have moderation. If you get your deepest satisfaction from your ideals rather than from your sensual pleasures, you are practicing moderation.

Young adults who are concerned about being independent should be encouraged to think about how they leave themselves open to manipulation by failing to have a spirit of moderation. If seeing an advertisement on TV makes them want to run out and buy whatever was advertised, is that really freedom? Or have they just been masterfully manipulated?

Resisting impulses to self-gratification can be aided by building favorable habits. But the habits have to begin young. David Isaacs, a wise student of human virtues, suggests that a family should ask itself the following questions before embarking on a significant purchase. Get the children involved in thinking through the hidden costs of indulging desires and thinking the differences between needs and wants.

- How does this advance our goal in life? A family should have a sense of its unique purpose, just as individuals should.

- Are we creating new needs by this? For example, buying a VCR means that soon we'll have to join a tape rental club, then we'll need to buy tapes, then we'll need a place to store them, then we'll need to make rules about who can tape what, and so on. Are we planning for those new needs as well?

- Why are we really doing this? Have we wanted this for some time, or is it just because we saw our cousins playing with one that made us suddenly want one of our own?

As youngsters begin to have their own money, they should be taught to put each spending decision under such a magnifying glass. The same scrutiny should be applied to decisions about courses of action (signing up for this sport or that, joining this club or that).

- Will this satisfy a deep, long-term longing of mine? Or is it just a short-term, impulsive desire?

- Is getting this (or doing this) yielding to an appetite that should be controlled? For instance, does a boy want to take up boxing because he wants to learn how to beat up other kids? Or is he genuinely interested in the sport?

TEMPTATION

What is the origin of temptation? "Your adversary the devil walks about
like a roaring lion, seeking whom he may devour" (1 Pet. 5:8). Strong
temptations roar at us; others merely meow, hoping to seem so harmless
that we feed them so they can grow up to roar at us.

How does temptation grow? "Each one is tempted when he is drawn
away by his own desires and enticed. Then, when desire has conceived, it
gives birth to sin; and sin, when it is full-grown, brings forth death"
(James 1:14–15).

Temptation itself isn't sin. Sin comes in yielding to the temptation. If
young people don't understand this distinction clearly, they are going to
wear themselves out feeling guilty over temptations they couldn't help.
And sooner or later they will be so frustrated and feel so powerless that
they'll be ripe for real danger.

Of course young people are going to be tempted. Male physiology is
such that during the early years of puberty, the most fleeting glimpse of a
woman can provoke a sexual response in boys. The most remotely sug-
gestive song may evoke a sexual temptation, a reaction of the involuntary
nervous system. But these are temptations. As long as the boy moves his
mind on to something else, he has incurred no guilt. As long as he didn't
deliberately look at that magazine to see those pictures in order to enjoy
the temptation, his conscience is clear. The thought is no sin so long as he
didn't invite the thought. If he purposely continued the thought, savoring
it in his imagination and embellishing it, getting the voluntary nervous
system into the act, however, that would be yielding to the temptation.

Girls aren't so readily stimulated. They're more likely to be tempted by
their fantasies about relationships that aren't real. A girl may let her
imagination embellish one or two words or glances from a fellow until
she's convinced herself that he loves her. Then, with this mental work
done, she has prepared herself to be stimulated by him sexually. For her,
the first temptation was the romantic fantasy. The indulging in that
thought was the first sin. The sexual actions, whatever they may be, only
follow some complicated mental preparation.

Since imagination is a vital part of intelligence and creativity of all
kinds, and since using imagination is so much a part of a day's work, it is
perhaps a more difficult challenge for girls to resist the first temptation.
That's a good reason for mental discipline to have been learned before

hormones start coursing through the blood stream, and for daydreams to be left behind in childhood.

Whatever forms it comes in, temptation is to be both avoided and resisted. Scripture contains guidance on controlling temptation. The first control, naturally, is prayer: "Watch and pray, lest you enter into temptation. The spirit is willing but the flesh is weak" (Matt 26:41). Those were among Jesus' last words to His disciples. We should cherish them as among His first words to us.

If the temptation seems too great and we feel tested beyond our strength, there is this thought to strengthen us and snap us out of our self-pitying impulse to indulge ourselves: "No temptation has overtaken you except such as is common to man; but God is faithful, who will not allow you to be tempted beyond what you are able, but with the temptation will also make the way of escape" (1 Cor. 10:13). When His own Son was tempted in the desert by Satan, how did God provide a way of escape? With His Word, with Scripture. As we read, "For in that He Himself has suffered, being tempted, He is able to aid those who are tempted" (Heb. 2:18).

One closing, practical thought. John Chrysostom, that ancient father of the Church, once stated that "no one can harm the man who does himself no wrong." More than one politician has lost his chance for higher office, or forfeited a favorable mention in the history books, because of his marital infidelities. It wasn't their political foes who brought them down, but their own sin. A Christian must know what he ought to believe; must know what he ought to desire; must know what he ought to do. And in the case of temptation, what one ought to do is to flee from it. This is one of the most important and practical things we can teach our children.

Chapter 11

EMOTIONS
AND FASTING

I n the preceding chapter, I talked about how love of God is the ultimate motivation for self-control, but that this self-control does not come naturally. It has to build upon a foundation of grace and rightful self-esteem. All the self-esteem in the world, however, and even a good prayer life, will not guarantee self-control if a person is not in control of his or her thought life and, more importantly, of his or her emotions. So in this chapter, we'll look at how we can help our children develop control of their emotions. We'll also consider how the great traditional fasts and feasts of the Church can be of great assistance toward that end.

EMOTIONS: WHO'S IN CHARGE HERE?

Who controls our feelings? If you asked a representative cross-section of American teenagers that question, an astonishing proportion of them would indicate that when feelings come on strong, there's just nothing they can do about them. As the two lovers in *West Side Story* sang, "When love comes so strong, there is no right or wrong." A lot of people believe that. It isn't just teenagers, either.

Of course, Christians know better—in our brains. If you asked us on an examination paper, we'd say that the mind dominates the emotions. But how do we actually live? How well we stack up in daily practice gives us some indication of what we're really teaching our children. Do we go around controlled by our moods, or do we control our moods? I'm challenging you to some rigid, and perhaps painful, introspection of the type I have to put myself through regularly.

Where do emotions come from, anyhow?

They come from attitudes, and attitudes come from thoughts, and thoughts come from ideas. If I read an article about being overweight, soon I'll think about being overweight. And as I think about it, I'll develop a certain attitude toward it. And then I'll have a feeling about it. Now, the feeling in and of itself is probably neither right nor wrong. It is a pretty powerful indicator, however, of something else. When I get to that stage, if my feeling happens to be negative and my husband says something friendly about my apple cheeks, I may just snap at him. He'll look at me confused, and rightly so. The negative emotion was in me, not in what he said.

An idea that becomes habitual becomes an attitude. The attitude, then, over enough time, becomes capable of influencing or controlling our behavior. In order to control the behavior of rational human beings, of course, the idea has to have the consent of our wills. But the dangerous thing about emotions is that they can be so subtle that we don't even realize when we have consented to one. Have you ever wakened in the morning feeling sad? Maybe you had to think for a while before you remembered why you were sad. Once you remembered what had happened the day before, you then could decide whether you wanted to stay sad or wanted to forget it. But some people go through days, weeks, and months of life dominated by certain attitudes, never stopping to ask themselves why they feel that way and whether they want to continue feeling that way.

Michelle never learned how to be critical of her own emotions. She heard a lot about "being in love" from her girlfriends, on the radio, and in the movies. The idea of being in love began to take hold in her. She thought about it a lot and imagined how it would feel to have Charlie—the tall, handsome quarterback who smiled at her in math class—in love with her. Without realizing it, she had developed a romantic attitude toward Charlie. Her thoughts about Charlie—her fantasies, really—were controlling her. Then he asked her for a date. For several weeks she had been indulging in vague feelings of warmth and what she called "love" for Charlie, so when he began to make improper advances on their first date, she readily sank into the current of the emotions and surrendered herself to him. Actually, in other respects Michelle is a sensible girl. But she never stopped to think about her feelings toward Charlie. If she had, her thoughts might have given her some pause, and in that pause might have been her protection.

What emotions are the most likely to undermine sexual virtue?

Actually, just about any emotion can dominate our thinking so that we see the world through the filter of that feeling. And it doesn't have to be just the negative emotions, either. Positive emotions can cause us to lose our sense of reality just as completely as negative ones.

For example, resentment can contribute to immorality. Not resentment against the boyfriend or girlfriend, but against parents. A parent may have been overbearing, and the child is full of deep resentment and anger. Then along comes an opportunity for forbidden sexual behavior. *Aha,* say the emotions, *here's a way to get back at Mom for all those harsh words from her. She can't stop me now.*

Rational? No. Emotional? Yes. Emotions ruled the day.

Guilt is a frequent factor in sexual sin, because if allowed to flourish it can kill hope. Laura may not like sleeping around. But her attitude may be one of, *Why bother to resist? I'm already tarnished, so what difference is another night going to make? Why not? That's the way I am, I guess.* These thoughts may be far from the level of consciousness and self-analysis, mind you, but the dominant attitude may well be one of hopelessness induced by guilt.

As Christians, we know we need not carry guilt around forever, and this is one of the most important truths we can instill in our children. Indeed, we are commanded to put our guilt far from us once we have repented. When we first notice a sense of guilt, we must pause, examine our lives, and decide if we're doing something wrong. If we are, we change our hearts and repent, and then we change our lives. Then we're free, with no room for guilt. Not that it's as easy as it sounds, but it works exactly as it's supposed to, and it's why Christians have peace in this troubled world.

The very first step in this process is to notice the sense of guilt. One mustn't be oblivious to it or it may, as in the case of Laura, control us. But guilt can be a helpful emotion as long as we recognize it and seek to rid ourselves of it, because it signals that we're in a danger zone.

Self-pity is another subtle, ruinous emotion that can take hold so gradually that we don't realize we're viewing the world through pity-colored glasses until it has already led us to indulge ourselves. Extramarital affairs frequently have self-pity at their root: "My wife just doesn't understand me." "I love my husband, but he just doesn't appreciate me." People who say such things don't realize they are wallowing in self-pity. They think they've analyzed their emotional needs quite well.

Young people are certainly not immune from feeling sorry for themselves. If one isn't doing well in school, is losing hope of achieving things beyond school, and isn't getting much sympathy at home, self-pity can become a dominant attitude. Pigging out on a box of candy is one way to indulge in self-pity; guzzling the beer at a party and throwing caution to the wind is another.

Not that self-pity can be avoided. It lurks in all kinds of nooks and crannies, waiting to sidle up to us and take root in our vulnerability. So do most emotions. Very few of them announce themselves and seek the conscious consent of our minds. Self-pity happens to be more lethal than some because the deeper we sink into it, the more we isolate ourselves from other people and from God's Word. If we're fortunate, by the time we're adults, we have a friend who will tell us flat out when our emotions are getting the better of us. But with adolescents, usually the only people who perceives that they are being victimized by emotions are observant parents, and they're the last ones adolescents want to hear criticize anything about them. Furthermore, there aren't enough observant parents in the world. That's all the more reason we must teach our children, in our homes, Sunday schools, and youth groups, to be able to recognize and control their own emotions.

One last thought about self-pity is that there is such a thing as legitimate grief. And tragically, many, many teens have every right in the world to legitimate grief when their parents' marriage breaks up. The grief over the sundering of the union that begat them and gave them love and security is a real one. Young people enduring a divorce should know that they have every reason in the world to feel all the wild emotions of grief, and they should be prepared for those emotions. Any bereaved person is always warned: Don't make any drastic changes for at least a year, and expect the emotions to trouble you for years to come. It's good advice for a child suffering through parental divorce, and it's protective advice, because it helps the child to analyze the feelings she is going to have. For the custodial parent to say "What are you so down about? He's gone, and that's good riddance" betrays an enormous self-centeredness on the parent's part. It's about as *un*helpful as anything could be. Not only does it create an instant Grand Canyon of communication between the grieving child and the parent, but it also, by denying a legitimate right to mourn, invites self-pity. The bereavement is real. But if the victim doesn't know it's real, she will feel the pain and not know why, leading to a generalized feeling of self-pity.

It's no accident that so many teenage girls who become pregnant are without fathers. In fact, not living with both biological parents is a predictor of early sexual intercourse among adolescents, according to some recent research.[1]

Another large area of human emotions where we are led astray by our unexamined feelings is the concern over having the respect of our fellow human beings. Coming to grips with this is a real test of maturity, since as children, the approval of our parents is something we should want very much. Somewhere along the line, we must substitute that external approval for the internal approval of our own rightly formed consciences. If parents make it clear that chastity is the way to go, we hope children will concur and make their parents' standards their own. On the other hand, if a mother pressures a daughter to go with Chauncey Walsingham because she wants her to marry a rich man, the daughter should be able to resist that pressure, just as she would resist pressure from Charlie the quarterback to do something immoral. For a young woman to make the distinction between the "right" kind of parental pressure and the "wrong" kind is asking for a lot of objectivity and maturity on the part of the young woman. It's not asking too much, however, if the parents have given the child the tools of judgment, objectivity, and self-control through the years.

Peer pressure, of course, is a dominant feature of the adolescent landscape, far more real to the victims of the rock culture than parental pressure. I devote a whole section to that in the next chapter. For now, let me just observe that fear of what other people might think of us can compel us beyond our own intentions, and we may not realize it until it's too late. "Will he still love me if I say no?" is probably more real a fear to many young people than "Will I go to hell if I say yes?"

EMOTIONAL CONTROL IS POSSIBLE

Emotions or no emotions, it's clear from Scripture—both Old Testament and New—that God expects us, as He expected far-more-primitive people than we, to control impulses. Witness Leviticus 20 and Deuteronomy 22: the death penalty for fornication, adultery, and sodomy would not have been imposed unless God knew that the people were capable of controlling the emotions that would compel them to break the law otherwise.

In Matthew's Gospel, Christ explained that Moses had allowed divorce "because of the hardness of your hearts." But then He went on to set a higher standard for us: He expected us not to put asunder what God has joined together (Matt. 19:6). He expects us to have our emotions more under our control than our ancestors'. Jesus let the woman taken in adultery go free after telling her to "sin no more," because after He wrote on the ground, all her accusers were convicted by their own consciences (John 8:9–11). He expected our consciences to convict us more than the law.

The early church certainly expected control of the emotions. Timothy preached that "God has not given us a spirit of fear, but of power and of love and of a sound mind" (2 Tim. 1:7). What a clarion call to us to control our thoughts and emotions! How else can we achieve a "sound mind"?

One aid to a sound mind is to keep good company. Not only were the early Christians expected to avoid fornicating, drunkenness, and extortion, but they were exhorted to avoid even keeping company with a person who engaged in such things (1 Cor. 5:11). Why would that be? Well, I find I'm prone to absorbing even unconsciously the attitudes of others. If I spend an afternoon with a real complainer who criticizes everything and everybody, when I get home again I'll see a lot more to criticize. It's the same with any weaknesses. You know the saying: if you lie down with the dogs, you'll get up with fleas. The apostle Paul clearly expected us to avoid picking up emotional fleas. If a marriage had gone on the rocks, the partners were to "remain unmarried or be reconciled" (1 Cor. 7:11). Despair and self-pity were not to be tolerated.

Much of the spirit of the early church has been distilled into one prayer, that of Ephrem the Syrian:

> O Lord and Master of my life, take from me the spirit of sloth, faint-heartedness, lust of power, and idle talk. But give rather the spirit of chastity, humility, patience and love to thy servant. Yea, O Lord and King! Grant me to see my own errors and not to judge my brother.

It is one of the most ancient Lenten prayers, dating back to the Fourth Century. A close reading shows the prayer to be a highly condensed plea to God for precisely what we most need to control our thoughts and emotions.

What does sloth have to do with self-control? Self-control requires much spiritual energy, and sloth is the sin that sucks away that energy. Imitating

Christ, doing things for His sake, carrying His cross in our lives. None of this comes easily, and we can lose our will for the struggle. It's sloth when we say to ourselves, "Why bother?" It's sloth that makes us put off the exertion of repentance. It's sloth that causes faint heartedness.

And lust of power? That's sloth directed at other people instead of at myself. It's the lack of respect that enables a boy to lie to a girl so she'll have sexual intercourse with him.

Idle talk was the tool used by the Deceiver to tempt Eve. The gift of speech, that distinguishing crown of human beings, is the weapon through which we inflict perhaps more harm on our fellow human beings than any other. In idle talk are launched many of the sins of the world.

The prayer asks for chastity, but it means much more than sexual continence. The Greek word *sofrosini* could be more literally translated as "whole-mindedness." It's the ability to see ourselves as whole persons—body, soul, and mind united as God intended, controlled by His spirit. Grasping and maintaining that vision is an essential task of a Christian. Not only are we to *see* ourselves as whole, but we're also to be whole with the grace of Christ's restoration. Humility, patience, and love are the virtues that most enable us to see God's working in our lives and to cooperate with His grace on the one hand, and at the same time they're the most difficult for fallen humanity.

Significantly, after saying this prayer every weekday of Lent, the Eastern Christian bows deeply twelve times and prays, "O God, be merciful unto me a sinner and have mercy upon me." The prayer defines precisely the needs, and then it begs God to meet them.

While we're asking God to meet our needs, we can also take steps to cooperate with the grace He will give. Emotional control precedes self-control. Just as self-control grows from being submissive to authority, so also control of the emotions grows from the feelings' being submissive to the mind. The mind will not take control of the emotions unless it is both taught and motivated. Impulsive self-indulgence and perpetual self-excusing do not provide either the teaching or the motivation. But steady discipline and gradually increasing understanding provide both.

Steady discipline from age one, thus, is the surest foundation for chastity at age sixteen. Don't despair, however, if your child is approaching adolescence now and never had the steady discipline that's ideal. Neither did most of us, truth be told. Yes, discipline is harder to begin at age ten than at age five, at age fifteen than at age ten. But as reason becomes stronger in the young person, the necessity for more discipline can be explained, which is an advantage over dealing with a two-year-old. The child may not agree with the parent's logic and may not see the need for discipline, but with experience will come understanding. And if the explanation is given often enough and the discipline is loving enough not to antagonize, yet firm enough to command respect, the stage is laid for the child to submit his will to authority, even belatedly. When that happens, the benefits, even belatedly, are wonderful to behold. They are far better than the alternative.

REMEMBER FORTITUDE?

The virtue that summarizes much of what I've said here is that old-fashioned one we don't hear much about anymore. It used to be called a gift of the Holy Spirit and was defined as the virtue that enables us to do what is good in spite of difficulty. It's the virtue that enables us to say no to our desires and still be happy. It's the one the psychologists forget about when they say you have to avoid frustration, and it's called fortitude. Sometimes I think it was designed by our Creator precisely to enable us to defer gratifying our impulses.

With fortitude, a boy can watch his friends go fishing but cheerfully reconcile himself to mowing the lawn because it's his job and he didn't do it sooner. Fortitude keeps us going when everything is against us. It strengthens a young person to preserve his or her virginity no matter how much ridicule gets piled on because of it. Endurance, which enables us to see the advantage of a disagreeable situation and thus persist in our course, is a close relative. So is prudence, which gives us the discernment to control our fears but nonetheless allows room for justified caution.

Perseverance is a precursor of fortitude. In fact, it's a precursor of almost all other virtues, because all other virtues require perseverance to be developed. Children are too young to learn stick-to-itiveness, as its worldly application is sometimes called, before about age eight. And by age thirteen, the learning curve moves on to other things. The window of opportunity for learning perseverance is those golden years after early childhood and before early adolescence. During those years, a child can see that what he applies himself to brings forth fruit that is useful to himself and others, and he develops the ability to discriminate between what is proper and what is less than proper.

Another virtue that stems from perseverance and fortitude is optimism. Not the naivete of a Pollyanna—though I didn't think Pollyanna was a bad role model for little girls, despite how her name has become a common synonym for foolish optimism. I'm talking about Christian optimism, which is realistic. It sees problems, difficulties, and obstacles and assesses their seriousness with full cognizance of the inherent risks. But Christian optimism also sees the positive elements and the opportunities for improvement that are to be found in them. Even if the only good to come from a situation is a stronger virtue in oneself, that's something— enough to justify one's patient toleration of an unpleasant situation.

The sexual impulse has a high level of demand and insistence. A teenager who has never had the experience of denying himself a comfort or an indulgence is a poor candidate to deny a sexual urge when hormones are running full-steam ahead and circumstances are convenient. The frustration level will be very high.

Some schools of psychology, as we've already seen, preach that frustration levels must be kept low, that impulses, particularly sexual ones, cannot be denied without harm to mental health. Don't frustrate your children, such counselors advise; give them what they want. Well, if you're talking about a nursing infant, I agree: don't deny a crying baby food and warmth. But by six or eight months, even a baby can understand, albeit in a vague sort of way, that too much kicking and squirming at diaper-changing time is not what Mommy wants. If that baby abandons his squirming to please his mother, he has learned an important first lesson in controlling his impulses—though he doesn't see it that way, and usually the mother doesn't think of it in those terms, either.

We can understand and be sympathetic with an infant's demands for absolutely immediate gratification. After all, survival depends on getting that gratification. But you can certainly see the Fall of mankind in the self-centered desires—no, demands—built into a two-year-old. A two-year-old who has not been properly disciplined will be running the household. Maybe a doting grandmother thinks he's so adorable and hates to see him cry, so she frowns when Mom tries to get some authority established. Mom and Dad may not realize how much they're dancing to his tune until a new baby comes along and they find their lives controlled, not by the demanding new one, but by the undisciplined toddler. It isn't inevitable that two-year-olds run households, but our culture has so completely lost its sense of discipline that the "terrible twos" are a cultural phenomenon we have come to expect and accept.

The fact remains: If from before age two children are getting whatever they want and controlling other people, and if this pattern continues pretty much unchanged until adolescence, it is asking a great deal of the Holy Spirit to change a lifetime of habits, expectations, and behavior patterns when their maturing bodies propel them toward the other gender at high speed. But this is the way most of us were raised. And despite our best efforts, it's the way most of us are raising our children. We are indeed asking a great deal of the Holy Spirit to preserve us and our children from temptations that we are so poorly disciplined to meet.

TEACH CHILDREN TO FAST

"If you love your children, you will teach them to fast, and show them how." Those are the words with which Father Joseph Francavilla, pastor of Holy Transfiguration Melkite Church, always begins his sermon on the first Sunday of Lent. The Melkites are the descendants of the apostolic church of Antioch, where the followers of Jesus were first called Christians. They are the Christians of modern-day Syria and Lebanon. Among Melkites and Antiochian Orthodox, the teachings and customs of the Church of the first several centuries have been preserved more intact than perhaps anywhere else. And one of the characteristics of the spiritual life of this church is a strong emphasis on fasting.

Father Joe's reason for exhorting parents to keep the Great Fast is simple: if you can't say no to food, how in the world can you say no to sin? Self-denial teaches us and our children to say no. If we can't or won't deny ourselves for our own benefit, then let us deny ourselves at the behest of the Church. Fasting teaches us that we, not our appetites, can be in control of the body, mind, and spirit. There is no better way, and perhaps in this society there's no other way at all, to learn that we can deny our senses and live to tell of it.

The tradition of fasting is ancient. Even amid the abundance of the Garden of Eden, Adam and Eve were expected by God to fast from one tree. They failed to keep that fast, with dire consequences. As Father Joe says, Adam and Eve could not remain in Paradise without fasting—how can we regain it without fasting?

Throughout the Old Testament, God commanded fasting: "'Now, therefore,' says the Lord, 'Turn to Me with all your heart, with fasting, with weeping, and with mourning'" (Joel 2:12). It was always practiced by God's servants. The book of Ezra provides just one example. When Ezra and his family felt in danger in their travels, what did they do? "We fasted and entreated our God for this, and He answered our prayer" (Ezra 8:23).

Fasting in and of itself moves God to mercy for those who fast. Consider the Ninevites who had heard Jonah's messages. What did they do? "The people of Nineveh believed God, proclaimed a fast, . . . from the greatest to the least of them. . . . And [the king] caused it to be proclaimed . . . saying, 'Let neither man nor beast, herd nor flock, taste anything; do not let them eat, or drink water'" (Jon. 3:5–7). And what did God do? "God saw their works, that they turned from their evil way; and God relented from the disaster that He had said He would bring upon them, and He did not do it" (Jon. 3:10).

Christ Himself fasted forty days and nights in the desert to set an example for us (Matt. 4:2). It was during His fasting that He was tempted by Satan and taught us how to resist temptation by calling upon the Word of God. In His teaching, the Lord taught us how to fast: "When you fast, do not be like the hypocrites, with a sad countenance. For they disfigure their faces that they may appear to men to be fasting. . . . But you, when you fast, anoint your head and wash your face, so that you do not appear to men to be fasting, but to your Father who is in the secret place; and your Father who sees in secret will reward you openly" (Matt. 6:16–18).

Not only will our Father in heaven reward us for our fasting, but the fasting in and of itself is efficacious against evil. Remember the story of Shadrach, Meshach, and Abednego? The three young men first attracted the attention of Babylon's King Nebuchadnezzar by refusing to eat his rich food, preferring instead to keep the Jewish dietary laws. Offered red meats, delicacies, and wine, they preferred vegetables. Part of their regimen was fasting. "And at the end of ten days their countenance appeared better and fatter in flesh than all the young men who ate the portion of the king's delicacies" (Dan. 1:15). But their fasting was strengthening them for a future they could not know. For then Nebuchadnezzar made his golden idol and commanded all the people to fall down and worship it.

Shadrach, Mishach, and Abednego, strong for having fasted, refused to worship the idol, though they knew the punishment. Nebuchadnezzar ordered them thrown into the fiery furnace. They were not afraid to die for their God, but even in the midst of the flames, He protected them. Witnesses reported to the king that four men, not three, were walking unhurt in the midst of the flames: "I see four men loose, walking in the midst of the fire; and they are not hurt, and the form of the fourth is like the Son of God" (Dan. 3:25). The king ordered them released, and they came forth, and "the hair of their head was not singed nor were their garments affected, and the smell of fire was not on them" (Dan. 3:27). Likewise will our God reward our fasting and protect us in the fires of temptation.

The early church knew the efficacy of fasting. Acts 13 tells how before Barnabas and Saul were sent out as missionaries, the community of Christians, "having fasted and prayed," laid hands on them and sent them away (Acts 13:3). Whenever the special help of God was needed, fasting was the first resort of God's people in Old Testament and New.

Since God's help is always needed, the Church in her wisdom established a regular series of fasts. The customs grew up independently—different ways of observance, different schedules—in the different regions where the Church was, but by the Council of Nicea in the year 325, the concept of Lent was universally accepted. And a forty day fast of some kind before Pascha, or Easter, was the universal custom for centuries throughout the Church.[2] In some places, baptisms could not take place during those forty days, indicative of how seriously held were those days of fasting and abstinence in preparation for the joy of Easter. Other fasts, preceding other major feasts throughout the year, were added to flex the spiritual muscles year round.

A hymn (sticheron) of Vespers for Tuesday in the second week of Lent captures the beautiful spirit of consecrated fasting:

O Christ, Thou hast stretched out Thy sinless hands upon the Cross, gathering together the ends of the earth. Therefore I cry unto Thee: Gather together my scattered mind, taken captive by the passions; cleanse me in every part through abstinence, and make me a sharer in Thy sufferings.

And later in the same service, another hymn (sticheron):

Fasting gave strength to the Children in Babylon of old and made them, as it is written, mightier than the flames of fire. Fast then, my humble soul, kindling within thyself love for the Master, and thou shalt escape from the Gehenna to come and burn up the destroying passions.

Whatever ancient, anonymous holy man wrote those words centuries ago, he understood profoundly how urgent is our need for divine help in controlling our minds and emotions if we're to control our passions. He also understood how fasting has a unique power to bring that divine help.

BRINGING IT HOME

"But I'm not an Eastern Christian," you say. "This is all very beautiful, but it's not my tradition. My church doesn't fast at all. I can see the point, the wisdom of those ancient prayers. But they are precisely that: ancient. Nobody really fasts nowadays, do they?"

Oh yes they do! One might even say that fasting is coming back. Many intercessory groups, led by the Spirit, have begun encouraging their members to fast, even though it is new to them. They're not necessarily following the strict Byzantine fast—which forbids meat or dairy products the forty days prior to Easter—but they're adopting some form of consecrated fasting.

We can fast without our friends' and neighbors' even noticing it. That, of course, is the best way. After all, if we fast so everybody notices it, we already have our reward. Wednesdays and Fridays are traditional days of fasting for the church. It's not hard to plan meatless meals for those days. Before Vatican II, generations of Catholic children practiced "giving up candy for Lent." But that's something easy to live without. And again, we are benefitted by our sacrifice physically as well as spiritually. The proliferation of medical findings about the harm of too much meat and too much sugar makes it tempting to fast from those items for purely secular reasons.

But maybe you have young children and you want to make sure they get a superior diet, and you don't have the time to learn how to balance proteins in meatless meals. There are still other things that can be avoided. How about fasting from television and radio for a period of time? Maybe forty full days seems a lot if you have never gone without it, and that *would* be a long time for a first effort. Since it's important that the first effort succeed, set a modest goal, one that can be achieved. Try no television on Wednesdays and Fridays. Or how about no radio except for the news? Maybe the problem in your family right now is backbiting and complaining. "For every idle word men may speak, they will give account of it in the day of judgment. For by your words you will be justified, and by your words you will be condemned" (Matt. 12: 36–37). Maybe you and your wife will want to resolve to give up your idle talk, your complaining, for a few weeks before Easter. Maybe you couldn't go forty days that way, but surely you could manage a couple of weeks. Each family can decide how best it can begin.

But watch out! Fasting will grow on you, because you won't just be avoiding meat, sweets, television, idle talk, or whatever. It's so much more than just "giving up" something. You will be increasing your prayers and your almsgiving, even as you fast. Mere abstinence from food does not win the favor of God; notice how many times when fasting is mentioned in Scripture, it is accompanied by prayer. The two go together. If you deny yourself food—and maybe even with slightly mixed motives, you *could* do with a few pounds less—you may just end up crabby, and that doesn't do you or anybody else much good. But if you increase your prayers at the same time, you are calling upon God to bless and reward your sacrifice. And He will. Historically, the Church has also urged an increase in generosity toward the needy at the same time we are calling on God to increase His generosity toward us. What is really going on with fasting is that we are re-affirming the goodness of creation. Man has become a consumer in this day and age, and we forget to be the priests of creation, we forget to offer back to God that which He has given us. Fasting restores this function to us.

The offering of our passions to the Lord can bring unexpected spiritual benefits. One reader of *Theosis,* the newsletter of Orthodox spiritual renewal, wrote this letter to the editor: "I gave my life to Jesus nine years ago, and the Holy Spirit led me back to the Orthodox Church. In my search . . . I found Lent. Lent is fantastic! It is like looking through the eyes of Christ at the Church and seeing how He guides frail humanity closer to Himself. Who, on their own, would fast to draw closer to God? God, through the Church, is holding us in His hands, teaching us how to draw near, how to pray, how to worship."[3]

Through fasting, God offers to teach us and our children how to control our passions, making it a valuable resource in the struggle with temptation. It's yet another part of His marvelous provision for our needs.

Chapter 12

MODESTY, PEERS, AND DATING

R osie was a girl I knew at college. A girlfriend invited her to a party one night, and Rosie spent most of the evening talking to Jose. She didn't do too much dancing, because she could feel a severe head cold coming on. In fact, as the evening progressed, the cold got worse and worse. Jose said he had some cold tablets at his apartment, and he offered to get her some. When the party was over, the girlfriend took Rosie by the dorm to drop her off, but Jose repeated his offer of cold tablets if she would come to his apartment. Knowing she didn't have any cold remedies in her own room, Rosie agreed. The girlfriend was astonished but didn't say anything.

Of course, Jose had motives far beyond medications. When they arrived at his apartment, he showed her to the bedroom, put his arms around her, and declared passionately, "Te quiero" ("I want you"). At that point she decided there was something about Jose that she didn't trust. She asked for the cold tablets, and he produced them. But then he wouldn't take her back to the dorm. He claimed starting the car would upset his landlady, who would look out the window and see Rosie, and then he'd be in trouble because he wasn't supposed to have girls in his apartment. Since she was feeling pretty sick by now, Rosie didn't argue. Instead she wrapped up in a blanket and spent the night in a chair, having decided to herself that if Jose took a step toward her she'd scream at the top of her lungs. As the day was breaking, Jose took her back to the dorm, leaving her wiser but unharmed—except in reputation.

Rosie had been so naive that she didn't know even the basic groundrule, which is that consenting to go to a man's apartment means consenting to have sex. She had had no idea that when she failed to get out of the

173

car at her own dormitory, she was signaling Jose that she was willing to go to bed with him. Most of all, she had no idea that Jose's offer of cold tablets was anything other than it seemed. So inexperienced was she that she didn't realize that while she had been making a real effort at conversation all evening, being nice to a foreign student, Jose's mind had been running in an entirely different direction.

Rosie's story vividly illustrates the fact that our job as parents doesn't end with moral and intellectual instruction. Those two jobs, along with equipping a child with the desire to do right, are indispensable and have been the focus of this book so far. But there's a fourth level of training necessary to raise virtuous young people. Our kids need to know how to formulate strategies and tactics to protect their virtue. As children move more and more into the world, beyond the protection of the home, our instruction must assume more and more practical shape. It should even include outright strategies and tactics for handling social relationships. Those are the subjects of this chapter.

CHANGING TIMES

When a young woman went from her parents' home straight to her husband's home—with perhaps a stop at a proper ladies' college in between—knowing how to behave and wanting to behave properly were usually enough. Within the controlled confines of social circles, a young person had to look hard for the opportunity to stray. Other people were around to supervise her and protect her from difficult situations. Chaperones and rules protected her everywhere she went.

Until the 1960s most colleges had stricter curfews for women than for men, as well as rules about the hours that men were allowed even in the lobby of the girls' dorm. But with the youth revolution and women's liberation it became "repressive" to protect women. So not only did curfews disappear, but men moved into the same dorms, even sharing shower facilities. For the after-college job situation, the respectable boarding houses and Christian young women's homes disappeared, too, as career women scorned the idea of living in such sheltered atmospheres.

The burden of protecting her virtue now falls on the shoulders of the young woman far more than it fell on the shoulders of her mother or grandmothers. Likewise, the burden of resisting temptation falls on the young man's shoulders far more than it fell on his father's. At least his father (probably) and his grandfather (most probably) would have faced some measure of social stigma if they had conducted themselves too improperly with a girl. Not so in this generation. Today the stigma comes from conducting oneself properly!

Consider the case of Sally and Jim. They were nice Christian kids, the kind you'd be proud to have raised. They were strongly attracted to each other when they first met at their public high school. Because they both were Christians, they were glad to have each other so they'd be free from the ridicule of their friends for not having dates. They felt comfortable with each other, and from the beginning of their relationship they found themselves sharing the secrets of their souls. Soon they found themselves spending every free moment together and being more physical than they wanted to be. They seemed to have run out of things to talk about. They recognize they were far too young to think about marriage, so they don't talk in terms like that. They also knew it was wrong to be so physical, but even though they prayed about it, they couldn't seem to stop it. What was wrong?

Sally and Jim's problem was, for the most part, caused by that all-American institution: casual dating. The response to it may be found in some old-fashioned concepts called respect and modesty.

RESPECT AND MODESTY

Jim had enormous respect for Sally, and she for him. If you asked them, at least, they would have told you that. And Sally didn't dress provocatively at all. So what's this about respect and modesty?

In fact, Jim *didn't* have respect for Sally, despite his words and intentions. As David Isaacs says, "A person who has respect for others acts or refrains from acting so as not to harm, or indeed so as to benefit, himself and others, according to their rights, status, and circumstances." If Jim had real respect for Sally, he simply would not allow an evening to get "too physical." Period. If he allows to happen things that he realizes are harmful to her, spiritually or otherwise, he is not showing respect. I'm not saying Jim is deliberately "using" Sally—on the contrary, most likely, he is doing his level best. Most likely, neither he nor his parents ever thought about respect the way David Isaacs has phrased it.

Note: Remorse is not respect. Just because a guy feels sorry the next day, when he's thinking clearly again, is not a sign of respect. Also, civility is not respect. It's nice that Jim did not make anti-woman jokes about Sally or talk fresh to her. But respect is more than talk; it is deeds. It's a two-way street, of course: Sally did not show respect for Jim because she allowed him to act in a manner that was harmful to him, spiritually and otherwise.

Sally was so eager to keep Jim's friendship and his social availability as protection from the ridicule of her peers that she forgot her own self-respect. She didn't have to be a doormat, however; there are worse things than the other kids' laughing at her. These are lessons she may have learned as a child but had forgotten. In the course of forgetting her self-respect, she should have asked herself if she was using Jim for her own purposes. If she was, that was not respect for him, either.

What is the source of respect? In childhood, justice is the source of our respect for our parents. In adulthood, our respect for our parents is based on love. But our respect for our peers is based on love, too—a different kind of love. In C. S. Lewis's *Four Loves,* he described the kind of love we have for our peers as *phileo* (friendship) or *agape* (generosity), and the love for our parents as *filial.* Only for a potential marriage partner does *eros* love—romantic love—have any place. And eros should be saved for the life's partner chosen.

Modesty is more than covering yourself, too. Covering your body is an elemental instinct that begins before age six, and that, if not interfered with, will continue through life, to be suspended for the marriage partner but no other. Physical modesty is easy to understand in principle. I realize it's hard to practice when all the other girls are wearing G-string bikinis.

But there's another kind of modesty—a habit of mind and soul. It can be seen beginning in adolescence, as teenagers begin to distinguish between what they will tell the world and what they want to store away in their hearts. Sometimes when this begins, parents—especially mothers—feel they are being deceived and react with hostility and accusations. It's true that if the child is disposed to deceiving his parents about some wrongdoing, that will also happen at about the same time, which makes the situation confusing. But with obedient children, who are not prone to wrongdoing and not scheming enough to cover their tracks, the ability to separate the private from the public is really a sign of growing in control of oneself. It's good that a young person no longer has the compulsion to tell everything he knows to everybody.

This kind of modesty is the beginning of the ability to "be oneself," a major milestone in the achievement of self-respect and maturity. The dawning need for privacy should be respected by parents. If private space, for instance, is possible within the home, now is the time to provide it, even if it's only a sacrosanct portion of a room. Parents, after all, have their private space in the house. Far from signifying a breakdown in communication, the granting of "breathing room" at this time will ultimately make firmer the ties of affection between parent and child.

What should be emphasized to the youngster in every way possible is that it may become necessary for him to emerge from his privacy to seek help with an occasional problem. Teach your child how to know when she needs help, and teach her who, besides you and your spouse, is an appropriate source of assistance. A Planned Parenthood counselor, for example, is not an appropriate person from whom to seek counsel on relationships. The youth minister might be. Express willingness to always be available to provide help, but don't express the willingness in such a way that the child gets the impression you will be offended if she gets the advice of others as well. Especially don't frighten the child into thinking that if he or she makes a mistake, you are going to rant and rave. Make sure you do anything but that!

As the privacy impulse gains strength, you can see the fruit of years of work. The sense of right and wrong will be strong now; the young person's vision of goals will be apparent from time to time. The lessons you tried to teach one way or another in earlier years will have been absorbed, and occasional moments of delight will come when you hear your child repeating to you with conviction what you once taught. You'll see evidence of fortitude.

You'll also see the fruit of your earlier teaching about standards in music, dress, and behavior. The lessons you gave long ago that ingrained a contempt for drug usage and the rock culture will begin to come to fruition, though it may be a few more years before you can see the full effect. Don't be surprised if you see some self-righteousness in your child, popping up occasionally amid the perennial defense of the peer set. As a teenager observes the mistakes his peers are making and can see for himself how his course of action is wiser, it is natural for him to feel a little smug, and it's impossible for him to avoid expressing it. For most people, experience in the near future will adjust this superior attitude. In the meantime, a little smugness is a small price to pay for preserving personal integrity.

How did Sally and Jim violate the rules of modesty? They did not have private areas apart from each other. From the beginning, they confided their whole hearts to each other. That's tender and romantic, but not wise—nor modest. Privacy is a buffer zone. They deprived themselves of it. And, they dated.

PEER PRESSURE AND CASUAL DATING

America invented casual teenage dating in the same generation that the youth culture came into existence. What previously had been a custom that signaled entrance into maturity, and betokened a person's readiness for matrimony, became something very different.

The normal age for beginning dating is around fourteen for girls and sixteen for boys, though both ages are steadily declining. By age seventeen, almost every teen has dated, and probably close to half have had "steady" relationships like Jim and Sally's. Do boys and girls of these ages really prefer each other's company most of all? No, they don't. In one study, when asked their preferences for associates, the first choice of twelfth-grade boys was boys their own age, and ninth-grade girls chose girls their own age.[1] This is what common sense would predict; after all, the interests of girls and boys are still quite divergent in adolescence and there's a great discrepancy between the respective maturity levels. So why do they inflict themselves on each other and pretend they enjoy it?

The answer, not surprisingly, is status with their peers. Youth culture, that stranglehold on the minds and behavior of youth, has made performance with the other sex the ultimate criterion of status. The favorite topic of conversation among teenage males is sex. If a particular boy doesn't have dating experience, he can't join in the conversation. If a boy has respect for women and does not engage in lewd conversation or pretend to experiences he has not had, he is uncomfortable with these conversations. That will show. Then he is deemed a "nerd" and excluded from the "neat" and "cool" set of kids.

Looking back on my high school career, I guess I was the female equivalent of a nerd. One day in my senior year, the class male intellectual and I both happened to not be present in one class when attendance was taken. We were both in school that day and had been seen by the other kids. Somebody, I am told, wondered out loud whether we were together. Said another kid, "If they are, they're talking philosophy!" That produced, I was told, roars of uncharitable laughter from the class. When I was informed about it, I took it as a compliment. It wasn't intended that way, and most kids, who were more sensitive to peer pressure than I was, would have suffered the intended sting. Fortunately, I think I missed a lot of intended stings in those days because nobody had told me how important the opinion of my peers was supposed to be to me.

I know I was a nerd in the eyes of my first roommate at the University of South Carolina. Her friends would gather in our room on Sunday night and talk about their sexual experiences of the weekend in graphic detail. I would sit stubbornly at my desk, trying to study or write a letter, but internally be aghast and disgusted. I didn't know that "good manners" should have impelled me to leave the room. As far as I was concerned, it was my room and they were the intruders. I never said anything out loud to that southern belle roommate, but she moved out the next semester, and we never had any contact with each other again. I can imagine what she thought of me. But you know, I never gave it a thought at the time. *Because I didn't care. And why should I?* I had so much fun with the kids I did associate with, who were wholesome and interesting, and treated me with personal and intellectual respect, that I never paid any attention to the kids whose values were so radically different from my own. I wasn't rude or condescending toward them, and I'd like to think my higher standards were some kind of Christian witness to them, but that's another subject. My point here is that my social standards and self-esteem were strong enough that I didn't need to try to win popularity with peers who celebrated immorality.

As my children began to cope with the pressures of adolescence, I thought about the baneful influence of peer consciousness, and wondered why my eldest son has so much of it when I had none (and his father had none, either, from what I can tell). My husband was browsing through a book on home schooling one night and came up with a fascinating idea. Dr. Raymond Moore, godfather of the modern home schooling movement, wrote in *Better Late Than Early* that children who are subjected too early to a peer group—such as preschool—tend to be more peer-dependent all the rest of their lives. It's true that when Pearse was four years old he went to a preschool, and then he had about six months in a family day-care situation several days a week. I began to feel guilty thinking I may have contributed to his affliction with peer dependency.

At the time my income was needed, however, so I need not blame myself too much. I have confessed any sin I may have committed and sought the Lord's forgiveness. I have also prayed for the healing of Pearse's memory. But I think my husband is on to something, and I mention it to you now so you can factor this information into any decision you may have to make about putting your young child into unnecessary group situations, especially with non-Christian peers.

I didn't care what other people thought of me, and why should I? That attitude was deeply ingrained in me from the time I can remember. Whether by deliberate stratagem of my parents, accident of circumstance in growing up a Navy junior and changing schools and homes every couple of years, or the sheer grace of the Holy Spirit, I know not. But I can see now that the attitude was a blessing. If I respected people, and if I knew they were worthy of admiring, I would care what they thought of me and would allow myself to be influenced by their ideas. Otherwise, I wasn't swayed by people's opinions. Civility, proper manners, and courtesy toward all was drilled into me, so at that superficial level I was respectful—but internally, in my heart, my attitude to peers per se was not one of subservience.

Now, some Christians could read this and be appalled. "How uncharitable, how insensitive, how closed of you," they might say. But I think my attitude was providential. I was getting Christian education, and I knew I should love my fellow men. But children aren't capable of very much practical love of their fellow men in any case. Hanging up the laundry when my mother asked me to was the extent of practical love of which I was capable—which is true for most children.

In order to love our fellows properly when we're mature, we must first have learned some of the other virtues explained and discussed in this book. But if a child is all wrapped up from the youngest age in what other kids think of him, and if he spends time worrying about what he's wearing and how his hair is cut, those preoccupations drive out the proper preoccupations of childhood: How am I progressing in virtue and goodness? Why was I disobedient yesterday? How can I be more obedient tomorrow? How come I'm crabby so often? These are the thoughts that lead to self-knowledge and improvement of the soul. Being influenced by virtuous role models encourages this growing process. Being swayed by frivolous icons of the peer culture militates against it.

And when adolescence comes, if a childhood has been spent in anxious desire to please peers, then the date is not likely to be an exploration into building a relationship, but an exercise in exploitation.

THE DATING BATTLEFIELD

Most Americans have a "steady" dating relationship by age seventeen. Such frivolity is unheard of in Orthodox Jewry, whose adherents object strenuously to steady dating of any kind, at any age, short of preparation for matrimony. "Ethnic subculture," sociologists say, dismissing the practice as quaint. Maybe. But unwed pregnancy is practically unheard of in Orthodox Jewish communities.

Actually, the restriction of dating to a preparation for matrimony is not an Orthodox Jewish idea at all. Until the post-World War II generation, dating was seen throughout Europe and America as courting behavior intended to result in marriage. Today, that expectation is different. To console the broken hearts along the way, we tell ourselves that dating is just a social custom, not intended to be serious, and so on. But hearts do get broken as emotional attachments get cast aside. This may be the "normal" way to behave, but it leaves emotional scars on those who play this game, particularly with girls. Scar tissue is weak, and many a girl has gotten pregnant with a new boyfriend while her heart was still suffering the pain of the previous one's rejection.

When we tell ourselves dating has nothing to do with marriage, in fact we are lying. It's wise to remind ourselves of the connection, for several reasons. Just for fun, ask all your married friends to think back to how they first met. Didn't most of them start their acquaintance on a date? So then, isn't dating a first step to marriage? All dates certainly don't lead to marriage, but just about all marriages began with dates. Thus, "Don't date anybody you wouldn't be willing to consider marrying" is the most minimal advice for coping with the dating battlefield. When you go on a date with somebody, you are indicating a willingness to explore a relationship. How many marriages between Christians and non-Christians begin with casual dates?

Better yet, don't engage the battle. Because dating *is* a battlefield. Consider what goes on in the dating scene. Immature boys and girls are seeking to have some emotional needs met by each other—the incapable nurturing the incompetent, ego feeding ego. Without preparation, they are thrown together in unstructured situations, entirely on their own, mindful only of the eternal watchword "Be cool." One girl, now in graduate school, explained to her father why she had never dated in high school: "I didn't want to screw, so I didn't date." This girl knew the rules of the battlefield better than her father, because that's the basic rule today. If a date doesn't end up like that, there's nothing to boast about to the guys on Monday. Oh, some schools and some communities may be a little more guarded, but casual high school dating is basically a game to see how much sex a guy can get from a girl for the price of a movie and a pizza.

At its best, its most innocent, the dating routine camoflages real communication. It prevents real growth in the skills of intimacy and interpersonal communication because the nature of dating is to wear a mask, to put on a front. There are roles to play, expectations to meet—stressed-out adolescents want to date someone who will be "everything in the world" to them. Knowing that the expectation is so high, it is only natural for a girl to be the person that her date wants her to be—and that means, to almost intuitively disregard, and disguise, her own thoughts and feelings, to take on his, in order to please him. Isn't that what psychotherapists call co-dependency? That's a sign of emotional problems—not a sign of maturity! If our children have gotten to adolescence without learning that kind of behavior, we should rejoice—and we should certainly avoid putting them into situations where they are going to learn unhealthy ways of relating to others. Parents, be aware that contemporary dating teaches unhealthy relationship patterns.

Parents often may instinctively resist wanting their vulnerable daughter or son to date. And at the beginning, the adolescent may not realize the ground rules either—about sex or deception—and may argue vociferously, "Everybody does it" and "Oh, Mom, you exaggerate so much!" or the real clincher: "Don't you trust me?" So the parent fears being overprotective, fears alienating the child, and gives consent. Once the child is caught up in the dating scene, however, his ego is invested in it, and even though he may not like it, he now fears he will be a "supernerd" if he leaves it. So he makes sure his parents don't find out what the ground rules are. This is whence come the figures that, while 80 percent of parents believe their children are telling them the truth about their sexual conduct, only 30 percent of children really are.

In high school, then, there should be *no* one-on-one dating. Period. If I sound radical, maybe I am. But, slogans like "Everyone does it" and "It's the American way" don't sway me. I see no need to be conformed to this world, but instead prefer to try to prove what is the good, acceptable, and perfect will of God (See Rom. 12:2). If your children are still small, consider this standard. If your children are already in the thick of adolescence, this may not be for you. It is unrealistic to impose such a high standard on a teenager who has not been brought up to it. And if you and your spouse do not agree on the standard, forget it and go with some compromise that both of you do agree on and can enforce without a hint of division between you.

In saying that no dating should be allowed, I am not advocating that boys and girls never see each other. On the contrary, I realize how important it is for young adults to develop appropriate social skills with the other sex. But I emphasize the word "appropriate." Figuring out fifteen ways to get a girl flat on her back within three hours is not an appropriate social skill.

Appropriate social skills are things like having long, long, open-ended conversations with people in order to learn about them. Or like helping other kids work together, play together, think together, worship together, and serve humanity together. Organizing a group of friends to do Christmas caroling. Helping at a soup kitchen, mission, or an old age home. Working on a political campaign. Joining walk-a-thons for worthy causes. Using their time and skills to fix cars, help paint somebody's living room, fix a little brother's bike, and so on.

In the years of senior high school, there are lots of things boys and girls can do together, and lots of reasons why they should associate with each other in structured environments. They need to develop the art of conversation, learn how to read each other's moods and signals, learn what the other gender acts like, and discover a zillion other things that make up successful social skills. These skills are needed so that they can be whole human beings, capable of empathizing with their fellow human beings, and of helping their neighbor. They need to know many members of the opposite gender, and have lots of interaction with them, so they can begin to settle in their own mind what kind of traits they want their eventual spouse to have.

The skills that can be learned in a couple of years of non-dating fun in large groups can be picked up later only with more difficulty—or they may get missed altogether. And don't feel you're depriving your kid of something important if he or she doesn't date—think of it as alternative growth.

The dating may come once they leave home anyway. But at least, if they agreed to avoid the dating scene in high school, they can enter into new relationships in college with more maturity and sense of purpose than if they had had aimless dating experiences for years thinking they were having "fun." While the trend of leaving home to go live on campus seems to be in decline, most kids who do move onto campus are going to date.

That brings up another area where even non-dating kids need help from parents. Remember Rosie? Nobody is more vulnerable than a girl who goes to a college campus away from home without previous experience of any kind with boys. She didn't know the informal rules of social interaction, because she had been too sheltered from it before going to school, and now she was trying to be responsible in an environment she was not prepared to cope with. The analogy that comes to mind is the people who raise wild animal cubs as pets, then have to let them go into the wilderness unprepared to survive.

If you want your kids not to date, and yet be able to cope successfully with a secular environment, they have to want the same thing too. Rigidly forbidding dating in high school can make a kid who is determined to rebel the minute he or she gets away from home do so. Not a good prognosis. Even a kid who can see the dangers and the harm in dating, and agrees not to date because he or she genuinely believes it is the best choice for high school, needs some preparation for the time that she will begin seeing other people one-on-one, whether it's age 20 or age 30. The same principles still apply.

KNOW THYSELF . . . AND EACH OTHER

Rosie, who was just beginning to date as a junior in college, didn't know the first thing about the difference between boys and girls in sexual stimulation. Neither, unfortunately, do most girls at any age. How can this be? Don't their mothers know? Maybe not. Typical is the woman who sits with her husband in front of the fire, tired on a Saturday night, resting her head on his shoulder, enjoying his arm around her, billing and cooing softly—and then she's surprised when the husband wants to make love! To the woman, the billing and cooing were satisfying in and of themselves. To the man, they were nice, but they stimulated a desire and an impulse for more. Some women get offended at this and decide their husbands are "sex maniacs" or something similarly ridiculous. It's absurd to expect men to respond like women.

The shoe fits the other foot, too. The husband who had been billing and cooing may expect his wife to be just as eager as he is to continue the action when they leave the fireplace and get to the bedroom. He might be angry, feel rejected, and decide his wife is "frigid" when he finds she has sleep on her mind. That would be equally ridiculous. They're just mis-reading each other's signals, that's all, just as Rosie was misreading Jose's signals in a different context.

It may take married couples years to realize that they love each other the same but react differently to stimuli. And if it takes them years, how can they expect their just-out-of-childhood kids to be able to know it, and cope with all the multitudinous levels of subtle interaction it implies in the dating scene? This is another reason why a no-dating policy makes sense. As children approach marriageable age, however, this is informa-tion they need to know.

I don't mean Mom should take her daughter aside and say, "Watch out for men. All they're interested in is one thing. Don't believe anything they say. They're just waiting to attack you." If the girl believes that advice, she will approach the opposite sex with something amounting to terror. If she doesn't believe it, she will, at best, discount any further advice her mother may offer on the subject.

God made females with an instinct to establish a relationship with another person's mind and heart. In anthropological terms, this is so their children will have a father. Males, on the other hand, are aggressive and not innately interested in relationships; they seek sexual satisfaction.

Realizing that basic difference, explain simply that girls want to know and enjoy the personality of the fellow before they want to be touched at all, and then they consider simple contact awkward (a little squeeze on the hand, resting a head on the shoulder) to be adequate expression of affection. A kiss on the first date is not something a girl would ordinarily want. If she thinks it's expected of her, of course, she may delude herself into thinking she likes it. A girl can understand that a little squeeze on the hand may be taken by the boy as an invitation to squeeze somewhere else, some place she does not want to be touched at all.

Understanding the tyranny of the flesh can help teens see the wisdom of no dating. Boys can understand the demands that their bodies make on them. The adolescent male body is so demanding that even if a girl says, "No, I don't want you to do that," the boy can't believe what he's hearing. His body certainly isn't saying that to him! He needs to have a conscience that shouts louder than his body. Girls can realize that they are not stimulated physically until their affection has been won, but that boys are stimulated by sight or touch, without affection needing to be present. Thus, early in the relationship, while the girl is just (in her opinion) getting to know the fellow and has dressed up pretty so he'll like her, he may take the fact that she dressed up special to mean she's crazy about him and ready to give him whatever he asks for. And since the next date begins where the last one left off, if she let him kiss her on the last date, he'll expect to begin this date with a kiss and go from there. Like the unwary frog placed in warm water that is gradually heated to boiling, his passions will increase slowly and steadily, and he may not realize what's happening to him until it's irreversible.

This is not to say that boys are especially depraved, but merely to describe the nature of the male sexual response. Boys can, of course, with discipline, control their physical urges and direct the energy into building healthy relationships with women. But it does take time and will. Structuring the circumstances in which a boy comes into contact with girls so he learns by degrees how he is going to react to what contact—and so he can then build his self-control by degrees—makes eminent good sense. And it's one more reason why unstructured casual dating in the early teenage years is such an invitation to mishap.

Adolescents are people who are on their way to being adults. Half the time they're still kids, but hopefully they are moving toward adulthood in body, in status, in ability to function productively in society. And in spirituality. It seems harder and harder for each generation to attain maturity at the ages their predecessors did. That's true with respect to career preparation, for sure; but it is even more so with spiritual matters. The enormous flood of input, both idea and sensate stimulation, from endless radio, television, movies, newspapers, magazines, and so on, produces a mind that races from one idea to another, rarely stopping to examine one thought.

Spiritual growth comes with stillness and quiet, and focusing the mind on God. A person has to know himself (or herself), know how to examine his conscience, know how to repent, learn how to hear the Lord—all of which is a combination of skill and grace that is hard even for adults. But for teenagers, it is next to impossible. Only the most unusual will have prioritized holiness while still in the teen years—and I'm not completely sure that it's good to skip over the other stages of adolescent development that have to be skipped to get to sanctification in youth, lest the foundation built be flawed.

Immaturity is inevitable for teenagers. It's part of the definition. That means emotional extremes, unpredictability, carelessness, mistakes, poor judgment, rebellious attitudes, thrill-seeking, and more are just part of the territory: all to be expected. Therefore, a wise and loving parent will want life to be as simple as possible, as focused as possible on the real imperatives of growth in wisdom and knowledge. Including American-style dating into the mix adds many levels of complications—complications which could be avoided, and which should be avoided.

And the mix gets so complicated, and so out of control, that sexual purity is likely to be only one casualty.

So why allow your teenagers to date? Dating does not have to be inevitable. If you don't want your children dating, make up your mind early, stick to it, and give a lot of thought to an effective marketing strategy. If your children know from the time they're ten that they won't be allowed to go out alone for an evening with a member of the opposite gender until they achieve a level of maturity that Dad and Mom agree is sufficient, and for sure not until after high school—then they know it. The fact that they won't date is as normal as the fact that they're expected to graduate high school. On the other hand, if you wait until your daughter is fifteen, and then tell her she won't be allowed to date for another two years, you will probably have a problem on your hands.

GUIDELINES FOR CHRISTIAN RELATIONSHIPS:VIRTUES

If young Christians spend their entire lives within a Christian subculture—Christian elementary and high school, Christian college, employment with a Christian organization, and marriage to a Christian—it is theoretically possible to avoid the secular dating scene altogether. But few Christians are so sheltered, and that's probably just as well. If one is not prepared to cope with the world, one is at its mercy when the protections are gone. Besides, we aren't called upon to cower in our caves, hiding our lights under bushels. We are commanded to be Christ's witnesses unto the ends of the earth. And that doesn't mean wait until you're safely married and then be a witness. It means here and now in whatever circumstances you are in.

The college women who go into high schools as guest lecturers in an abstinence-based sex ed program report that they are always gratified by the impression they make on the high schoolers—"Wow! You're in college, and you're a virgin!" Because the high schoolers know the social mores so well, their awe over an attractive girl's proclamation of chastity is not only sincere, but very significant. There's a witness worth its weight in gold.

Many Christian young adults do not have the privilege of living their lives in the shelter of a Christian community. They will be working in the world, and they will be finding social life in the world. They want to keep pure—but they need lots of help. Parents don't arrange marriages any more. Maiden aunt chaperones are scarce as hen's teeth. Few people go from home to marriage any more. Friends from college and the workplace are the main social circle for years. When I was a young career woman, I occasionally babysat for my boss's children. One of those is today a dynamic young career woman. Once every couple years, she comes to stay at our house with our children, so Bill and I can get an overnight away together (*bless you, Diana!*). From her I realize that the young adult universe is very age-ist. Her parents live in the area, so she has dinner with them once every couple of weeks. But most of her friends have come to Washington on their own, and don't know anyone who isn't their own age. Even if they're churchgoers, they stick with the people their own age. There's just little opportunity to interact.

Washington may be a little worse than most places in this regard, but I'll wager that all big cities are the same, and more and more small cities too. Parents need to be practical about preparing their children for leaving the nest. How do you teach your daughter to be wise as a serpent without losing her gentleness?

First, facts. She needs to know what the male animal is like. Understanding the differences in sexual response inherent in males and females is basic knowledge. Being in possession of a few virtues is also basic knowledge, and one of the most important is sincerity.

Second, sincerity. This means letting your yes mean yes and your no mean no. It means, if you don't like a guy, you don't go out with him—not to please a friend, not to avoid boredom, not because you want to see the play he has tickets for. Let your *no* mean *no.* So many dates occur because a girl doesn't want to be alone on a Saturday night! So she wastes God's precious gift of time to spend with somebody she knows is a total loser, for a frivolous reason. Sincerity would prevent that waste of time. Sincerity also means that if a girl says she doesn't go to certain places, then she doesn't go. Not on the first date and not on the fifth, either.

It means thinking about what you want to do before the situation is out of control. If a girl wants a ground rule that she doesn't kiss after a date, she shouldn't wait until the fellow has his arm around her to tell him that. She needs to work it into the conversation early on, perhaps humorously, before she even entertains the idea of spending an evening with him. When he says: "Are you serious?" she can say, seriously now, "yes." He may stop there, but if he's interested in her as a person, chances are he'll now be more intrigued.

Sincerity also means being able to communicate clearly, without ambiguity. A girl shouldn't say, "I want to be home early." Early to him may be 2 *a.m.* She ought to say, "I want to be home by 11:30." She also needs to know how to spot ambiguity in what somebody else says. "We'll go home after the movie" does not mean "I will take you directly back to your apartment after the movie, without stopping at a restaurant or anywhere else."

A young person would also do well to develop what the Germans call the "third ear"—learning to listen not only with the ear, but also with the mind. What are the words he just said? And what did she really say? They're not always the same thing. Rosie didn't have a "third ear" at all; she thought Jose was offering her some cold tablets.

Sincerity includes the honesty to recognize and admit your own weaknesses. A great tendency of our age is to intellectualize things and fail to recognize the physical and emotional side of one's own nature. It's a dangerous shortcoming.

Third, flexibility. This is another desirable virtue. A rigid person who cannot adapt to different circumstances can give only a very limited witness. This doesn't mean a young person should be easily led. It's possible to adapt one's behavior to the circumstances around you without abandoning your own personal principles of behavior. If a girl accepts an invitation to an Oktoberfest and she didn't know what an Oktoberfest was beforehand, she shouldn't be so appalled at the sight of all the beer that she starts lecturing everybody in sight about why drinking is evil. Rather, she needs to be flexible enough to ask for a soft drink but enjoy the company of the other merrymakers. Later on, she can have a conversation and give her witness about alcohol. But if she tries to do it in the Oktoberfest hall, she'll just give Christians a bad name as killjoys. This is the kind of flexibility our young adults should have.

Young adults need to know how to be interested in the other person but aware of their needs simultaneously. That way, they can be building the foundation for friendships that may last long after the dating is over. For example, teach your son to notice when he's talking too much or when the other person is. Encourage him to trust his instincts when they indicate something doesn't "seem right." If something doesn't seem right, chances are it's wrong. He should never be so full of himself that he fails to be sensitive to his environment. Women, too, need the same awareness.

Fourth, goal-oriented. Young people should keep in mind at all times what their goal is in socializing with each other: it's to become better acquainted with a person because they want to get to know a lot of different people, and in the process getting to know themselves better. A date should be an exercise in *phileo* love, not in *eros*. *Phileo* is the kind of love learned as one spreads one's wings and leaves the *agape*-love nest of home. *Eros* may come naturally, but it must be restrained.

A good verse to use as a guide is 1 Corinthians 8:12: "When you thus sin against the brethren, and wound their weak conscience, you sin against Christ." Even if you don't do something contrary to your conscience, if you make somebody else do something contrary to his or hers, you have committed a sin. If one is beginning to look for a lifetime partner, one is capable of understanding that our salvation is not easily separable from our choice of spouse. One better be mature enough to understand that love is not a feeling but a decision to want what is best for the other person.

Fifth, time-conscious. Unless a young person is serious about one particular individual and has determined that that person is worth being serious about—that is, would make a good partner for life—he or she simply ought not to spend vast amounts of time alone with that one person. As Sally and Jim discovered, that's not the way to deepen a new relationship. Besides, when groups get together, it's more fun. So urge your grown children to at least double date until they are indeed preparing for marriage.

A young person should understand the wisdom of limiting the amount of time she spends paying particular attention to any one particular person. If she sees only one person, several times a week, and then in addition she talks on the phone with that guy another five or more hours a week, they are spending too much time together for the relationship to remain casual. Things take on a momentum of their own with such time invested in them.

And when they begin to focus attention on one particular person, it's time for activities that will increase knowledge of that person. Try balancing each other's checkbooks if you want a real eye-opening initiation into how somebody else's mind works! Take a class together at the local adult ed extension program of the public school system. Repair a car together. Write a letter a week to each other, explaining your feelings about some area you're not comfortable talking about. Make a list of things each of you has never done, and plan how to do them. When you find a difference of opinion about something, both should do a separate Scripture search on that topic to see if they can find God's opinion on it. An exercise like that reveals a great deal about how submitted a person's heart is to the Lord. Whatever you do—do not just "hang out." Plan time—it's too precious to waste. The more time together is planned, the more fun everybody has, because the shared activity will provide a focus for everyone's personality. Besides, they'll also have a sense of objective accomplishment at the end of the activity, and that's important. One of my strongest high school friendships originated in painting an office together on a weekend, and deepened through cleaning a basement—with comic relief provided by a broken pipe on a fuel tank so that we all were sloshing around ankle-deep in kerosene.

If they run out of organized projects they can get involved in, help them organize some. The adult singles group at the Bethel Full Gospel Church in Rochester, New York, organized a pro-family political coalition as a singles activity. They arranged for hookup to the satellite transmission of National Empowerment Television, and now sponsor monthly meetings to be catalysts for pro-family political action in their area. Now there's a meaningful contribution, as well as fulfilling interaction among those involved.

If singles make their plans as a group, it's easy to gather at one person's place to watch a thought-provoking video, perhaps a movie like *The Mission* or *Man for All Seasons,* with discussion and refreshments afterward. They can organize gourmet parties, where each couple has to cook a different international dish, and plan surprises for each other's birthdays.

Focused activity with a specific purpose is the easiest, least risky way for singles to expand their circle of acquaintances and to deepen particular relationships. Remember, it's only in an atmosphere focused on other people and free from the stimulation of sexual urges can personalities really shine.

DEFENSIVE DATING

Working women in urban areas have a particularly unenviable dilemma when it comes to social life. When I first graduated from college and went to work in Washington, D.C., there was a small circle of conservatives with whom I worked. At that time, it was distinctly unfashionable to be a conservative in Washington, but at least among conservative youth the odds were pretty good of finding "decent" fellows with whom to socialize.

By the late 1980s, conservatism had become fashionable (President Reagan had been in office eight years), and the supply of available, eligible males was a lot larger than it had been in my single days. But my single friends would confide in me their horror stories about trying to have a social life. Even the supposed conservatives were not to be trusted in matters of morals. "They expect you to go to bed on the first date, or at least the second. If you're not willing to do that, they forget you," one attractive girl who worked at the White House complained to me one time. Rather than endure constant challenges to their virtue, these girls contented themselves with sparse social lives. That gave them more time and energy to invest in their jobs and helped them get promoted and acquire high salaries and political power of their own. That, in turn, made them seem intimidating to anybody who hadn't known them back when they were "nobody," which meant there were now obstacles in the path of men trying to socialize with them.

It's a vicious cycle, but it's not unique to Washington. It goes on in every profession, every career, in every city in the country. Traditionally-minded girls find themselves becoming high-powered career women because they won't compromise their standards in their social lives. Of course, there are also high-powered career women who are quite willing to compromise values in their social lives, and their ready availability makes it possible for the men to forget the girls who won't go to bed on the second date.

What's a girl to do? Well, since this book is directed at parents, let me rephrase the question: What's a parent to do? Understand what a jungle your daughter is walking into when she gets a job. Make sure she knows you trust her. If she's working close enough to home, make Fridays or Sundays family night, and have a big dinner with everybody there. Otherwise, on the Sunday night telephone calls, ask her about her social life. Just having your shoulder to cry on, and having the benefit of your understanding will help her. Commiserate with her, but not so as to encourage self-pity. Reassure her that there are lots of good fish in the sea. Pray that she will find the one who is somewhere waiting for her. For goodness' sake, don't ask why she hasn't gotten married yet. If she thinks you're pressuring her to get married, and she hasn't yet found anybody with whom she wants to spend her life, you're only going to add to her miseries.

Realize that her social life is one of defensive strategies and tactics. She knows that fornication doesn't just "happen"—except in the case of rape. It is planned for, scheduled, and arranged by at least one of the parties. Usually, the girl just goes along without realizing the trap being laid for her. But your daughter has learned to be wary and is constantly alert. She considers every invitation critically, looking for the loopholes in the plans. She asks a lot of questions: who else will be there, when will we leave, where is it, what will we do next, and so on. If the answers don't add up, she asks herself, *Why am I going out with this character I don't really like and can't trust? Can't I afford to buy myself a movie ticket?*

The key to defensive dating is structure, structure, structure! A young woman shouldn't live alone (chances are she can't afford to anyhow). Under no circumstances or any pretext should she ever go to a man's apartment, even to set off on a date. She should insist that he come to her apartment and call her from the lobby (if she has one). If he comes to the apartment door, unless her roommates are obviously in the living room, she does not invite him in. He can stand in the hallway while she gets her hat and coat. If this sounds extreme, it's because either the man's or the woman's dwelling is the most likely location for a date rape to occur. According to the Justice Department's Bureau of Justice Statistics, 25 percent of the violent crimes against women are committed by men they have dated.[2] The first time a good, virtuous Christian woman I knew was date-raped, I was astonished. She was a sensible, prudent woman—she wouldn't have been in his apartment if she hadn't felt she knew him well enough to trust him. Yet it happened. She, commendably, was brave enough to press charges against him—but the emotional cost of the whole experience was devastating to her.

Obviously, a young woman shouldn't go alone with a fellow on over-night jaunts. Advise your daughter to insist that other couples be included and see to it that a girlfriend she trusts is included. She should also make sure somebody knows where she'll be and when she's due back, and the license plate of the car she's going in.

Teach your daughter how to structure situations for her own protection, and how to get out of a tight situation. If the car won't start as she comes out of the movie at midnight, she can pull out her own AAA card so help can be procured or produce her own money for a cab. If her date suggests going out dancing after the planned activity, she can remind him that she promised to pick up her roommate when her shift ends, and she was counting on him to do that. In other words, she should have alternative plans ready in her mind if he suggests something unacceptable.

Young women also need to be keenly aware that they may be sending unintentional signals. Maternal concern for a date's difficulties with job or friends may be misread as a deep personal involvement. Urge your daughter to be careful: she'll have ample objects for her maternal con-cerns after she becomes a mother. On a date, she's nobody's mother, and she wants to keep it that way. Besides, if her date needs spiritual counsel-ing he should be getting it from another man. "Missionary dating"—the idea of dating an unconverted fellow in order to lead him to the Lord—produces few sincere converts and more than its share of unequally yoked, ill-advised marriages.

Awkward moments are almost unavoidable, but especially if they are between people who don't know each other well. When the end of the evening is in sight, the urge to romance may be strong. Engaging in deep philosophical conversations about right and wrong is not going to get your daughter out of the car and into her apartment expeditiously. Com-mon lines need quick answers. Some suggestions:

The guilt trip: "You don't know how to have any fun."
"Yes, I do; I've had a delightful evening. Let's leave it that way, shall we?"

Nature-as-omnipotent I: "You don't understand. Guys have to have sex."
"Nonsense. Nobody ever died of celibacy before, and you won't be the first."

Nature-as-omnipotent II: "It's only natural."
"So is death, but I don't want to practice that either."

True love excuses passion: "I love you so much that I want to give you something more."
"OK, so give me your self-control, and let me keep what I cherish, control over my own body."

Guilt trip II: "Don't you love me?"
"Well, frankly, if you're that kind of person, not at all."

Peer pressure: "Everybody does it, you know."
"I'm not everybody."

Taunting: "I'll bet you're just scared."
"Of going to hell, yes. Of venereal disease, yes. Of illegitimate pregnancy, you bet."

Coaxing: "But I'll take care of you."
"Thanks, but I can take care of myself for now."

Pleading: "I won't hurt you."
"My soul is more important than my body, and that you would hurt seriously."

The ultimate "come on," of course, is the threat of physical violence. A girl needs to know from childhood that it is no sin to die to protect one's virtue; it is, indeed, a form of martyrdom. That doesn't make it any the less tragic, of course, but it is a morally defensible choice for a woman to make. The fact of having thought it through in advance gives a woman moral certainty in responding strongly should the issue ever come to this. On the other hand, being raped doesn't mean life is no longer worth living. Obviously, this is an area in which there are no easy answers. But the strategies and tactics in this chapter should help to reduce the likelihood that a date would result in such an attack.

The long and short of the dating ritual among adults is this: There is no substitute for being a good judge of character. And how is the skill of judging character acquired? By accepting wisdom from a teacher, a parent, an older person in some capacity. By acquiring experience. Or, to sound like a personnel manager, through a lot of multi-faceted interaction with many people of diverse backgrounds. Just like what church youth groups ought to be doing: lots of different projects, with lots of different people, in a safe environment. Just what Christians on campus ought to be doing. Just what successful large families usually do without realizing it.

If one is well-formed in virtue, and understands virtue, one will know whether or not it is present in another. Objectivity, remember, is a virtue in itself.

Chapter 13

THE TALK: SOME QUESTIONS AND ANSWERS

W hen I was doing research for this book, I prepared a questionnaire that I circulated informally among as many different people as I could get to take it. This was by no means a scientific survey, but I was struck by one thing that kept emerging: the people whose parents had never spoken to them about sex were the ones most likely to engage in fornication and promiscuity. It was too obvious a pattern to be ignored.

It is the thesis of this entire book that whether or not there is a single event known as "the talk" is of secondary importance in the formation of values and virtues that motivate and empower a young person to practice chastity. The values of fidelity, chastity, and self-control can be taught without ever breathing a word about sex; this is true. The virtues of fortitude, modesty, and prudence can be developed without mentioning the fact that there are two sexes; this is true. Remote, but true—not likely, but possible.

Nonetheless, if your child is ten years old and there has been no communication between the two of you about reproduction, sexuality, or male-female differences, there is no time to waste. Why? Because if he hasn't heard it from you, he will certainly have heard it from somebody else. And if he hasn't heard your values, he has accepted somebody else's attitudes and values and may have to be reeducated. It's that simple—unless you live in the country and your child plays with nobody but siblings (and they're all the same sex) and you have no farm animals that reproduce and he does not go to school with ordinary children and you haven't

197

got a television set and you don't receive a newspaper or any magazines. And if you're that isolated, you're not reading this book anyway. The point is, don't wait to inform your child, or somebody else will do it for you. Don't trust that innocence can survive past ten years in our decadent and sex-saturated society.

To help you discuss sexual issues with your child, I address some of parents' most common questions in a question-and-answer format for the rest of this chapter.

THE TALK

1. How can I be an approachable parent?

Have you talked with your spouse about your desire to be the primary sex educators of your child? Was the conversation comfortable? If it was, you can probably stop worrying, because you're probably relaxed and self-confident enough with the subject not to be nervous around your child. If that conversation was tense, you need to relax.

Before you'll relax, however, a couple of things have to happen: you must feel confident of your information, and you must feel comfortable with the subject. The former is easier to achieve than the latter. Read some adult-level books that fill in all the information gaps you may have—marriage manuals, biology textbooks, and so on. Read up on the subject to *more* than your heart's content. Immerse yourself in the subject for a couple of weeks. The idea is to get yourself surfeited with the topic to the point that it isn't strange or mysterious to you. In my case, this kind of total immersion can best occur if I devour the information by myself and don't discuss it with anybody while I'm still reading. Talking about it seems to diminish the effect for me.

As you are absorbing information, be checking your values. If it makes you uncomfortable to read about the subject, ask yourself why. You know this is part of God's creation, and that He made it for His wonderful purposes. Why are you uncomfortable with His creation? You have already shared in it by marrying and, most likely, begetting a child. What is it that makes you uncomfortable? Keep asking yourself that question. Ask the Holy Spirit to show you the source of your discomfort and to help you to deal with it now in a way that will give Him glory.

You will have to probe your own mind for things you may have heard from your parents or experiences that weren't pleasant, either in the distant or the recent past. It may be a difficult probing. You may uncover something painful that you have buried under your psychological rug for years. If it's too difficult, talk to your spouse. Perhaps he or she can help you to talk through the barrier. If you can't resolve it, perhaps you and your spouse will decide that it is best for the other spouse to be the primary educator on this subject.

If you find something that's bigger than you, you may need to consult with your pastor or other counselor. The fear of finding something big should not dissuade you from the effort, however. Usually what you find are small things—overreactions from your own parent, perhaps, when you were first starting to mature. But if you do find something big, it's a blessing to bring it to your consciousness and deal with it now. If it isn't good for you and it stays buried under your rug, it's not going to go away. It will keep growing unnoticed until one day you trip over it and it knocks you down. Better to dig out the garbage under the rug while you are strong and best able to deal with it.

What sort of things under the rug am I talking about? It could be as simple as an unexamined, and unhealed relationship—perhaps every time the subject of sex comes up, inside the well of your mind, you have the image of a stern, judgmental, even cruel teacher, or preacher, or relative, scolding you, belittling you. God wants you to forgive, and to outgrow that burden—and maybe thinking through sexual morality may be the tool He wants to use to accomplish that healing.

Lurking under the rug could be smugness with a life lived according to a certain pattern, a pattern that you don't want to examine. It could be a behavior that you know is inconsistent with your belief—but one that you are not willing to let go of, and so you avoid thinking about it. It could, of course, be a psychological trauma, such as molestation, that might have occurred to you in your childhood, or later. It could be unresolved guilt about your lifestyle before you gave your life to the Lord.

2. I don't really know much. Won't it make me seem dumb in front of my kids if I say "I don't know"?

No, it won't, because you won't leave the matter there. Whatever the question is, you'll find an answer. Then, at an appropriate moment, you will bring up the subject again. "Oh, Mary, remember last week we were wondering how twins get made? I found out the answer for you."

When parents first say, "I don't know," children usually assume that means the end of the subject. If *you* bring up the subject again, they'll be really impressed, and they'll know that your "I don't know" was genuine. This will indicate the sincerity of your desire to answer their questions and to have open channels of communication on the subject. That's why if you do leave a questioned unanswered, you must be very sure that you get the answer and deliver it later. Write yourself a note if you have to, but don't let your child think you're trying to avoid the question.

3. I'm so embarrassed by sex, I just know that my discomfort will show when I try to talk with my child. I'm not very good at pretending. What should I do?

If you've done everything I suggested in question 1, and you're still embarrassed, just accept it. We'll assume your spouse is even more embarrassed or he or she would be doing the job for you. Where do we go from here?

The younger your child is, the easier it will be, because he won't read anything into your embarrassment. Just tell him straight out: "I want to talk to you about something very special and very holy. I've never talked about it before to anybody, so if I seem a little nervous, that's why. Grandma and Grandpa never had a conversation like this with me, so this is the first time I've talked about it with anybody." And then plunge right into it and get the focus of attention off you and onto the topic. The next words out of your mouth should be, "Do you know how a baby gets made?"

If your child is close to puberty, she's going to be embarrassed herself about the subject. She's probably been agonizing in private over the physical and emotional changes she's noted in herself, and wherever she is right now, she may be wondering, *Where were you when I needed you?* You might start out by saying, "Sally, I can tell that your body is well on the way to womanhood by now. I probably should have talked to you sooner, but you know the motto, 'Better late than never.' Before you grow up any more, I wanted to make sure you understood why God made your body the way He did," Then proceed candidly. Again, get the focus on the information you are imparting, in this case, emphasize God's plan for sexuality. Even if Sally is a senior in high school and you can reasonably expect that she studied human reproduction in tenth grade, she'll be interested in hearing the biological information again. She may not show it, mind you.

In fact, Sally may frown and say, "Mom, I've known all that for years." In which case you say, "Well, good, I wanted to make sure you knew it somehow. I want to make sure you have accurate information. Your future happiness will depend in part on how you use the information, you know. And more than anything else in the world, I want you to be happy. I just wanted you to know that your Dad and I have lived through twenty years of marriage, and we've learned a few things. If any of our knowledge can help you, we want you to ask."

4. My children are six and seven. They seem so innocent. I don't think they need to be burdened with all this yet.

What is "all this?" Is knowing that God made every part of their body for a special purpose a burden? It shouldn't be. Is knowing that some day they will probably get married a burden? It shouldn't be, and they should already be absorbing some basic principles. For example, they can know that marriage is forever, one of its major purposes is to take care of the children God causes to be born, and that a lot of self-sacrifice is involved in marriage. Children need to learn these truths from the very first time they start thinking about marriage and the differences between mothers and fathers. They start noticing those differences by age four, whether they tell you about it or not.

You are not "bothering" them to tell them they are temples of the Holy Spirit, created by God for a special purpose. In fact, if they get to be fifteen or sixteen and don't know that yet, they will have a real burden in trying to understand why they are the way they are.

Let them know God's plan of creation as soon as they begin to look for it. And let their questions come naturally as their minds absorb the information and need more.

5. What kind of language should I use in talking with my child about sexuality?

Use correct, clinical language. Begin when he learns the parts of his body as a tiny child. Nothing is gained by teaching "private" language for body parts or functions; it only causes embarrassment to the child sometime sooner or later.

6. I know my child is hearing things on the streets, but he hasn't approached me. I don't know how to bring up the subject, but I want to. How do I handle that?

Remind yourself that the child who doesn't ask questions is more a concern than the one who does. The exception to this might be the child who is younger or youngest and who will have heard it already from older siblings. The noninquisitive child may be harboring secret anxieties. Only and oldest children, for example, are anxious to please their parents, and other kids might have told them that moms and dads get mad if they get asked certain questions.

Create a situation involving both you and the child in which the subject at hand is reproduction. You might make it a point to watch a wildlife program on TV that includes reproduction. Or take the child with you to pay a short social call on a new mother. Driving there and back alone with your child, start a conversation about where babies come from. Conversations like this can be helpful in telling you what your child already knows. You have to know what your pupil already understands, if you're going to be an effective teacher.

If you know somebody whose cat has kittens, ask if you can come to see them. I've never known a child who didn't think kittens were adorable, and the sight of nursing kittens gives a tranquillity and reassurance to the subject of reproduction in a child's mind. I was always grateful to the neighbors who convinced my mother that we should be allowed to see kittens being born. One fine day, I went down to their house when labor began. It was reassuring to watch, because cat labor is relatively simple, and my previous impressions had come from watching *Gone with the Wind,* which was more dramatic, and hence more frightening.

7. My mother was visiting us and heard me answering my four-year-old's questions in the bathtub about the different parts of the body and what they do. I was giving simple but frank answers. My mom hit the roof. She says I never knew anything until I was a teenager, and why should I do anything different with my daughter? What do I say?

The first thing you need to say is, "Mom, I love the way you raised me," or something similarly positive about your upbringing. Once you've reassured her that you're not subliminally critical of *her,* go on to explain,

"But Mom, the world I grew up in was so much simpler. My husband and I have talked about how dangerous it is today, and we've decided that we should answer all our child's questions as they occur. We think this is the best way to protect her against getting wrong ideas. If this were a perfect world, and everybody in it were perfect, well, then, perfect innocence would be appropriate. But she's going to be hearing wrong information sooner or later, no matter how we try to shelter her for a little while. And we believe that giving correct information and values ahead of time is the best way to counteract wrong information and values."

If the subject isn't laid to rest that easily, point out that children whose parents talk to them are *less* preoccupied with sexuality than children whose parents stay mum on the subject. You can both agree that you want a child in whom innocence reigns as much as is humanly possible. This is the way you believe you can achieve that goal, and since you're the parents, you had to make the decision, and this is the one you've made. As a last resort you say, "If you're not sure we're right, Mom, well, pray for us. We're only doing the best we can."

8. I'm divorced, but my ex-husband sees the children regularly. My ten-year-old son seems to get along much better with his father right now than with me. I'm afraid that if I try to talk to my son, he'll reject it. Should I go ahead anyhow?

Assuming that your husband is a Christian and that you pretty much have the same values—chastity, self-control, and so forth, and that he would exhort your son to abstinence—there's something to be said for asking your husband to bring up the subject, since he has the stronger relationship right now. On the other hand, if you don't know what your husband's values are, I'd say think not twice, but ten times, about asking your husband to bring up the subject. You might try leaving a book lying around the house, such as Jamie Buckingham's *Let's Talk About Life,* and hope your son picks it up. When he does, say something that indicates you don't mind his reading it and that you're willing to pursue the subject further. (If you're really shy, slip a note inside the book, so he'll find it as he's reading). Use a light touch, but be straightforward. Explain that your love for him is the reason you want him to have the facts, both about the body and about the moral consequences of behavioral decisions.

TOO LITTLE, TOO LATE, OR TOO MUCH, TOO SOON?

9. What are the rules of safety and self-protection that a first-grader should be taught, and how can I teach the rules without frightening my little boy?

You can avoid frightening the child by keeping it all on an impersonal level. "Some people kidnap children" is negative enough without being terrifying. Don't say, "You know Martha Smith? Well, one day she was walking home from school alone. . . ." That brings fear too close and too immediate. Kidnappings have occurred in fairy stories, and after some tribulations, things turn out all right. When I was young and heard the parental warnings against strangers, the example that brought it home to me was the Lindbergh baby kidnapping, which had occurred decades before I was born. My parents had a book about that, from which I learned the baby was later found dead. That was frightening enough for me. It wasn't until years later that I learned there were any sexual connotations to being wary of strangers, and thus I had the benefit of genuinely motivated caution without the planting of seeds of sexual fear.

Some of the rules for self-protection are simple: don't talk to strangers; don't go anywhere alone; don't be out after the street lights come on; avoid lonely places like wooded areas unless you're with a trusted adult or several friends (who are of a certain, responsible age). These rules are necessary, but not sufficient. The typical child molester, unfortunately, is not the seedy-looking character who lurks in the woods. It is more likely to be a friend of the family or a person in a position of trust. This makes the job of teaching self-protection more difficult.

You want to be able to say freely and fairly, "If Mom says you must obey So-and-So, then you must, and that's the end of it." But child molesters look for the obedient children and gain their trust. They compel children with bribes and threats—frequently threats that unless the child complies, the parents will suffer dire consequences. How can a parent possibly provide against this kind of viciousness?

From the beginning, as you are teaching the parts of the anatomy, include self-protection. "We have another name for the vagina and the anus together. We sometimes call them the private parts. Do you know what that means? It means that nobody ever touches these parts except you, a doctor, or Mommy and Daddy when they're giving you a bath. But absolutely nobody else at all. You mustn't ever let anybody else touch you in your private places. If somebody tries to, you tell Mommy or Daddy right away, and we'll make sure it doesn't happen again. Whoever would try to touch you there is being very bad, and they won't want you to tell Mommy and Daddy, but don't believe *anything* they say. You tell Mommy or Daddy or another grownup in the family just as soon as you can." By the way, Daddy probably shouldn't be washing his little girls' private parts much after they're potty trained, or about age three, anyhow, though it's all right for him to help them dry off and get their jammies on after a bath.

That's a lot for a four-year-old to pay attention to, so the input may have to be spread out over several weeks, or even months, to make sure the small doses are effective. Before the first sleepover at someone else's house, mention it again. Mention that people who look at pictures of people's naked bodies are most likely to want to touch other people's bodies. This is an important warning if it turns out that his friend's big brother has a pornography collection. If a neighborhood adult starts showing unwarranted interest in your child, get a conversation going with the child about what goes on when they're together, and make sure the child understands that physical contact is not allowed. Before your child goes on a first Scout outing, repeat the warning. Before he goes away to camp, say it again.

By now, the child will be old enough to have some glimmers of what you're really talking about, or even a definite idea. But even though the exterior may be bravado, the reassurance that Mom and Dad will always help is welcome. Make it clear to the child: "If somebody does something to you that you don't like, just call us and we'll come and get you. We won't be mad at all. We just want to make sure nobody hurts you." Always add the reassurance about "we won't be mad," because children fear their parents' getting mad at them more than parents realize, and pederasts are not above intimidating a child by saying, "If you don't do what I say, your parents will be really mad at you."

Understand, in this as in all things, that we do the best we can—we take precautions. As children get older, that is all we can do. My son's first camping experience was when he was ten, and I gave him the precaution about dirty pictures. It was only when he was seventeen that I found out my warning came a year late. The camp was well-run, and had no dirty pictures—but certain kids had been bringing them to his Christian school a year earlier. I'm sure the staff would have been horrified to realize that—which proves my point that *you* must take responsibility for inculcating values in your child. At seventeen, this son had a healthy attitude toward porn—"It's stupid," he said, "It's gross." That attitude does not reflect any teaching particularly about porn—it stems from an overall attitude toward sex, and, though my seventeen-year-old doesn't realize it, he has a deep underlying sense of the sacredness of sex. Thanks be to God.

10. My daughter is thirteen, and I think some of the girls in her crowd are pretty fast. Every time I try to talk to her about Christian values, she pooh-poohs me. She says that the "new morality" gives women what men have always had, equality in sexual behavior, and that she's not going to be bound by some medieval standard of morality. How do I respond?

With prayer, to begin with—incessant prayer that the Holy Spirit will touch her heart. But you also need some practical tips.

Such a girl seems to be a victim of women's lib-Planned Parenthood propaganda. Somebody needs to tell her that the sexual revolution is the worst joke ever played on women by men. There are prominent feminists who say this. Read *Ms.* magazine at the public library for a few months until you find an article that says that, then bring home a photocopy. And don't present it to her with a flourish and an "I told you so." Just leave the article lying around in a very findable location—like her pillow.

Is there anybody in your circle of acquaintances whom she respects? Might one of them be of any help to you in talking with her? Does she still go to church? Or have any respect for the pastor? If so, perhaps you could clue the pastor in on what's going on, and have him over to the house for dinner when she's present.

A college-age young woman as a boarder might show her that it's not "cool" to be free and easy, and in casual conversation she might come to understand how a promiscuous lifestyle can be more dangerous than fun. A slightly-older but still non-adult person, like a college student, might be best able to inform her that what she calls "medieval morality" is still the best recipe for mental and physical health.

11. I've never talked with my boys about homosexuality, but one of my sons sings in the county youth chorus, and I'm a little concerned about some of the adults involved. What should I do?

This is really hard, because what you have to do is teach your son to distrust other people. That sounds un-Christian—but instead, look at it as a survival skill. It's part of being wise as serpents.

I have observed that adolescents who are very much in the world are very aware of homosexuals nowadays, and straight guys are usually very militantly so. But a boy who has been sheltered may be too trusting. My reading in sexual identity development has just about convinced me that every boy goes through a stage in early adolescence where there is spontaneously some attraction to the same sex. The danger is if a homosexual looking for sex establishes a relationship with your son at that stage—and you can't know when that stage is occurring.

Homosexual *inclination* may not be completely voluntary, because of the complexity of our psychological development, and the interplay of body and mind. But homosexual *behavior* is voluntary. This is why it is possible to love the homosexual, but to hate the homosexual behavior.

I don't doubt that there have been and are many saints with homosexual inclination—and that was their cross to bear. They did not allow the defective inclination to manifest itself in action. That was their heroism. (I do doubt, by the way, that we will ever know these past or present saints—because almost by definition their struggle is a silent one.) There are many people who have terrible tempers—but if they control the anger, having the defect of a disposition to anger is not a sin. The temper that rages uncontrolled and leads to murder is a sin. Heterosexual inclination is essential to the family and to society and culture. But uncontrolled heterosexual inclination is lust—which is clearly a sin, and which, if allowed to, destroys the family and society and culture.

Similarly, with homosexuality. It is the crusading, militant mode that is synonymous with "gay": "gay pride," "gay lifestyle," and so on. The militancy we, as Christians, reject. The individual who may be disinterested in the opposite sex is not the same as a crusading gay. He may be a gifted musician. He may be an inspired teacher. Our lives may be enriched by knowing him, as indeed our lives may be enriched by knowing any other person God has created.

If you think I sound like a wimpy liberal, relax—here comes my next sentence. *But that is not a judgment for children to make.* As parents, our job is to protect our children. Not from knowing people who are homosexual, but from being harmed by them. If the music is an important part of your son's life, and he isn't able to satisfy his musical yens in the church choir, say, then let him continue in the choir, but arm him with discernment to protect himself. Teach him to be aware of how people manifest their sexual inclinations. Make sure he understands that God's word explicitly prohibits homosexuality. Repeat your love and trust, and repeat the first-grade cautions about "good touch" and "bad touch." More importantly, psychologically equip him to choose heterosexuality.

The common psychological history of a homosexual male is one who grew up with a controlling, but not very loving, mother, and a distant or rejecting father. Make sure that your home does not fit that description.

12. At church, the pastor said that abortion is a matter of personal conscience, and that it's OK sometimes. We firmly believe it's always wrong. I can tell that my daughter, thirteen, is confused. What do we do?

Change churches.

I don't mean to be flippant, but the choice you have to make is clear. In your family, you believe in the sacredness of life. If your church doesn't, you are closer to the mind of the Lord than your church. Do not subject your children to conflicting loyalties.

13. The daughter of a close friend of mine just found out she's pregnant. Fortunately, abortion is not even being considered. I'm wondering whether that teenage girl is ready to raise a child, though. Her mother says it'll be good for her, and will make her grow up, so she doesn't discourage her daughter's idea of keeping the baby. She says it's her daughter's problem, not hers. Don't you think adoption might be a better option?

Any pregnant woman contemplating single motherhood should ask herself some very tough questions. What does she want out of life, longterm? Is giving total care to a helpless infant compatible with those goals? Would education be abbreviated? How's her income level? If it's government child support level, can she give the baby what she herself had? Don't assume the baby's father will contribute a dime.

Remember, a baby is a total, 24-hour a day responsibility, entirely on her shoulders. What previous responsibilities has this young woman handled successfully in the past—school? job? Is she ready to do with a few hours sleep a night and not lose her temper the next day? How good is she at controlling her impatience and temper now? Does she like children? Has she spent a lot of time around babies and toddlers, so she really knows what she's getting into? Is she good at teaching children? Is she ready to do with no social life of her own for long periods of time? Can she tolerate not seeing her favorite TV program if the baby is crying?

Children need loving discipline. Is she a disciplined person herself? What does discipline mean to her? How would she discipline a toddler if she were tired and angry? What makes her think she will be able to avoid making the mistakes her parents made?

Try to get your friend to face these questions honestly. If the answers aren't encouraging, I'd suggest somebody start thinking about adoption. Going through the pregnancy and giving up the baby will be a tremendous "growing up" experience, you can be sure of this. There is no painless solution to an unwed pregnancy, that's a given. But your friend is a grandmother now, whether she wants to be or not, and she's got to focus on what's best for that grandchild. You and I both know that very few unmarried teenage mothers are able to give a baby a good start in life.

And don't fall for the cop-out that "nobody wants to adopt." That's a lie. There are waiting lists for even bi-racial and handicapped babies. Adoption is usually the most loving decision, consistent with the baby's long-term best interests. It's the pro-abortion lobby which has encouraged the notion that adoption is too painful to endure, because if girls believe that, then they really do think they have no choice but abortion.

You might want to encourage that daughter to look into a shepherding home, where she could stay for the rest of her pregnancy, with loving Christian houseparents, who would help her to take responsibility for her life and her child's, and to see some things she may never have seen before about family life. You can find out more about shepherding homes from Loving and Caring, 1905 Olde Homestead Lane, Lancaster, PA 17601, phone (717) 293-3230.

14. I just found out that the school nurse gave my daughter's fifth-grade class a lecture on "safe sex" last week. My daughter is wondering why I never told her about family planning.

"Family planning" for children is a euphemism for giving a false sense of security to fornication. Sex education advocates imagine (or pretend to imagine) that by giving out contraceptives and encouraging young people to use them, they are protecting fornicators against any consequences of their actions. Nothing could be further from the truth. Armed with a false sense of protection, young people plunge into promiscuity, and we end up with the highest teen pregnancy rate in the world.

Did you know this lecture on "safe sex" was coming to the fifth grade? If you didn't, you might want to talk to the school principal and your school board to protest this invasion of your parental rights. You might also ask what surprises they have in store for your daughter in the future.

15. My son is away from home, and recently he gave his life to the Lord. Now he wants to live a chaste life, but he's afraid it's not possible to reform so totally. His bad habits go back almost ten years. Is there any hope for him?

Of course there's hope. If he's a Christian, while there's life, there's hope! No golden road, maybe, but hope. Habits are hard to make and hard to break. If it took him ten years of sinning to make the habits, it could take him ten years of resisting temptation to fully break the habits. But he can break them. He is a new creature in Christ. Give him Psalm 51; the passage about "wash me and I will be whiter than snow" tells graphically how real the Lord's forgiveness is. "The bones that were broken shall rejoice" speaks directly to him. In following Christ and forsaking his old sins, he is breaking the bones of those habits. But with God's love, those broken bones will stop hurting and will ultimately rejoice.

New Christians are particularly vulnerable to despair. Once the demon has been cast out and the Lord admitted to one's heart, seven more demons come to torment us. The habit of prayer is not well-established; emotion may be primary in the mind, and your son may not realize that a tough discipline is necessary to keep the fervor in his heart. Even though he's away now, perhaps some things you didn't know when he was twelve, you can teach him now. And rejoice! He's ready to learn now, whereas it seems he wasn't then.

You might want to pray particularly for God to bless him with good companions, and to provide friends who will help him make the right choices.

16. What you say about modesty on dating is all well and good—for the 1950's. Is it really possible nowadays to avoid kissing on dates and not be a nerd?

If it isn't, you don't want to date.

It is always possible to do what is right. Maybe some people are going to think you're a nerd—but you don't care what those people think of you anyway. They don't want what's good for you. You certainly don't want to share your life with them, so you wouldn't be wanting to date them anyway.

Along this line, I received a beautiful letter from a listener to Dr. Dobson's "Weekend" program, who had heard my request for personal stories. This is a contemporary story that I think is worth sharing with everyone who has expressed this concern:

"When I was in my early teens, my mother made a family rule there would be no more kissing on the lips within our family. She taught us that our lips were reserved for our husbands and that we weren't to kiss a boy on the lips until we were engaged. . . . At the age of 23 I was living in an apartment with three girls. One night Kathy looked at me and in her soft, Texas drawl asked, "Ruthie, you mean you're sweet 23 and never been kissed?" How embarrassed I felt, and I gave it some thought.

"Here I was, 23. I no longer had to do everything my parents told me to do. However, I realized, I had put up with boys scoffing at me this long. If I changed my standard now, it would mean all that ridicule for nothing. So I decided to keep on with the rule. . . .

"When I was 24, Andy came into my life. . . . He proposed on a Sunday afternoon, and we went to a nice, private place for our first kiss. That night, I told him that now that he could kiss me, that was about all we were going to do until we got married. And since we both were in agreement that we would go no further, our five-and-a-half month engagement was not a time of extreme temptation for us.

"It took several days for the excitement of our beautiful wedding to wear off. And it was in that emotional climate that we began our sexual involvement. We have no bad memories or guilt to deal with."

17. I still think you're being unrealistic to expect such high standards for kids in today's world. Fact is, I wasn't a virgin at my own wedding. Why should I expect my daughter or son to be at theirs?

Because you love them, and you want them to have a better, happier, more virtuous life than you have had. And because there is such a thing as self-fulfilling prophecies. Your children will expect themselves to act as they believe you acted. Listen to this story from a "Weekend" listener:

"When I was about 15 years old I was having a conversation with my mother. She told me no one was a virgin when they got married and I wouldn't be either. Up until that time I thought my mom—a born-again Christian—expected me to be a virgin until I was married. To me her comment was like a license to go ahead and give up my virginity. . . . A short time after my conversation with my mom I lost my virginity. I'm not putting the blame entirely on my mother. I just want you to understand the implications of what a child thinks of his/her parent's expectations. . . . I nearly lost my mind with the guilt and I could never put down on paper the pain and suffering I went through with the one I gave myself to. . . . The main thing I want to convey to you is for parents to be careful what they say to their kids and don't ever let them know that you don't have the highest expectations for their purity."

Chapter 14

CONTINUING
THE DIALOGUE

O nce the values have been laid down, the framework of character built, and the basic facts taught, the task of the parent trying to raise chaste children becomes less obvious. In some respects it's more difficult, because it requires a great deal more subtlety, which is hard to achieve when the vigilance has to be even more constant. The character is far from formed, but the hand of authority has to be less and less evident lest it invite rejection.

With the coming of puberty, the desire for privacy becomes strong, and the need to find one's unique identity is real. "I'm finding myself" was used as a liberal excuse for burning flags and blowing up buildings a few decades ago, and it was so much psychobabble that it was an abuse of the language. Teenagers will experiment with different interests, fads, ways of behavior, and even loyalties. Most experiments are just that: experiments. They will go on a little while, and then they will end—provided parents have not made such an "issue" out of them as to spark contrariness, and providing the love and concern of the parents predates the storms of adolescence.

Generations ago, the problems of parent-teen conflict were avoided by a simple, ancient device: about the time that adolescence was imminent, children were separated from home by apprenticeship, by boarding out to learn a trade, by going to school far from home, by going to work. This prevented the parents from being the ones with whom the inevitable conflict of that "identity formation" stage occurred. The cruel master took the rap for administering discipline, leaving the adolescent with a fond memory of mother and father's kindness and acceptance. It made it easy to cherish fond feelings for your parents.

213

I suppose the last vestige of such cultural arrangements is the boarding school. But few can afford them, and all too often they are dumping grounds for the unfortunate children of the divorced wealthy, with all the problems that implies. So most of us, then, have the blessing and the burden of shepherding our children through adolescence. If it's any encouragement, know that recent studies[1] suggest that the heightened tensions coincide with the arrival of puberty. If that comes early, perhaps between the ages of ten and thirteen, those years will be the toughest. If it arrives late, the worst may be delayed. In any case, by age fifteen or sixteen, things have usually calmed down. My first son began adolescence at twelve, with emotional excesses I never thought possible, and it was not until seventeen that reason could again, if the circumstances were right, reign in his mind. My other son had only a few rough spots until age sixteen, and then was impossible for six months straight. That's where he is as I write these words, but I can face the future with equanimity, because I know that, sooner or later, it will pass.

Other studies[2] suggest that it's the brain, not the body, that causes the turmoil: it is during the pubertal years that children's cognitive capacities develop, and the ability to think abstractly emerges. There are even differences in right-and left-brain hemispheres noted in connection with the timing of puberty. During our long and difficult siege with our first son, I myself was greatly comforted by Maria Montessori's opinion that the intellect essentially shut down at age twelve, not to re-emerge until age eighteen. I think Montessori was brilliant with her observations of how young children learn, and I regret that she died before she could complete her writings on adolescence. What little of it I know, I'm inclined to agree with.

These findings are worth mentioning because they suggest that it is something other than Mom and Dad and Johnny that is causing the turmoil. The bickering of adolescence can become so personalized that all parties to it feel it's their own fault when things get rocky. Mothers who are full-time homemakers are particularly susceptible to feelings of failure and the consequent depression that invites. Not that parents are not tremendously important. But take heart and console yourself that you are not everything. And if another child is entering the difficult stage at the time one is getting over it, not to worry: your ability to cope grows with experience, so it probably will not be harder each time. Parents of large families have suggested to me that the first and second children's adolescence were the worst, and that with subsequent children there was less tension.

If this is true, part of the reason may be that the younger children observed which limits their pioneer siblings could force the parents to yield on, and which ones they could not. If Oldest Girl whined and complained about the family dress code enough, did she succeed in getting Mom and Dad to modify it? If she did, Second Girl will repeat the effort. If she didn't, Second Girl probably won't bother to undertake a losing campaign. If Oldest Boy wheedled and cajoled and deceived parents into allowing rock albums in the house, Second Boy is sure to try. But if Oldest Boy lost that battle, Second Boy will look elsewhere for his cultural experiments. Clearly, this is a good reason to be consistent at all costs.

The real challenges of adolescence continue to be those of childhood: developing virtues. Learning selflessness is a lifelong task, one that can become a serious, personal challenge as the abstract reasoning capacity grows. By then, it isn't so much the parent's teaching as it is the young person's learning. With the guidelines in place, virtue can be learned by applying informed thoughtfulness to one's experiences. How else do people who grow up in godless, totally undisciplined households become virtuous adults? Somewhere along the line, they learn something about virtue, and from that point on, they form their character according to the knowledge. If they happen to be nineteen or twenty before they grasp the higher ideal (usually it is the Word of God that is first heard), they have already made plenty of mistakes. The goal of Christian parenting is to prevent as many mistakes as possible by instilling good training until maturity enables children to be motivated independently for the good.

Faith, hope, and charity are the key virtues. Purity, or chastity, is an extension of these virtues. Nonetheless, sexual sins are the ones most likely to cause a person to leave the church or to isolate him from Christian fellowship. The burden of guilt sexual sins cause makes a person liable to not even try to practice the other virtues. The danger of this happening is a tangible reminder why children should be taught from a young age that forgiveness is always possible, that God will help one repent, that God wants to forgive.

The danger of sexual preoccupation's causing other ill effects is also a reason why parents must not keep the subject on the front burner after the natural curiosity has been satisfied. Of course, respond as asked, and offer practical help as needed in the development of relationships with the other sex. But wait to be asked. Remember the ultimate goal of sexuality. Remember that the teaching now should be geared toward preparing the young adult for marriage and eventual parenthood.

CELIBACY? WHOLLY FOR CHRIST!

There is always the possibility, of course, that God's call on a young person may be to the single state. This is an area where even Christians have a hard time today, but it was not always thus. In the ancient Church, of course, singlehood consecrated to the Lord was historically understood as an honorable call. An excellent tradition grew up around that call. In a sex-saturated world, the idea of voluntarily refraining from what is a good thing in itself seems strange. But when one realizes how much God has done for her, what can be wrong with the impulse to take everything that she would have given to a husband, and give it wholly to Christ?

Consecrated celibacy is best understood not as a rejection of sexuality, but a leaping over the body, so to speak, to free oneself from the earthly cares that family and children entail, in order to more completely seek union with God. A vow of chastity historically went hand in hand with a vow of poverty—the person who was giving his or her heart to Christ was striving to become more detached from all the things of the world, in order to become more attached to God. Another thing that went hand in hand with consecrated celibacy was the communal life. Think of Mother Teresa and her sisters. Poverty and chastity, a life of service to the poorest of the poor in the worst slums on earth—how do they endure it? Because they pray together, deeply and regularly, and because they share their lives with each other, deeply and regularly. In a marriage, the primary food of the relationship is communication; in a celibate life, the primary food of the relationship with God is prayer. And the kind of profound prayer that sustains this life can only flourish in a communal environment. This is an aspect that must not be minimized. Celibacy is too difficult to be lived alone, and the much-publicized failures in celibacy on the part of those who have consecrated themselves to it are proof of as much. Mother Teresa's institute was organized in our lifetime; religious institutes that were organized in the Middle Ages are dying out in our time, even as new ones arise. The tradition is associated with Catholicism, though in fact it is far older than the Roman church, but it is no longer unique to Catholicism any more. The impulse to dedicate one's whole life to Christ will last until the end of time.

It is a difficult call to discern in the sensuous society of today, of course, but my observation has been that God leads those who have it to find those who can guide them. It's entirely possible that many people never find their call, because we are programmed as a society to anticipate marriage and children. As our children become adults, it's probably wise to discuss the celibate state sometime early on, in a theoretical way. Don't wait until spinsterhood seems inevitable before letting your daughter know it's all right with you that she stays single if it is God's will. If you have given her the idea early, you will save her a lot of grief and sorrow if opportunities for marriage elude her. And boys can feel pressured to get married, too, because "everybody's doing it," even if it's not the right thing for them. So they need the same assurance.

MARRIAGE AS SACRIFICE

Even allowing for the possibility that God will not call every person to the married state, the training of children in sexuality focuses essentially on education for marriage. Marriage is for most of us the highest imitation we can achieve of Christ: as God loved His bride, the Church, we love our spouses. "Therefore be followers of God as dear children. And walk in love, as Christ also has loved us" (Eph. 5:1–2). And how has Christ loved us? This passage continues, ". . . and given Himself for us, an offering and a sacrifice to God for a sweet-smelling aroma."

Christ's love for us is a love of sacrifice, of offering Himself to the Father, as incense rose when the apostolic church offered its sacrifices of praise and thanksgiving. As a child, I thought that sacrifices were painful instances of self-denial, unpleasant things, things that entitled me to feel like a martyr if I did them. For years I was baffled by phrases in hymns like "a sacrifice of praise." I knew praise was not uncomfortable for me, and I thought that in order to be a sacrifice, it had to be painful.

Now I know that the word comes from the Latin *sacrificium,* which literally means "doing the holy thing." In practice, it means giving something to God in order to be in harmony with Him. Sacrifices do not have to be unpleasant, tedious things. Baking an apple pie can be a sacrifice to God if I do it with a cheerful spirit and tell Him I am doing it for Him. Yes, denying myself meat during Lent is also a sacrifice, because I am doing it in order to draw closer to God. Denying myself in order to lose weight is most likely something for me, however, and thus not necessarily doing a holy thing.

We know that Jesus Christ sacrificed Himself in a painful way for us: He allowed Himself to be nailed to the cross as an offering to the Father on our behalf. He denied Himself the physical and emotional comfort He was entitled to as a human being (and which with His power He could have claimed) in order to suffer unspeakable agony. He sacrificed Himself for us, His Church, His bride, that we might be radiant and spotless.

Why is this an apt analogy for marriage? Because that is what we are called to do in marriage: offer everything to God. The apostle Paul was explicit about the analogy later on:

> Husbands, love your wives, just as Christ also loved the church and gave Himself for it, that He might sanctify and cleanse it with the washing of water by the word, that He might present it to Himself a glorious church, not having spot or wrinkle or any such thing, but that it should be holy and without blemish. So husbands ought to love their own wives as their own bodies; he who loves his wife loves himself (Eph. 5:25–28).

On the honeymoon, things are easy. We are in love, we're full of joy, and it's easy to offer thanks to God for making such happiness possible, for choosing this spouse for us. Five years and two children and half as much income later, things can be quite different. Tempers are short and all we can see are the faults of our spouses and the demands and shortcomings of our children and the problems with our lives. What is there to offer to God now? Actually, a lot more, but we, in our self-pity and preoccupation with mundane concerns, often don't see it.

Here Ephesians 5 is our roadmap: "Walk in love, as Christ also has loved us, and given Himself for us." When the going is tough, that's the best time to imitate Christ, to keep offering to Him all the things that frustrate us. When the spouse is difficult, that's the time when we can be most like Christ and continue to love, and to love deeper, based not on our desires but on the needs of the spouse. The spouse may be unlovable then, but God is always lovable. And the more we love God, the more we are capable of loving our spouses. We aren't always lovable, either, but God always loves us. Husbands and wives should do the same for each other.

Many people (Christians or otherwise) have endured unhappy marriages for years by sheer dint of discipline and willpower. All too often, for these people, the words of poet Padraic Pearse apply: "Too long a sacrifice can make a stone of the heart." There's that word again, this time used in its secular meaning of self-denial. Self-denial on the human level, without the redeeming practice of supernatural love, without the "doing the holy thing" element of it, can indeed freeze the heart. And then the possibility of future love for the spouse becomes more and more remote, as long as the willpower-motivated discipline focuses the person more and more on himself, because the person is, in an ironic sort of way, more and more wrapped up in himself. I'm not criticizing people who have taken this course; in fact, I admire the discipline they have practiced. And without doubt they are doing the right thing by their children to hold their marriages together. But I weep for them, seeing they are unable to taste in their marriages the love their heavenly Father would want them to have.

These are the ultimate truths we want our children to know before they enter upon the sacred estate of matrimony. But obviously it cannot be taught all at once. For most of us, it takes a lifetime to really learn anyhow. So how do we break it down into bite-size pieces?

PREPARATION FOR MARRIAGE

We can challenge young adults to think about how Christ loved. Was it selfishly, making sure His affection or commitment to us did not interfere with His pleasures and desires? Or was it despite the cost to Himself that he pursued what was good for us? If we are to imitate Him, we must be able to focus on the best interests and needs of the other person—not on what we *want* to be their needs, but on what really *are* their needs. The ability to be objective is the first prerequisite of love.

Young adults need to know that "falling in love" is so much balderdash, a creation of medieval poetry immortalized by seventeenth-century dramatists, perpetuated by eighteenth-and nineteenth-century novelists, and exaggerated by twentieth-century Hollywood. As any competent high school teacher of *Romeo and Juliet* can point out, Romeo wasn't so much in love with Juliet as he was in love with the idea of love. Contemporary youth culture doesn't even bother with much pretense of romantic feelings. I suppose, in its frankness about sexual conquest for the sake of conquest, it is at least honest. Unfortunately, it's easy to see this message and reject it without being immune to the lure of infatuation.

Infatuation is not love; romance is not intimacy. True love is not "fallen into"—it is achieved by dint of effort. If people who think they "fell in love at first sight" examine what really happened, they're likely to discover that an infatuation with each other struck them at the same time they were prepared to love, and so simultaneously they grew in love. That's a great way to discover love, but it's a far cry from catching a glimpse of a girl on the street and deciding to marry her.

Not that the sudden infatuations do not hit; they do, sometimes to the most unlikely person and in the least expected manner. And powerful emotions can sway even the most analytical mind. All the more reason, then, why a young adult should have thought through the important things in life before Cupid's arrow strikes. Throughout adolescence and young adulthood, a person is wise to be self-analytical to the extent that he or she knows the following: his goals in life and a plan to achieve them; his personality, his tastes; his expectations; his toleration level for frustration; and his emotional vulnerabilities. We all wear masks at least some of the time. What's his? The macho, Humphrey Bogart type? Is hers a charming southern belle facade to disguise her will of iron and desire to control everyone around her? Better to know one's own weaknesses than to ruin relationships one cares about.

We must teach our children that marriage is a vocation, just as surely as a call to ordained ministry is a vocation. It should be entered into only in such a spirit, not merely because "everybody does it," and not to "make the best of a bad situation" such as premarital pregnancy. Premarital pregnancy is a misfortune; compounding it with a doomed marriage makes a tragedy. Because marriage is a vocation, a sacred calling, all the steps leading toward it should be covered abundantly in prayer. By all means, young people should give their love lives to the Lord, and they should regularly pray about their relationships: "Lord, Your will be done. If You want something to develop in this relationship, I will be pleased. If You want nothing to come of it, I accept that as Your will also."

Especially when interest is growing, should prayer be a constant companion. Your goal is to be certain that as your daughter begins to get really interested in one man, she will, of her own accord, ask God whether this is the person He is calling her to share her life with. Your goal as a parent is that, by the time your daughter is old enough to be asking the Lord that, she will also know how to hear from God, and know how to distinguish her desire from God's answer. And that she will be wise enough that, if she doesn't receive a clear answer, she will not commit to it.

Remember: even on the way down the aisle, it's not too late to call off a wedding. Forget the reception, the presents, the guests, and all the other temporary concerns. Fathers, as the march begins and your daughter is holding on to your arm, turn to her and say, "Sweetheart, are you sure you want to go ahead with this? If you don't, it's OK with me." If God wants your daughter to marry someone else, you want to cooperate with Him by giving her every chance you can to avoid making a mistake.

THE SCANDAL OF DIVORCE

Why do I place so much emphasis on avoiding a mistake? With no-fault divorce, it's easy to remedy a mistake, isn't it? No, it isn't. And to whatever extent Christian people buy into the "easy marriage, easy divorce" mindset of our day, to that extent we are giving scandal to the world.

Several generations have now grown up with divorce increasingly available and utilized. Today, 5 out of 1,000 marriages end in divorce. "Well, that doesn't sound too bad," you may say. But think of it this way: suppose there were 1,000 marriages in your town. At this rate, in two years, there will have been ten divorces; after three years, fifteen; and after four, twenty. Five years of this rate means 25 divorces. And meanwhile, suppose the rate should go up? That means the number will increase even faster. Among women who marry at age sixteen or seventeen, for instance, the rate of divorce has been noted as high as 38.9 per 1000 couples! It used to be that once a couple had been together fifteen or twenty years, they were pretty much out of the danger zone for divorce. Not so anymore. Since 1960, the divorce rate for men and women aged forty-five and older has doubled.[3] The perennial optimists at this moment will point out that many of those people remarry. About 83 percent of divorced men do remarry, usually women a few years younger than they and often never-before married. Prospects for divorced women are not so bright. But even in the case of re-marriages, their chances of success are no better than they were the first time around.

But that's a public policy concern, you say. Who cares if people get divorced and remarry? I answer on two levels, the personal and the public. On the personal level, every divorce leaves in its wake a larger or smaller number of walking wounded—children, women, and men—

whose lives have taken a serious turn for the worse. Feminist ideology may provide some cold comfort for a while to the women if they embrace it—as many do in the wake of a divorce. Pop psychology that emphasizes how "resilient" children are may reassure a mother's conscience, but it cannot give the child the comfort or psychological protection of two parents. Selfishness may be rewarded as a man enjoys a 73 percent increase in his standard of living the year after a divorce—while his former wife experiences a 42 percent decline—but even that will provide small comfort in the wee, still hours when the conscience can be heard.

The most vicious undermining of the Christian family today is divorce. Christian couples seem just as susceptible to the pressures working to destroy marriages as anyone else, and easy divorce delivers the fatal blow. The mindset of divorce is natural for an age that has exalted selfishness to the highest good. What's the solution to the "problem" of not getting the gratification I want? Try a new partner! Christians who have endured rocky times in their marriages—and anybody married longer than five years has—know that the rough times can draw us closer to God and teach us to love one another because God loves us. Those who succumb to the easy out of divorce usually have not discovered this great secret of love.

People are hurt by divorce. If there are 1.2 million couples divorced each year, that is 2.4 million men and women, and probably another million children, who are being added to the category of high risk for psychological instability. That means they are vulnerable to depression, loneliness, guilt, and promiscuity. All this in and of itself ought to be enough to make us want to avoid it.

But these are temporal reasons still. There is also eternal reason to avoid divorce. It is contrary to God's will. Are we so enamored of our own pleasure that we refuse to take up our cross if the cross happens to be a spouse who fails to provide us with bliss every day? The world says, "You have a right to be happy. If you are not happy, it's somebody else's fault. Change the situation."

Christ, on the other hand, challenges us to *change ourselves* and *stay married*. He said, "Moses, because of the hardness of your hearts, permitted you to divorce your wives, but from the beginning it was not so. And I say to you, whoever divorces his wife except for sexual immorality and marries another, commits adultery; and whoever marries her who is divorced commits adultery" (Matt. 19:6–9).

Exactly what is meant by that exception for "sexual immorality" is a subject of debate among scholars; the most authoritative research seems to suggest that it is a poor translation of what would better be called today "consanguinity", or too close a kinship relationship. But the spirit of the Lord's teaching is unmistakably clear. Even if your spouse sins against you more times than you can count, what do you do? We have sinned against God more times than we can count. What does He do? He forgives us and pardons us when we repent. And so ought we to forgive and pardon our spouses. Occasionally, as in the case of physical abuse, one spouse has truly wronged the other, and it's necessary to separate. I don't mean to minimize the seriousness of such situations. But it's amazing how many times changing yourself will cure what you saw wrong with your spouse.

Christ sees us, His Church, spotted and blemished. We see the faults of our spouses. But does that excuse us from loving them? No, it does not. God will help us to love the spouse for whom our feelings have grown cold. We have established a covenant with that spouse, a covenant in the eyes of God. It is not ours to break it. "So then, they are no longer two but one flesh. Therefore what God has joined together, let not man separate" (Matt. 19:6).

SOME RESEARCH FINDINGS

Part of the role we parents must play as our children pass adolescence and become adults is to help them prepare for marriage by teaching them some critical thinking about what are the ingredients of marital happiness. Much of what makes a marriage work or not can be spotted ahead of time by a wise counselor. It is one of the perennial griefs of a pastor's heart that he can tell in a brief interview when a requested marriage is practically doomed from the start. But he's often the only one to raise a hand in caution, and the young couple are so much in love that they don't hear him at all. If he drags his feet, they may go elsewhere.

Well, we parents must be such counselors. We know our offspring better than anyone, both the hidden and the visible characteristics. We love them and want their happiness more than anyone else in the world. And through years of living, we have learned something about evaluating the character of other people. Through years of marriage, we have learned a thing or two about what makes a marriage work. Our practical wisdom is considerable and should be brought to bear as the dating and courting process goes on—not in a heavy-handed, interfering way, of course, but in the form of dialogue and conversation.

Psychological and sociological research accumulated over the years has also helped identify some predictors of marital success. Age is an obvious one, because maturity tends to come with age. Maturity must be present before a person is ready for the self-effacement of parenthood. There's no point to pretending that parenthood is anything other than a demanding, absorbing calling. A person who has not outgrown his or her own need for abundant attention is not going to be optimally suited to give patient, abundant attention to a child.

Arthur Norton and Jeanne Moorman, the Bureau of the Census specialists in marriage and divorce data,[4] have found that for women who first married before age twenty, divorce rates throughout the 1970s were roughly twice the comparable percentages for women who first married in their twenties. Their analysis of the data suggests that women who marry after age thirty may actually have more stable marriages than women who marry in their twenties (though if a divorce is going to occur, it will likely occur sooner in a late marriage than in an early one).

On the other hand, we all know marriages that began in the teen years and have lasted for thirty years and more. This emphasizes the point that statistics are simply guidelines: they tell us how most people in a certain age group are likely to behave, not how any particular individual is likely to fare.

In our materialistic culture, the hardest thing about a young marriage is the low living standard that frequently accompanies it. The mindset that "we have to own a house before we have any children" causes many children to be denied life at all. If a young couple are capable of resisting the materialistic lure of the age, however, and are willing to accept the children that God may send, there is reason to think they can succeed despite the statistical odds. A young man approached me one time to ask my advice about whether he was too young to get married. I suggested that he go for four weeks without buying a single unnecessary thing for his own pleasure: no newspaper, no item of clothing, no taxi fare, no soft drink on impulse, and so on. If he could do that for four weeks without feeling sorry for himself, and if his intended young lady could do likewise, they might be mature enough.

How close in age should the partners be? Common sense suggests caution in dealing with too great a difference in ages. Might one of the pair be attracted to the other because of maternal or paternal qualities? That isn't necessarily fatal, mind you, but it can be if the older partner doesn't realize it. Some difference in ages can actually be advantageous: an immature woman, for instance, who marries a somewhat older, more stable man will have a rock to lean on as she weathers the storms of her own growing up. Her appreciation for him can increase enormously as she looks back on how emotional and childish she was and how steady he was in dealing with her immaturities.

Another factor to consider is what the impact of the parents' ages will be on future children. To have a father sixty years old when one is in sixth grade can be a matter of no concern, but it probably means Dad is not likely to be eager to play a game of ball after work, and if that is Mom's idea of what a father should do, it could present a problem. On the other hand, Dad's earning ability will probably be at its peak then, so that could compensate for some things. Then again, to have a father who has retired when you're in high school presents another situation. The valedictorian of my son's high school graduating class began her speech by saluting her father on this, his 72nd birthday. Everybody applauded, of course, and I had a twinge of jealous thought: if my husband had been retired, and had had lots of time to spend helping my son do his homework, my son might have been valedictorian too. Which goes to show how Satan can implant jealous thoughts anywhere, because of course I know that God has a unique plan for my son's life. That age gap would have some advantages (Dad may be infinitely more patient at sixty-five than he was at twenty-five), but it might also have some disadvantages (Dad may have poor health). These and other factors can best be considered well while the relationship is approaching the seriousness that will lead to a proposal of marriage; some objectivity is still possible before the love has been declared.

What about length of acquaintance? On the one hand, the longer the pair know each other, the fewer surprises they will have about each other's character, tastes, family, and so on. On the other hand, a long engagement presents a real challenge to virtue. So perhaps a long acquaintance followed by a short engagement might be optimum. My friend Louis Gasper has a One Year Rule: A couple should have known each other for a year before they are married, but should not be seriously dating after a year. In other words, a year is long enough and more than a year gets dangerous for the morals of a healthy young man and woman.

DEVELOPING THE MARRIAGE BOND

Marriage counselor Dr. Donald Joy has enumerated twelve stages of courtship that he argues are essential to developing a strong marital bond, or pair-bond, as he calls it. He emphasizes that these stages should be followed sequentially, one at a time, over the course of many months. Stage one: when we meet anybody, we do this: eye-to-body. Stage two: eye-to-eye. This is the level at which most casual interaction among members of the human race occurs—with salesmen, delivery men, and so on. If a person cannot make eye contact, we instinctively distrust.

When love is growing, the next stage is voice-to-voice contact. Long telephone calls will abound during this stage. The pair will be able to pick out each other's voices from a crowd. Stage four is hand-to-hand; the couple will naturally want to touch each other, and hand-holding is the obvious way to do it. A handshake is a frequent social exchange, but that's not what is going on here. After a period of holding hands, the couple progress to his arm around her shoulder. Then the next stage is arm-to-waist. Dr. Joy notes that by the time this stage has been reached, the couple have begun to keep secrets from the rest of the world. Intimacy has begun, though they still face outward together. At the next stage, they begin to exclude the rest of the world and to face each other. This face-to-face stage is the first stage of courtship at which a kiss should be exchanged. According to Dr. Joy, it is premature to kiss before the intimacy has grown steadily through all the earlier stages.

And what do couples in love do after they have begun kissing? They sit side by side and touch each other's hair. Dr. Joy calls this next step in bonding the hand-to-body stage. The following stage brings more familiarity with each other's bodies, but still in a nongenital way. Here may be friendly, fully clothed neck or back rubs after a stressful day or a game of touch football. At this stage, if she falls and skins her knee, she will not be embarrassed to have him lift her skirt and put on the antiseptic and bandage. They will be comfortable with each other's bodies now.

There are three more stages, but they become progressively more physical and are reserved for marriage. They are mouth to breast, hand to genital, and finally, penetration. Dr. Joy emphasizes and reemphasizes:

Don't get these stages out of sequence. Don't go from the dance floor to the bedroom and expect to be able to build a marriage out of it. Couples who skip stages are not properly bonded with each other. He urges couples to take it slow and easy. And he suggests that married couples repeat the sequence from the beginning to help keep their bonding secure and strong.

Notice how chastity is presumed by Dr. Joy's anthropological and psychological research. It is no surprise that divorce-statistic experts Norton and Moorman also find that having borne or conceived a child before marriage increases the likelihood of eventual divorce. When sexual intimacy precedes emotional intimacy, the bond is undermined. This research simply proves what the Ten Commandments taught ages ago and what our grandmothers may have taught us, that respect precedes love. Love cannot flourish where there is no respect; and where sexual excess has occurred, respect cannot inhabit.

The need for sexual control continues after the wedding day. This again is something that needs to be understood before the wedding occurs. Lots of young men enter marriage expecting that now, finally, they are going to be able to get all the sexual indulgence they want, whenever they want it, legitimately. And when they discover that their wives get headaches, they feel shortchanged, sorry for themselves, and angry at her. Such men may have believed that as long as you were married, anything went. They weren't prepared properly for marriage. Matrimony is not a license for sexual self-indulgence. It is a license to love completely, which is not the same thing at all. The essence of marriage is seeking the Spirit of God in partnership with another soul. A sensual man cannot perceive the things that are of the Spirit of God, Paul told the Corinthians (1 Cor. 2:14). Even within the bonds of matrimony, we must strive to be spiritual men and women. And that means sacrificing—offering to God for holiness—our insatiable physical urges.

OTHER PREDICTORS OF SUCCESS

Do the romantic stories of the kid from the wrong side of the tracks marrying the wealthy social butterfly have much truth in them? No. It's nice to think that true love conquers all, and of course there are cases where it does. But more realistic is the problem of cultural incompatibility. The girl who has vacationed at the finest international resorts may be infatuated with the fellow who thinks the restaurant in the Holiday Inn is uptown, but infatuation doesn't last. His lack of social graces may be amusing at first, but it rapidly becomes an embarrassment. If she thinks she'll change him after marriage, she has succumbed to one of the oldest lies love can tell. All the willingness in the world to please her cannot enable him to stop being himself, though he may try. And the more he tries, the more he imperils his own self-acceptance.

The advice not to date anybody you wouldn't want to marry is sound. I would like to add Marshner's Corollary to that rule: Date people who are your social and intellectual equals and you will have a head start on happiness.

There are plenty of jokes about marrying for money, but they should be that only: jokes. What does money have to do with seeking a spouse? Money cannot buy love; it cannot buy happiness; it does not enable one to imitate Christ. In fact, Christ warned us many times about how being too fond of money may make it harder to follow Him. If a woman overlooks a man's faults because of his cash and convinces herself to be in love with him by thinking of his bank balance, she has not only deceived herself, but him as well. Marriage is between two hearts, two souls. On the Day of Judgment, we will be held accountable for how much we loved as Christ did, how much we helped our spouses to grow in grace. The bottom line on net worth statements will not count for much.

It won't count for much in this world, either, if it produces tension between husbands and wives, and if underlying guilt about having deceived self and others makes people miserable. What good is money if the heart has no peace? Virtue is the only wealth that lasts, because no matter what the circumstances of the world may be, virtue can bring joy to the humblest of dwellings. But a spoiled, undisciplined, materialistic heart can make the most magnificent of dwellings a prison.

THE REST OF THE FAMILY

When two people marry, they marry one another's whole families. Thus, before your child gets serious about somebody, encourage him to learn as much as he can about the rest of the family.

When Bill and I were first getting serious about each other (though neither of us had said anything to indicate it), he arranged for me to have his sister Susan as a roommate for the summer. I've often thought what a clever move that was on his part, because living with his sister told me a lot about the kind of family and home life the Marshners had, and I was pleased to find how similar it was to my own. Knowing that our basic family living styles were compatible removed one more question from my mind about this fellow I was starting to see so frequently.

Since children are normally a part of marriage, the more a prospective couple can know about how each of them would raise children, the more harmony they can have from the beginning. Bill and I did a lot of talking about how we wanted our children to end up, but we never talked about how we would get from here to there. Consequently, a few years later, when the fact of having to make a discipline decision faced us, we were both unprepared. It turned out we had some different ideas of what to do. And in the meantime, the children were our guinea pigs. I am sure the Lord in His wisdom and mercy meant for them to be the victims of our ignorance, and I believe He will use it to His purposes, but all the same, I can see how their lives and ours would have been easier if we had communicated better and been more consistent from the start.

Part of the dialogue a parent has with a marriage-age child, then, should be about such things as this: it's not just yourselves you have to think about, but the larger society you are fitting into, and the larger society you will be creating. The larger society of your in-laws is far too serious a matter to be relegated to jokes.

What are relations like with the extended family? Has a divorced parent been the only role model for years? Is there any relationship with the other parent, and what has it been? Is the girl dominated by her parents? Are they accustomed to making all important decisions for her? Will they resent her husband's making decisions?

One marriage I know began with the bride-to-be's mother bustling around with the husband-to-be and finding an apartment that she felt was appropriate for her daughter. The young man, anxious to please, went along with this scheme—though after making a deposit on the apartment, he and his bride chose one of their own after all. The bride's mother refused to ever visit that apartment, and it was the first of many power plays in the marriage. It was years before the wife was mature enough to tell her Mom and Dad to mind their own business, and as long as they lived, she was unable of her own strength to resist their demands. She needed her husband to be strong for her, but when he didn't feel up to a confrontation, he would let her make commitments they would both come to regret. And then she would find it hard not to resent him for not protecting her from her family, which wasn't exactly good for their marriage. Sort of a no-win situation, you could say.

Another marriage was destroyed because a big sister did not approve of little sister's choice of husband and spent hours on the phone pointing out all the husband's faults in minute detail, telling her how awful he was treating her. Eventually the little sister came to believe she had indeed made a mistake and began divorce proceedings.

The young couple cannot change the members of their families but they can know ahead of time what kind of situation they are walking into and be prepared to recognize the first challenge to the husband's authority or the first effort to sow discord. And part of their preparation should be an agreement between themselves about how they will handle it.

Do daughters grow up to be like their mothers and sons like their fathers? In many traits of character and behavior, yes. If the prospective father-in-law barks at his wife more than he talks to her, the prospective daughter-in-law had better note it well. Such will be the innate tendency of her husband in the future. If the bride's mother feels she is not enough appreciated by her husband, the daughter should beware of the same tendency in herself. At times of stress, we revert to the patterns and habits we observed unconsciously in our childhood. Even though we know better, are aware of our weaknesses, and have consciously rejected those behaviors, we still have the weaknesses somewhere inside us, needing to be controlled.

WORK AND MONEY

What about attitudes toward work? Is the prospective husband's father a workaholic? The prospective bride should read up on workaholism and realize that if she marries this promising medical student, she may spend many days and evenings with the children all by herself. This is one more thing to be talked through in advance. And it isn't just the man who might be the overachiever, either. The girl may have been taught by her parents to have professional expectations for herself. Though she wants to be a proper wife, she may not know how to find self-esteem in such an anonymous undertaking. Without realizing it, she may be a workaholic with regard to her own career.

At the other extreme, is one of the couple so excessively laid back as to be considered lazy? Is the man totally indifferent to the expectations of his job? Does he say, "Oh, who cares?" to any question about his lack of punctuality? That's a real warning sign. A prospective wife who takes a similar attitude toward fixing a meal or doing the dishes is likewise waving a red flag. It may seem cute before the wedding, but such a woman has major work to do in her habits and on her character in order to learn how to make a pleasant home.

What about finances? Do they both like to spend their money in similar ways? Do they have an organized approach to balancing their budgets? Do they share values about such things as savings? Do they have essentially the same aspirations about money and what to do with it? Are they agreed about whether she will continue to work outside the home when the first child comes? Do they have realistic expectations of what their position in the world will be?

In this instance, I speak from the wisdom of having made the mistake. I had always been reared to believe it was rude to talk about money, and so, I guess, had Bill. In any event, all during our courtship we never talked about it. When we got married, I didn't have the faintest idea what his income was! If my parents had told me in a heavy-handed way a few months earlier that I better find out his income, I'd have been annoyed at them and would have interpreted their interest as an implication that he wasn't earning enough. I would have married him no matter what his income. And that, I guess, is as it should be with true love.

Nonetheless, it would have helped us both to have had a more realistic idea of what his income could provide. Instead, we just blithely assumed we could buy a home in a couple of years. That turned out to be a totally unrealistic assumption, and it took me years of less-than-gracious living with the idea of being forever at a landlord's mercy before I finally sacrificed my desire for home ownership to the Lord. As it turned out, that's what the Lord was waiting for. Once I sincerely was able to tell Him I didn't want a house if He didn't want us to have one, He made it possible for us to get one. But I regret the years in between when I made myself (and consequently, of course, others) unhappy because I couldn't have what I wanted. It was my fault, to be sure, my lack of virtue. But having had information from the beginning of our marriage might have helped me to have more realistic expectations to begin with.

PRAYER AND POLITICS

I grew up in a family that talked about politics all the time. Bill and I talked about politics a lot before we were married, and we agreed. It was great that his parents had similar views to my parents'. And it was even more delightful when our children began to pick up our interests. When they brought up a political subject with any Grandpa or Grandma, they got essentially the same message. We haven't have to cope with much rebellion along political lines.

We weren't so fortunate where religion was concerned. Bill and I joined our church when we were married and have been perfectly contented there ever since. But when our children became old enough to bring up this subject with my side of the family, they got lectures on how their mother had extreme notions of religion. Let me tell you, it doesn't do a thing to encourage a ten-year-old's spirit of cooperation for a grandmother to tell him his parents are abusing him by expecting him to go to Sunday school on a cold winter's morning! My mother-in-law is of a totally different denomination from us but at least when the kids floated the trial balloons looking for sympathy from her, what they got from that grandma was a nice, gentle, but firm observation that "your mother and father have to follow their conscience, and you should go along with them." Bless her heart!

I mention this not only to point out how the most loving and well-intentioned grandparents can throw the biggest seeds of discord into a happy home by misdirected sympathy, but also to bring up the two subjects the etiquette books tell us are forbidden in polite discourse. Politics and religion are what make the world go round as far as I'm concerned. I can't think of any two areas where agreement would be more helpful in a marriage.

Agreement in religion is more than a matter of creed. The matter of practice is the one that has day-to-day ramifications. The creed, the statement of belief, underlies the practice, of course, and unless two people are in substantial agreement about the intellectual content of their faith, there will be no foundation for a real meeting of the minds. But even members of the same denomination can be miles apart in practice. So a serious couple need to discuss: Will we pray together every day after we're married? Will we have family devotions every day? Perhaps even more obvious, will we go to church every Sunday? A woman who has been a faithful church attender may find herself going alone after she's married, much to her dismay, since she assumed that by marrying a Christian she was getting a church-goer in the bargain. But she may not have asked the right questions beforehand.

Protestant-Catholic marriages can work beautifully when both partners really love the Lord and both understand ahead of time how the children are going to be raised, what family devotions will consist of, and so on. I even know of Jewish-Christian marriages that proceed smoothly because a similar understanding of the ground rules prevails. Yet between Christians of the same church, such harmony can be missing. Thus ground rules should *always* be discussed; expectations must harmonize with reality or everyone is just asking for trouble.

Politics is easier for most people to adapt to than religion. For me, a widely divergent political viewpoint suggests a widely divergent world view. At the very least, a rock-ribbed conservative should think twice before marrying a confirmed liberal. Most of us aren't really as tolerant of differing opinions as we like to think we are. On the other hand, an enthusiastic Republican can find true love with an enthusiastic Democrat, because party label doesn't matter so much as philosophy. It is the conflicting world views that preclude harmonious households, not the party label.

IN CONCLUSION

As I draw this book to a close, 1 hope that the dominant message you've received is that *you can succeed as a parent in today's world*. Despite living in a culture with values and expectations that work to draw your child into a sexually promiscuous, self-centered lifestyle, you can win the battle. You can create a Christian atmosphere in your home, discuss the sexual part of life openly and honestly, and instill self-discipline in your child. You can be the proud parent of a child who honors God in thought, word, and deed.

None of this comes easily, however, as I said earlier. I didn't choose the term "battle" lightly in describing the job of negating the influence of our secular culture. It takes planning and sacrifices, continual working toward agreement between husband and wife, conscious and constant efforts at more effective parenting, and periodic review to see how you're doing and make needed adjustments.

Keep in mind that the end goal is worthwhile. Don't ever give up hope that it is attainable. And when it comes to the task of parenting, not only is the goal worthwhile and attainable, but we also have this sustaining promise from Scripture: "And my God shall supply all your need according to His riches in glory by Christ Jesus" (Phil.4:19). On such a promise we can build families that overcome any challenge.

My children are not full grown and safely happily married yet, so I can't give you that definition of success. But recently I had breakfast alone with my son, the one who has had such a long and difficult adolescence, and who is going into the Marine Corps in a few months. We talked about his longrange plans for his life. Does he want to get married? Yes, eventually. What did he expect from marriage, I asked him.

"What do you mean, Mom?"

Well, do you expect it to last, for instance, that divorce will be out of the question?

"Oh sure," he said, without a moment's hesitation.

So, you're assuming you'll be faithful to each other?

"Oh, sure, of course."

So, you'll practice pre-marital chastity?

"Sure."

Won't that be hard, when you're in the service, and all your buddies are trying to get you into a contrary situation?

"Have I ever had trouble telling people to take a flying leap if I didn't want to hear what they were saying?"

The answer was so straightforwardly honest I had to chuckle. Indeed, he has never had that trouble. His noncomformity has been a source of much heartache over the years. Nonconformity with my husband's and my ideas of what a boy should be like, for instance, or his refusal to accept faith just because somebody said it was true. Here's a boy who is determined to chart his own course in life. It might have been wiser to hearken to his father's voice, and doing so might have given him an easier road ahead, but those are not the choices he has made.

Right now, he is at least wanting the right things for himself with his sexual faculty. He has seen the kids in his public high school try the other way, and, thanks to God's grace, he has seen results that he recognizes as undesirable. There's one baby alive today because he talked some friends out of an abortion. He could be a lot worse off. As he goes off to life outside our roof, at least he is intending the right things. He could be worse off. What he has to learn now are things that only God can teach him. Like the fact that his own strength is not sufficient.

What can I as a mother do now? For the past eighteen years, I have worked as if everything depended on me, because it seemed to; now, I must pray as if everything depends on God, because it does.

NOTES

Chapter 1: Nobody Says No Anymore

1. Otis Bowen, "Teenage Sexual Activity: Postponement as a Viable Alternative," *The Journal of Family and Culture*, Autumn 1986, p. 2.
2. Kristin A. Moore, "Birth Rate Trends," *Facts at a Glance*, March, 1993. Factsheet published by Child Trends, Inc., 2100 M St NW, Washington DC 20037
3. Kristin A. Moore, Ph.D., "Facts on Births to U.S. Teens," *Facts at a Glance*, published by Child Trends, Inc., Washington, D.C.
4. Betty Collier Watson, "Seven Myths about Teen Pregnancy," *The Evening Sun*, September 28, 1987.
5. "About 56 million in U.S. have viral venereal disease, study says" by Felicity Barringer, *The Dallas Morning News*, April 1, 1993, page 1A.
6. For a more thorough discussion of this sobering depopulation trend, see Ben J. Wattenberg, *The Birth Dearth* (New York: Pharos Books, 1987).
7. Robert O'Brien and Moris Chafetz, M.D., *The Encyclopedia of Alcoholism* (New York: Facts on File, 1982), p. 312.
8. Ibid., p. 314.
9. *Statistical Abstracts of the United States 1987*, (107th ed.), U.S. Department of Commerce, December 1986, p. 100, chart 159.
10. Robert O'Brien and Sidney Cohen, M.D., *The Encyclopedia of Drug Abuse* (New York: Facts on File, 1984), p. 380.
11. Bowen, p. 2.
12. U.S. Department of Health and Human Services, National Centers for Health Statistics, Centers for Disease Control, "Percent of Women 15–19 Years of Age Who Are Sexually Experienced, by Race, Age and Marital Status: United States, 1988," *National Survey of Family Growth*.
13. "Drugs, Premarital Sex Rejected by A Students," *The Washington Times*, September 15, 1987.
14. Mary Battiata, "Beverly LaHaye and the Hymn of the Right," *The Washington Post*, September 26, 1987.
15. Jacqueline R. Kasun, "Cutoff of Abortion Funds Doesn't Deliver Welfare Babies," *The Wall Street Journal*, December 30, 1986.
16. Interestingly, this pattern occurs only with traditional-value parents. The children of parents who hold liberal, nontraditional attitudes toward sexual behavior are equally as sexually active as children whose parents have not talked to them at all. This finding is reported in Kristin A. Moore, et al., "Parental Attitudes and the Occurrence of Early Sexual Activity," *Journal of Marriage and the Family*, 48 (Nov. 1986), pp. 777–82.

Chapter 2: The World of Adolescence

1. Martin Luther, *A Letter to the Mayors and Aldermen of All Cities of Germany in behalf of Christian Schools,* cited in Christopher J. Lucas, *Our Western Educational Heritage* (New York: Macmillan, 1972), p. 250.
2. *Sapientiae Christianae,* 1890.
3. The magazine I was looking at was *Seventeen,* May 1993, issue.
4. Joyce Price, "G-rated masses feel written out of script," *The Washington Times,* May 6, 1993, page A1.
5. Medved, Michael, *Hollywood vs. America,* New York, HarperCollins/Zondervan, Publishers, p. 4.
6. Ibid.
7. "Television Viewing" in *The Index of Leading Cultural Indicators,* William J. Bennett, Washington, D.C.: The Heritage Foundation, March 1993
8. This figure and others in this section come from Michael Keating's excellent series "The Stolen Generation" in the May, June, and July–August 1987 issues of *Pastoral Renewal,* P. O. Box 8617, Ann Arbor, Michigan 48104.
9. For elaboration on this trend, see the wonderfully well-written book *Why Johnny Can't Tell Right from Wrong* by William Kilpatrick, New York: Simon & Schuster, 1992.
10. Thomas L. Jipping, J.D.,"Volunteer labeling not working", *AFA Journal,* March 1993, p. 17.
11. John Wooten, "Dionysius Superstar," review of Robert Pattison, *The Triumph of Vulgarity: Rock Music in the Mirror of Romanticism,* in *National Review,* August 14, 1987, p. 51. Wooten's main criticism of Pattison is that after brilliantly analyzing the ideas inherent in rock, Pattison then lamely concludes that rock has little effect on behavior.
12. David P. Phillips Ph.D. and Lundie L. Carstensen, M.S., "Clustering of Teenage Suicides after Television News Stories about Suicide," *The New England Journal of Medicine,* September 11, 1986, pp. 685–89.

Chapter 3: The Wrong Kind of Education

1. Quoted by Constance Horner in "Is the New Sex Education Going Too Far," *New York Times Magazine,* December 7, 1980.
2. William Raspberry "'Don't Is the Proper Advice," *Chicago Tribune,* April 22, 1986.
3. In Melvin Anchell "Psychoanalysis vs. Sex Education," *National Review,* June 20, 1986, p. 33.
4. Letter to author from Dennis Smith, Director of Office of Family Planning, Department of Health and Human Services, February 23, 1988.
5. William J. Bennett, "Why Johnny Can't Abstain," *National Review,* July 3, 1987, p. 36.
6. Ibid.
7. "1 in 5 in U.S. Have Sexually Caused Viral Disease," Felicity Barringer, *The New York Times,* April 1, 1992, p. A1.

8. "Having abortion increases risk of breast cancer," by David Alan Coia, *The Washington Times*, April 2, 1993, page A3. This article lists four scholarly journal references.

9. Charles E. Irwin, Jr., MD, Mary-Ann Shafer, MD, "Adolescent Medicine," *Journal of the American Medical Association*, July 15, 1992, Vol 268 No. 3, p. 334.

10. Heidi M. Bauer, et al., "Genital Human Pappilomavirus Infection in Female University Students as Determined by a PCR-Based Method," *Journal of the American Medical Association*, January 23/30, 1991, Vol. 265, No. 4, pp. 472–477.

11. *Journal of the American Medical Association*, June 17, 1992, p. 3153.

12. William Marsiglio and Frank L. Mott, "The Impact of Sex Education on Sexual Activity, Contraceptive Use and Premarital Pregnancy Among American Teenagers," *Family Planning Perspectives*, vol. 18, no. 4 (July/August 1986), pp. 151.

13. Deborah Anne Dawson, "The Effects of Sex Education on Adolescent Behavior," Family Planning Perspectives, vol. 18, no. 4, (July/August 1986), p. 166.

14. In Judith Echaniz, *When Schools Teach Sex . . .* (Washington, D.C.: Free Congress Foundation), p.

15. Michael Schwartz, "School-Based Clinics: The Strategy," in *Family Protection Report*, March, 1987.

16. Joy Dryfoos, "School Based Health Clinics: A New Approach to Preventing Adolescent Pregnancy?," *Family Planning Perspectives*, March–April 1985, p. 71.

17. A speech delivered as "SBC's: Capturing Public Funds" and cited at p. 8 in Rita L. Marker, *Reshaping the Future: A Report on School-Based Clinics;* Steubenville, Ohio: The Human Life Center, 1987.

18. Richard D. Glasow, "Abortion and the Rise of School-Based Clinics," *National Right to Life News*, September 11, 1986.

19. "Mixed Response to Teen Study: Not All Schools Sold on Clinic Idea," *Chicago Tribune*, December 14, 1986.

20. *Family Planning Perspectives*, (September–October, 1980), vol. 12, no. 5, p. 230.

21. Rita L. Marker, "Too Much Too Soon—or Too Little Too Late?" *Human Life Issues* publication of the Human Life Center, May 1984, p. 4.

22. Stan E. Weed, "Curbing Births, Not Pregnancies," *Wall Street Journal*, Tuesday, October 14, 1986.

23. Quoted by Andres Tapia, "Abstinence: The Radical Choice for Sex Ed," *Christianity Today*, February 3, 1993, p. 29.

24. Horner, *op cit.*

25. The book is out of print now, and the publisher has gone out of business, so it would be hard to find. If you want to look for it anyway, here's the publication data: *Blackboard Tyranny*, Arlington House Publishers, 1978.

26. Eunice Kennedy Shriver, "Rx for Teen Pregnancy," *The Washington Post*, March 19, 1987.

27. Susan Newcomer and J. Richard Udry, "Parental Marital Status Effects on Adolescent Sexual Behavior," *Journal of Marriage and the Family*, May 1987, pp. 235–40.

28. Jacqueline R. Kasun, "The Economics of Sex Education," mimeographed factsheet in author's possession.

Chapter 4: The Origins of Conscience

1. F. Andre Leyva, PhD. "Raising Children: A Strategy of Affection and Discipline for Parenting", unpublished paper. Dr. Leyva is with the Pastoral Psychology Center in Gaithersburg, Maryland.

Chapter 5: Too Little Too Late

1. For the quotations and the historical account that follows, I am indebted to the excellent research of John Kippley in "Birth Control and Christian Discipleship," Cincinnati: Couple to Couple League, 1985.
2. "The Abortion Debate," *Journal of Current Social Issues,* Spring 1978, pp. 73–75.

Chapter 6: AIDS: Virtue Is Its Own Reward

1. Jean M. Carey, MS, *Heterosexually Transmitted AIDS in the United States.* Special Report of the American Council on Science and Health, August 1991, p. 1.
2. Figure cited in Fumento, Michael, "AIDS: Deadly Confusions Compounded", *First Things,* February 1992, #20, pp. 6–8.
3. Carey, *Heterosexually Transmitted AIDS,* p. 4.
4. Duesberg, Peter H. and Ellison, Bryan J. "Is the AIDS Virus a Science Fiction?", *Policy Review,* Summer 1990, pp. 40–51. Readers wanting to do further research should not fail to also see *Policy Review,* Fall, 1990, for the fourteen pages of letters-to-the-editor that Duesberg's article provoked, many of them equally well-credentialled scientifically.
5. For deeper understanding of the gay ideology, see *Gays, AIDS and You,* by Enrique T. Rueda and Michael Schwartz, Old Greenwich, CT: Devin Adair Company. That book is derived from *The Homosexual Network: Private Lives and Public Policies* by Rueda, (Old Greenwich, CT: Devin Adair Company, 1987).
6. For a list of Christian organizations that help homosexuals find an alternate way, contact: Exodus International, P.O. Box 2121, San Rafael, CA 94912, (415) 454-1017
7. Marcia Angell, M.D., "A Dual Approach to the AIDS Epidemic" *The New England Journal of Medicine,* May 23, 1991, p. 1500.

Chapter 7: Parents' Manifesto

1. Peter Uhlenberg and David Eggebeen, "The Declining Well-Being of American Adolescents," *The Public Interest,* (Winter 1986), 82: 25–38.
2. Martin Mawyer, *The Silent Shame* (Westchester, Il.: Crossway, 1987), p. 46.
3. "Soviets distribute Booklet in Major Anti-AIDS Drive," *The Philadelphia Inquirer,* September 15, 1987.
4. Jerome Greer Chandler, "Hard Questions About AIDS and the Traveler," *OAG Frequent Flyer,* October 1987, pp. 95–99.

5. For an extensive discussion of the nefarious effects on community of a modern technological society, a book well worth reading is Stephen B. Clark, *Man and Woman in Christ* (Ann Arbor: Servant, 1978). This book, as the title suggests, is about a lot more than the pitfalls of modern society, but Clark's analysis of that is brilliant.
6. For more elaboration on the trends to remove functions from the family, see my book, *Can Motherhood Survive? A Christian Looks at Social Parenting*, available from Word, Inc.

Chapter 8: Putting the Values Back

1. David Isaacs, *Character Building: A Guide for Parents and Teachers* (Dublin: Four Courts Press, 1984.)
2. Donald E. Greydanus, M.D., "The Teenage Girl Who Is 'Boy Crazy,'" *Medical Aspects of Human Sexuality*, August 1985, p. 122.
3. Gail Sheehy, "The Road to Bimini," *Vanity Fair*, September 1987, p. 136.
4. Karl C. Garrison, *The Psychology of Adolescence* (New York: Prentice-Hall, 1940), p. 170.
5. One of the classic works in child psychology is Arnold Gesell and Frances Ilg, *The Child from Five to Ten* (New York: Harper and Row, 1946). This book, while somewhat dated now and definitely secular in its orientation, nonetheless contains interesting observations of children's behavior, and since it is based on objective observations, it has validity as far as the observations go.
6. Sol Gordon and Peter Scales, *The Sexual Adolescent* (No. Scituate, Mass.: Duxbury Press, 1979), p. 63.
7. Gordon and Scales, p. 61, citing R.C. Sorensen, *Adolescent Sexuality in Contemporary America* (New York: World Publishing, 1973).

Chapter 9: Five Basic Concepts

1. In a letter to Sheldon Vanauken, cited in *A Terrible Mercy*.
2. Julian L. Simon, "Why Do We Still Think Babies Create Poverty?" *The Washington Post*, October 13, 1985. Simon has also written the definitive response to the "Global 2000" report: *The Resourceful Earth*, published in 1984 by Basil Blackwell, Inc.

Chapter 11: Emotions and Fasting

1. Susan Newcomer and J. Richard Udry, "Parental Marital Status Effects on Adolescent Sexual Behavior," *Journal of Marriage and the Family*, May 1987, pp. 235–40. This fascinating study is a pioneer of its kind. Besides this finding, Newcomer and Udry also discovered that households in which parents hold permissive sexual attitudes, do not hold traditional religious values, or engage in permissive childrearing

practices are more likely to have sexually active children than parents who are conservative and traditional, even in the absence of divorce.

2. For more reading on the tradition of Lent and fasting in the Eastern Church, I suggest *Great Lent* by Alexander Schmemann, one of the foremost Orthodox theologians in America. It is published by St. Vladimir's Seminary Press, 1974.

3. Letter to the editor from Irene L., Newport News, Virginia. *Theosis,* September 1987.

Chapter 12: Modesty, Peers, and Dating

1. John E. Horrocks, *The Psychology of Adolescence,* 3rd ed. (Boston: Houghton Mifflin, 1969), p. 315.

2. Tamar Lewin, "Women Found to Be Frequent Victims of Assaults by Intimates", *The New York Times NATIONAL,* January 17, 1991, p. A20.

Chapter 14: Continuing the Dialogue

1. Lawrence Steinberg, "Impact of puberty on family relations: Effects of Pubertal Status and Pubertal Timing," *Developmental Psychology,* Vol. 23, pp. 451–60. A popularized account of Steinberg's research appeared as "Bound to Bicker" in *Psychology Today,* September 1987, pp. 36–39.

2. Summarized in popular form in Anne C. Petersen, "Those Gangly Years," *Psychology Today,* September 1987, pp. 28–34.

3. "Breaking the Ties That Bind," *Insight,* October 13, 1986, p. 10.

4. Arthur J. Norton and Jeanne E. Moorman, "Current Trends in Marriage and Divorce among American Women," *Journal of Marriage and the Family,* February 1987, pp. 3–14.

RESOURCES

The following are publications, organizations, and books that expand on themes only touched upon in *Decent Exposure.*

Chapter 2: The World of Adolescence

For a better understanding of the youth culture, expecially how it has pervaded the public library: *What Are Your Kids Reading? The Alarming Trend in Today's Teen Literature.* Jill Carlson, 1991. Originally published by Wolgemuth & Hyatt, now available from Word Inc.

ea   ea   ea

To be better informed about the culture war in general, or in particular about the public policy war against the family, there are several resources to choose from:

American Family Association
Don Wildmon
P.O. Drawer 2440
Tupelo, Mississippi 38803

Originally begun to help orchestrate public resistance to the increasing smut on television, AFA is now branching out to do legal work in defense of the family.

ea   ea   ea

Family Research Council
700 Thirteenth St. NW, Suite 500
Washington, D.C. 20005
(202) 393-2100

Headed by Gary Bauer, this is the only organization in Washington that fights full-time for the family across the full range of policymaking activity: from research and think-tank work to actual lobbying, on the complete range of issues from abortion, to tax policy, to education, to health care—wherever the battle is, FRC will be there.

ʔʌ   ʔʌ   ʔʌ

Eagle Forum
Phyllis Schlafly
P.O. Box 618
Alton, Illinois 62002
(618) 462-5815

Phyllis Schlafly, you may remember, is the woman who defeated ERA. The *Phyllis Schafly Report* is an indispensable newsletter, one topic a month. And the annual Eagle Council is the best training a woman can get at being politically effective.

ʔʌ   ʔʌ   ʔʌ

Concerned Women for America
Beverly LaHaye
370 L'Enfant Promenade, S.W., Suite 800
Washington, D.C. 20024
(202) 488-7000

This is the largest Christian women's organization, and it specializes in linking prayer and action. *Family Voice* is a first-rate monthly magazine that will keep you informed on a broad range of current topics.

ʔʌ   ʔʌ   ʔʌ

Capitol Hill Prayer Alert
325 Pennsylvania Ave. SE
Washington, D.C. 20003

This is a hotline to call for updates on urgent national prayer needs. (301) 899-4063. Also available as a FAX alert.

ʔʌ   ʔʌ   ʔʌ

National Empowerment Television
717 Second Street N.E.
Washington, D.C. 2000
(202) 546-3000

NET is a 24-hour satellite broadcast alternative network, available to cable systems as well as to anyone with a satellite dish. It is a complete alternative to the current stranglehold on television news and policy discussion by the Left.

Chapter 3: The Wrong Kind of Education

To help you cope with sex ed curricula: *Families for Good and All,* by Judith Echaniz. A comprehensive resource manual to help you understand and deal with secular sex ed by scrutinizing all aspects of it in light of a traditional understanding of sexuality and marriage. Available from:

Family-Life Culture and Education Council, Inc.
P.O. Box 18466
Rochester, New York 14618

‌ ‌ ‌ ‌ ‌

Another organization that has useful resources for chastity education is:

Womanity
1700 Oak Park Blvd., Annex
Pleasant Hill, California 94523.

Some of their material (buttons, posters, etc.) is particularly catchy among kids.

‌ ‌ ‌ ‌ ‌

National Association for Abstinence Education is *the* source of information on all sex ed curricula that teach that abstinence is a reasonable, attainable, and expected behavior. Some of the curricula include abstinence from alcohol and drugs as well as from premarital sexual activity. Some are suitable for public schools, some are suitable for religious schools. If your school board is open to considering an alternative to the Planned Parenthood-SIECUS type of sex ed, contact NAAE immediately!

National Association for Abstinence Education
6201 Leesburg Pike, Suite 404
Falls Church, Virginia 22044.
Voice: (703) 532-9459. FAX: (703) 532-0654

‌ ‌ ‌ ‌ ‌

For a particularly Catholic perspective on raising children for virtue: *Challenging Children to Chastity: A Parental Guide* by H. Vernon Sattler, C. SS. R., 1991. Available from:

Catholic Central Verein of America
3835 Westminster Place
St. Louis, MO 63108-3472.

Chapter 6: AIDS: Virtue is Its Own Reward

Exodus International is one of several national ministries serving people who want to leave the homosexual lifestyle. Free information will be sent by contacting:

Exodus International
P.O. Box 2121
San Rafael, CA 94912
(415) 454-1017

Chapter 9: Five Basic Concepts

Regarding the fundamentals of marriage: *Sex and the Marriage Covenant: A Basis for Morality* by John F. Kippley, 1991. Available from:

Couple to Couple League International, Inc.
P.O. Box 111184
Cincinnati, Ohio 54211.

Chapter 12: Modesty, Peers, and Dating

To expand on the whole topic of dating for young adults: *Dating with Integrity: Honoring Christ in Your Relationships with the Opposite Sex* by John Holzmann, 1990, Originally published by Wolgemuth & Hyatt. Now available from Word, Inc.

ಜ   ಜ   ಜ

Along the same lines, I highly recommend a conversation between Dr. James Dobson and Dr. Neil Warren on a tape called "Getting Married: It's More Than 'I Do'." The ideas Warren suggests are something that kids beginning to notice the opposite sex should be taught, before their emotions begin to get involved with any particular person. Available from:

Focus on the Family
Colorado Springs, Colorado 80995

(Ask for Tape Number CS 741)

SELECTED BIBLIOGRAPHY

Brown. Victor L. Jr. *Human Intimacy, Illusion and Reality.* P.O. Box 25777, Salt Lake City, Utah 84125, 1981.

Buckingham, Jamie. *Let's Talk About Life, A Candid Discussion of Growth and Sex for Pre-Teens and Their Parents.* Altamonte Springs, Florida: Creation House (Strang Communications), 1986.

Chrysostom, John. *On Marriage and Family Life.* Translated by B. Catherine P. Roth and David Anderson. Crestwood, NY: St. Vladimir's Seminary Press. 1986.

Cirner, Therese. *The Facts About Your Feelings: What Every Christian Woman Should Know,* Ann Arbor. MI: Servant Books, 1982.

Dobson, Dr. James C. *The Strong-Willed Child.* Wheaton, IL: Tyndale House Publishers, 1978.

Gilder, George. *Men and Marriage.* Gretna. LA: Pelican Publishing Co., 1986.

Grant, George. *Grand Illusions: The Legacy of Planned Parenthood.* Franklin, TN: Adroit Press. 1988, 1992.

Hartley, Fred. *Dare to Be Different—Dealing with Peer Pressure.* Old Tappan, NJ: Fleming Revell Co., 1986.

Isaacs, David. *Character Building: A Guide for Parents and Teachers.* Dublin, Ireland: Four Courts Press, 1984.

Martin, Ralph. *Husbands, Wives, Parents, Children: Foundation for the Christian Family.* Ann Arbor, MI: Servant Books, 1978.

Mother Mary and Archimandrite Kallistos Ware, translators. *The Lenten Triodion.* Boston: Faber and Faber, 1978.

Meier, Paul D., M.D. *Christian Child-Rearing and Personality Development.* Grand Rapids, MI: Baker Book House, 1977.

Mosbacker, Barrett L:, ed. *School-Based Clinics and Other Critical Issues in Public Education.* Westchester, IL: Crossway Books, 1987.

Schmemann, Alexander. *Great Lent: Journey to Pascha.* Crestwood, NY: St. Vladimir's Serminary Press, 1974.

Talley, Jim and Bobbie Reed. *Too Close Too Soon.* Nashville: Thomas Nelson Publishers, 1982.

Wattenberg, Ben J. *The Birth Dearth.* New York: Pharos Books (A Scripps Howard Company), 1981.

You Can Help Get the Word Out about Safe (and Biblical) Sex Education!

You can help parents and others who teach children learn about safe and sane sex education methods and principles. Please order additional copies of *Decent Exposure* for your public library, your local school board, your Christian school library, your Congressman, or anyone else involved in public policy issues.

Please order from your bookstore or by writing to Legacy Communications, P.O. Box 680365, Franklin, Tennessee, 37068.

1 to 3 copies	$10 each
4 to 10 copies	$ 9 each
11 to 20 copies	$ 8 each
21 to 50 copies	$ 7 each
51 or more	$ 6 each

*Please add 4% of total order (minimum $1)
for shipping and handling.*